OUT IN AFRICA

Social Movements, Protest, and Contention

Series Editor   Bert Klandermans, Free University, Amsterdam

Associate Editors   Ron R. Aminzade, University of Minnesota
David S. Meyer, University of California, Irvine
Verta A. Taylor, University of California, Santa Barbara

For more books in the series, see page 257.

OUT IN AFRICA

LGBT Organizing in Namibia and South Africa

Ashley Currier

Social Movements, Protest, and Contention
Volume 38

University of Minnesota Press
Minneapolis • London

An earlier version of chapter 4 was previously published as "Deferral of Legal Tactics: A Global LGBT Social Movement Organization's Perspective," in *Queer Mobilizations: LGBT Activists Confront the Law*, ed. Scott Barclay, Mary Bernstein, and Anna-Maria Marshall, 21–37 (New York: New York University Press, 2009). An earlier version of chapter 5 was previously published as "Decolonizing the Law: LGBT Organizing in Namibia and South Africa," *Studies in Law, Politics, and Society* 54 (2011): 17–44; copyright *Studies in Law, Politics, and Society*, Emerald Group Publishing Limited.

Published by the University of Minnesota Press
111 Third Avenue South, Suite 290
Minneapolis, MN 55401-2520
http://www.upress.umn.edu

Library of Congress Cataloging-in-Publication Data

Currier, Ashley.
 Out in Africa : LGBT organizing in Namibia and South Africa / Ashley Currier.
    (Social movements, protest, and contention ; v. 38)
 Includes bibliographical references and index.
 ISBN 978-0-8166-7800-6 (hc : alk. paper)
 ISBN 978-0-8166-7801-3 (pb : alk. paper)
 1. Gays—South Africa—Social conditions. 2. Gays—Namibia—Social conditions.
 3. Gays—Political activity—South Africa. 4. Gays—Political activity—Namibia.
 5. Gay activists—South Africa. 6. Gay activists—Namibia. I. Title. II. Series: Social movements, protest, and contention ; v. 38.
 HQ76.3.S5C87 2012
 306.7660968—dc23
                                                                                2012008198

Printed in the United States of America on acid-free paper

The University of Minnesota is an equal-opportunity educator and employer.

19 18 17 16 15 14 13 12   10 9 8 7 6 5 4 3 2 1

Contents

Acknowledgments

A number of people and institutions made this project possible. Kathleen Blee has supported this project from its inception in her Global Feminisms course at the University of Pittsburgh. The National Science Foundation (SBE-0601767), Society for the Scientific Study of Sexuality, and University of Pittsburgh supported my fieldwork in Namibia and South Africa, and the Department of Sociology and Women's and Gender Studies Program at Texas A&M University (TAMU) gave me the time and space to finish this book. Portions of chapters 4 and 5 appeared in *Queer Mobilizations: LGBT Activists Confront the Law* and *Studies in Law, Politics, and Society*, and I am grateful to both publishers for permitting me to reproduce this material here.

I never imagined that established scholars would be so generous with their time and wisdom. I am especially indebted to Gretchen Bauer, Glen Elder, Joshua B. Forrest, Susan Glover, and Rodney Hopson for their insights about Namibian and South African politics, and Teresa Dirsuweit, Robert Lorway, Graeme Reid, and Amanda Lock Swarr shared their knowledge of southern African sexual politics. Teresa Dirsuweit facilitated my affiliation as a visiting researcher with the University of the Witwatersrand's School of Geography, Archaeology, and Environmental Studies. I want to thank Anthony Manion and Paul Mokgethi for patiently explaining the breadth of the Gay and Lesbian Archives and sharing their thoughts about LGBT organizing. Support from the Text and Academic Authors Association has also contributed to the publication of this book.

I extend my heartfelt gratitude to the welcoming staff, leaders, and constituents at Behind the Mask, the Forum for the Empowerment of Women,

Sister Namibia, and The Rainbow Project. Although I do not name you individually, in part to protect your anonymity, each person I met was willing to talk to me about LGBT activism nationally and transnationally. Your hard work and dedication to improving the lives of LGBT persons in Namibia and South Africa are truly inspiring. Staff allowed me to access records and to attend meetings and did not grow exasperated with the new questions that I asked.

My support system in Pittsburgh enabled me to conduct research far away from home. Kathleen Blee expertly helped me navigate the complexity of data and findings I brought back from Namibia and South Africa. I would not be a sociologist if it were not for Kathy and her careful feminist mentoring over the years; I hope it will continue for many more. Kathy has graciously read multiple drafts of chapters and allowed me to run outlandish ideas by her. Akiko Hashimoto's advice was crucial as I executed a comparative sociological study, and I have greatly benefited from our academic and methodological conversations over the years. Cecilia Green, Eric O. Clarke, and Paula J. Davis supported my research objectives and used their expertise in postcolonial feminist theory, queer theory, and African studies to improve this project; I am particularly saddened that Eric was unable to see how his work on publicity and queerness influenced this project. Susan Andrade got me interested in gender and sexuality studies in southern Africa in the late 1990s, and I appreciate her early interest in my intellectual trajectory. Participants from Kathleen Blee's Qualitative Methods Workshop and the Pittsburgh Social Movements Forum helped me sharpen my analysis. A wonderful cadre of graduate students of gender, sexuality, and social movement studies at the University of Pittsburgh also encouraged and prodded me along with this project. In particular, I would like to recognize María José Alvarez, Kathleen Bulger-Gray, Kimberly Creasap, R. Spencer Foster, Kai Heidemann, Lisa Ruchti, Margaret Kerr, Amy McDowell, Melissa Swauger, Veronica Szabo, Tim Vining, and Jane Walsh. Bert Klandermans, Ronald R. Aminzade, David S. Meyer, and Verta Taylor, the editors of the Social Movements, Protest, and Contention series, believed in this project for several years and offered suggestions that improved the book's coherence. Jason Weidemann and Danielle Kasprzak at the University of Minnesota Press have been a joy to work with. Jason guided me through the editing and publication process with ease.

Kathleen M. Fallon provided superb feedback as the project metamorphosed into a book manuscript and listened to my ideas; she is an incredible feminist sociologist. The members of my writing group, Donnalee Dox and Marian Eide, read and provided invaluable feedback on the entire manuscript and encouraged me to stay on track with my research; your intellectual generosity has sustained me in ways I cannot express. Many people read and commented on early drafts of chapters. I would particularly like to thank Susan Egenolf, Dongxiao Liu, Krista May, Linda Radzik, Michelle (Misha) Taylor-Robinson, Rebecca Hartkopf Schloss, Andrew Vaserfirer, Joan Wolf, and TAMU's Queer Studies Working Group for feedback on individual chapters. Misha, I cannot thank you enough for your feminist mentorship. Each day, my colleagues and students at TAMU provided a warm, supportive environment in which to study southern African gender and sexual politics in the global South. Marian Eide, Mark Fossett, Sarah Gatson, Claire Katz, Verna Keith, Claudia Nelson, Jane Sell, and Jyotsna Vaid at TAMU offered their wisdom at key points as I revised the manuscript, and Rebecca Hankins helped me locate secondary research materials key to finishing this project. Over the last few years, Jennifer Earl has served as a fountain of wisdom for all matters related to publication. Daniel Humphrey, Claire Katz, Robert Mackin, Nancy Plankey-Videla, Tanya Saunders, and Neha Vora were always willing to listen to my revision ideas. Conversations with Paul Almeida, Mary Bernstein, Hannah Britton, Marc Epprecht, Tina Fetner, Neville Hoad, Henning Melber, David S. Meyer, Oliver Phillips, Deana Rohlinger, Mikki van Zyl, and Laurel Westbrook guided my revisions at key points. Paul was my social movement studies guru while he was at TAMU. Graduate students at TAMU and elsewhere have been wonderful sounding boards for the ideas in this book. I especially want to thank Daniel Delgado, Lauren Joseph, April Plemons, Andrew Vaserfirer, and Chi Cheng Wat for listening to my ideas and offering their insights.

The friendship, support, and patience of Kai Heidemann, Veronica Szabo, and Veronica Lifrieri reminded me that I could complete this project; I am a better researcher and person for knowing you. Dean Gerber provided a stabilizing influence amid the sometimes unsettling changes that accompany transnational research. I hope that the next time I do this, you are by my side.

Acronyms

ABIGALE	Association of Bisexuals, Gays, and Lesbians (South Africa)
ACHPR	African Commission on Human and Peoples' Rights
ANC	African National Congress (South Africa)
ARV	antiretroviral
AWB	Afrikaner Weerstandsbeweging (Afrikaner Resistance Movement)
CAL	Coalition of African Lesbians
COD	Congress of Democrats
EC	Equality Clause (South Africa)
ECOSOC	United Nations Economic and Social Council
EU	European Union
FEW	Forum for the Empowerment of Women (South Africa)
GALA	Gay and Lesbian Archives (South Africa)
GALZ	Gays and Lesbians of Zimbabwe
GASA	Gay Association of South Africa
GLA	Gay and Lesbian Alliance
GLON	Gay and Lesbian Organisation of Namibia
GLOW	Gays and Lesbians of the Witwatersrand
IGLHRC	International Gay and Lesbian Human Rights Commission
ILGA	International Lesbian and Gay Association
JDA	Johannesburg Development Authority
JWG	Joint Working Group (South Africa)
KCR	Katutura Community Radio
LAC	Legal Assistance Centre (Namibia)
LAGO	Lesbians and Gays Against Oppression (South Africa)
LBT	lesbian, bisexual, and transgender
LGB	lesbian, gay, and bisexual
LGBT	lesbian, gay, bisexual, and transgender
LGBTI	lesbian, gay, bisexual, transgender, and intersex

NA	National Assembly (Namibia)
NAMBLA	North American Man–Boy Love Association
NANGOF	Namibian Non-governmental Organisation Forum
NCGLE	National Coalition for Gay and Lesbian Equality (South Africa)
NGO	nongovernmental organization
NP	National Party
NSHR	National Society for Human Rights (Namibia)
OLGA	Organisation of Lesbians and Gay Activists (South Africa)
OUT	OUT LGBT Well-Being
PLAN	People's Liberation Army of Namibia
POWA	People Opposing Woman Abuse (South Africa)
PPT	political process theory
RGO	Rand Gay Organisation (South Africa)
SABTS	South African Blood Transfusion Service
SACC	South African Council of Churches
SADF	South African Defence Force
SANBS	South African National Blood Service
SCOG	Social Committee of Gays and Lesbians
SFF	Special Field Forces
SMO	social movement organization
SWAPO	South West African People's Organisation (Namibia)
TAC	Treatment Action Campaign (South Africa)
TRP	The Rainbow Project (Namibia)
UDF	United Democratic Front (South Africa)
UN	United Nations
ZIBF	Zimbabwe International Book Fair

Introduction:
How Visibility Matters

Visibility matters to social movements. Public visibility imbues them with social and political relevance, enhancing activists' ability to disseminate their demands and ideas. Increasing a movement's visibility can enable activists to attract new recruits. Certain forms of public visibility afford movements credibility that improves their standing with audiences that activists want to influence. Invisibility also appeals to activists at times, especially if political circumstances become hostile to organized resistance or if activists must withdraw from public visibility to respond to internal crises. These examples illustrate the strategic aspects of movement visibility. Activists make strategic choices to promote particular public presentations of constituents, organizations, and movements to target audiences, and at times, they opt for lessened visibility, even withdrawing from interactions in favor of invisibility.

Not only does visibility matter to social movements but it also matters to scholars. Visibility brings social movements into scholars' orbit. Scholars gravitate toward studying publicly visible movement actions such as large protests, charismatic movement leaders who rally supporters around them, and the effects of observable repression on social movement organizing (Blee and Currier 2005; Earl 2003). Since scholars tend to study what they can see, visibility brings particular movements into the canon of social movement studies.

In this book, I regard visibility and invisibility as fluctuating qualities that Namibian and South African lesbian, gay, bisexual, and transgender (LGBT) movement organizations carefully cultivated over time as strategies.[1] Visibility strategies encompass multiple facets of movement organizations, from how activists publicly portray collective identities to the protest tactics they select.

Even mundane matters, such as how to use public spaces, composed activists' visibility strategies, as exemplified in the following two vignettes from South African and Namibian LGBT organizing.

In 2005, black South African lesbian activists became publicly visible in a former apartheid prison. The Forum for the Empowerment of Women (FEW), a black lesbian movement organization in Johannesburg, began renting office space in the Women's Gaol section of the Old Fort, an apartheid-era prison that housed women and men. Now renamed "Constitution Hill," the complex is home to the Constitutional Court of South Africa, the highest court in the country, and a museum documenting apartheid history. Once the site of hidden human rights abuses perpetrated by the apartheid regime, the Old Fort has been reimagined as a place in which all South Africans can seek legal redress for injustice (Gevisser 2004). The paradoxical quality of black lesbian visibility in the Women's Gaol was not lost on FEW's staff and members. Nomsa, a black lesbian and FEW member, stated, "Women used to be locked up here; now women are coming out and saying, 'We're free, and we're speaking our minds,' in the same place that people were locked up" (interview with the author, March 17, 2006).[2] Black lesbians' presence in this former carceral space confirmed the strides made by the new "democratic, nonracial, nonsexist" South Africa (Tutu 2000, 5). In the space of a few years, leaders managed to shed South Africa's international status as a political pariah for its apartheid policies and to usher in sweeping democratic reforms, including a constitution that protected LGBT rights.

The location of FEW's office in the Constitution Hill complex also afforded black lesbians' psychological respite from homophobic violence in townships. FEW aimed to stop *corrective* or *curative rape,* terms coined by activists to describe the sexual violence some black men used to punish black lesbians for their perceived gender and sexual transgressions (Muholi 2004, 118).[3] Jessica, a black lesbian and FEW member, affirmed that Constitution Hill's tight security made it "unlikely" that "any crimes [would be] committed there," making FEW's office "a really safe space for everybody" (interview with the author, February 17, 2006). Ironically, the former prison, a site of hidden human rights violations in the past, had become a space for black lesbians seeking safety.

Activists with The Rainbow Project (TRP), a Namibian LGBT movement organization that worked to obtain LGBT rights, navigated different sociopolitical conditions. Since the mid-1990s, TRP has struggled against ruling party leaders' denigration of same-sex sexualities.[4] Leaders of the South West African People's Organisation (SWAPO) threatened to increase penalties for sodomy and to expel gender and sexual dissidents from Namibia. In light of state hostility to gender and sexual diversity, TRP staff and members approached the public visibility of the organization and LGBT constituents cautiously.

In April 2006, TRP staff took their video project from the capital, Windhoek, to a rural township in southeastern Namibia. Staff used the video project as an opportunity for rural constituents to gather in safe spaces to discuss gender and sexual variance and obstacles to individual-level visibility. On this cloudless night, staff invited LGBT constituents who lived in the area to a shebeen, an informal township tavern, to screen *The Adventures of Priscilla, Queen of the Desert* (1994), a film about a troupe of white Australian drag performers. Owing to a lack of infrastructure in rural Namibia, staff had to string several extension cords together to plug into a nearby generator that powered a television and VCR. It was hard to imagine that any trouble might emerge in this remote, tranquil township, but TRP staff carefully watched their unfamiliar surroundings. Policing the shebeen's entrance, one staff member shooed away inquisitive passersby he presumed to be heterosexual. His vigilance provoked another TRP staff member to object to this exclusionary practice. She asserted, "We are actually chasing away people we want to accept us."

These vignettes about activists' monitoring of public spaces reveal some of the choices Namibian and South African LGBT activists made about their organizations' visibility in different sociopolitical fields. Along with other South African LGBT movement organizations, FEW navigated a complex sociopolitical field in the newly democratizing South Africa. Postapartheid, democratic leaders publicly endorsed LGBT rights. FEW's proximity to the Constitutional Court confirmed working-class, black lesbian women's claims to equality and citizenship in the new South Africa. However, violence and discrimination still encumbered LGBT persons' visibility, necessitating the creation of safe movement spaces with lessened visibility in which LGBT constituents could take refuge. In neighboring Namibia, TRP and Sister Namibia, a feminist movement organization that advocated for LGBT rights, defended their organizations and constituents against ruling party leaders' political homophobia,[5] which stood in contrast to South African leaders' support for LGBT rights. In the late 1990s, former president Sam Nujoma and other SWAPO leaders publicly scorned Namibian gender and sexual dissidents, alleging that they betrayed African cultures by choosing a Westernized sexual modernity over African heterosexuality (Currier 2010b; Lorway 2010).[6] Instead of forcing LGBT activists into invisibility, these repressive statements provoked the public formation of LGBT organizing. Political leaders' stances on gender and sexual diversity helped create sociopolitical fields that were receptive, in the case of South Africa, or hostile, in the case of Namibia, to LGBT activism. In turn, these fields influenced the visibility strategies Namibian and South African LGBT activists developed.

This book addresses the visibility strategies used by LGBT movement organizations in Namibia and South Africa.[7] My main research question in this book is, how, when, and why have Namibian and South African LGBT movement organizations chosen or been forced to become publicly visible or to withdraw from public visibility? Visibility is a robust quality that encompasses different features of social movements. It is not reducible to a movement's presence in the mainstream media or to its cultural popularity. By developing visibility strategies (making strategic choices), activists take steps to control public presentations of their movements, movement organizations, and constituents.

To understand LGBT movement organizations' visibility strategies, I engaged in ethnographic observation of four Namibian and South African LGBT movement organizations, interviewed fifty-six LGBT activists in both countries, and analyzed more than two thousand newspaper articles and organizational documents. Most of my data came from daily, intensive ethnographic observation of two LGBT movement organizations in Johannesburg, South Africa (September 2005 to early April 2006), and two in Windhoek, Namibia (mid-April to July 2006). In Johannesburg, I observed Behind the Mask,[8] an LGBT movement organization that monitors LGBT rights in Africa and media representations of LGBT persons throughout Africa, and FEW,[9] a black lesbian movement organization fighting to eliminate antilesbian violence. In Windhoek, I observed Sister Namibia[10] and TRP.[11]

Visibility strategies arise from activists' *strategic choices,* or their decisions to use movement organizations' emotional, cultural, and material resources to execute a task in the pursuit of a goal (Jasper 2004, 4). These choices influence the successive choices available to activists by constraining or facilitating them, altering the "likelihood of subsequent" choices (Oliver and Myers 2002, 1). Examples of strategic choices include deciding whom to recruit (Klandermans 2004), which protest tactics to use (Taylor and Van Dyke 2004), which audiences to target (Gamson 1975), how to present a collective identity publicly (Bernstein 1997), and whether and how to respond to perceived political opportunities (Blee and Currier 2006). I identify activists, instead of movement organizations, as making decisions, in keeping with James Jasper's (2004) location of agency with embodied social movement actors.

Daily observation of movement organizations' dynamics helped me decipher organizations' internal processes and priorities of leaders, staff, and constituents. Often, studying strategic choices poses difficulties for scholars because "although choices about targeting, timing, and tactics can be directly observed, the strategic 'frame' within which we make these choices—and provide them with their coherence—must often be inferred" (Ganz 2000, 1010). Additionally, dissecting strategic choices can require "vast research," but a narrow focus on types of choices or a finite set of choices can illuminate a movement organization's strategic priorities (Jasper 2004, 11). Therefore I concentrated only on activists' choices related to public visibility and invisibility. Through daily fieldwork with each movement organization, I examined the content of organizations' public profiles and how, when, and why they made themselves visible or invisible to the media, state actors, political parties, the public, LGBT constituents, Northern donors, and international LGBT movement organizations. I did not limit myself to observations that occurred in the office. If an organization staged an event or meeting elsewhere, I gained permission to shadow staff and members. I took detailed notes about staff meetings, informal conversations I had with staff members and visitors, and events that took place at and away from movement organizations' offices. I averaged twenty hours a week of ethnographic observation, and I often divided my time between organizations. This methodological approach enhanced my ability to see the complex strategic choices Namibian and South African LGBT activists made about movement organizations' (in)visibility.[12]

Visibility, Invisibility, and Power

The link between visibility and power tends to be dichotomized in contemporary social theory (Brighenti 2010). Social and feminist theorists often associate positions of being seen with powerlessness and positions of seeing with power (Haraway 1988; Mulvey 1975). Institutions target individual bodies for surveillance (Foucault 1977). Depending on individually ascribed characteristics, such as race, class, gender, sexuality, nationality, physical ability, and age, "some bodies are public and dissected while others are vulnerable to erasure and marginalization" (Casper and Moore 2009, 9). People and groups deemed nonnormative by hegemonic institutions may find themselves relegated to invisibility, which symbolizes their structural disadvantage. Paradoxically, invisibility can lead to hypervisibility, a condition in which visible traits become interpreted as excessive in ways that attract the derision and gaze of a privileged group (Winnubst 2006). In Western societies, affluent, white, gender-normative, able-bodied individuals escape into the privilege of invisibility as the default referents for personhood, whereas people of color, gender-diverse persons, and individuals with visible disabilities often become hypervisible and discredited as less than human (Beauchamp 2009; Bettcher 2007; Carter 2007; Frankenberg 1993; Hammonds 1994). Whereas hypervisible persons cannot control how others view them, as in Erving Goffman's (1986) theory of stigma, those in positions of seeing can close themselves off to public scrutiny, gliding into positions of less visibility (Foucault 1977). The privilege of invisibility can double as normative visibility in the sense that the privilege afforded to dominant groups is rarely openly acknowledged, yet evidence of this privilege is "overtly visible in social spaces" (Steinbugler 2005, 427). In some societies, opposite-gender couples can show their affection openly in public spaces, whereas same-gender couples who demonstrate their fondness for one another may risk harassment from disapproving bystanders.

Visibility confers intelligibility to individuals and objects in Western systems of thought (Mohanty 2003).[13] When individuals, as objects of a knowing gaze, become visible and knowable, they become subjects (Haraway 1988). If researchers can observe a collection of individuals, they can generate knowledge that consolidates individuals into a definable group. One of Michel Foucault's (1978) familiar examples of this process traces the scientific preoccupation with cataloging same-sex desire as a way of treating and curbing it. Meticulous documentation of same-sex desires created homosexuality and heterosexuality as definable human conditions, producing homosexual and heterosexual subjects (Katz 2007); these ideas circulated among white settler colonialists and Christian missionaries in southern Africa, who applied them to their interactions with African women, men, and children (McClintock 1995). According to Foucault (1977), subjects internalized an institutional gaze and disciplined themselves in accordance with prevailing norms in a particular society. In turn, individuals became the subjects of institutions. Sometimes individuals became unruly, disgruntled subjects, motivated to seize power surreptitiously. Colonized groups in African and South Asian contexts mimicked European colonizers as a way to expose colonizers' cultural insecurities (Bhabha 1994), and peasants in Southeast Asia employed disguise and gossip to subtly signal their resistance to domination (Scott 1990).

Visibility and invisibility are not completely separable from one another analytically. Invoking public visibility also implicates those who are not visible and structures that generate invisibility. Visibility is a "complex system of permissions and prohibitions, of presence and absence" (Gordon 2008, 15; emphasis removed). Eve Kosofsky Sedgwick (1990) captures this understanding in her theorizing of the structure of the "closet" for sexual minorities. Individuals come out and publicly disclose their nonnormative sexualities to overcome the isolation of the "closet," the ideological, social, and political mechanisms of heteronormative shame that force sexual minorities to remain silent about their sexual desires (Sedgwick 1990). U.S. LGBT activists used the coming-out strategy to transform private gender- and sexual-minority subjectivities into public LGBT collective identities around which they could mobilize (Armstrong 2002; Chabot and Duyvendak 2002). As a form of "identity deployment," coming out allowed U.S. LGBT activists to use identity strategies to contest how the dominant heteronormative culture perceived the movement and LGBT constituents (Bernstein 1997, 538–39). According to queer theorists, coming out relies on the existence of a closet elsewhere out of which gender and sexual minorities step when they disclose their identities to others (Butler 1991; Sedgwick 1990). Thus, visibility and invisibility are implicated in one another; where one is, so is the other. Visibility and invisibility are not static positions that a person, group, or social movement occupies indefinitely. They are fluctuating conditions that correspond to changes in the sociopolitical fields in which individuals, social groups, and social movements are embedded (Ray 1999).

Many marginalized groups in the global North and South desire visibility, which can double as a desire for political and social recognition (Fraser 1997; Hobson 2003). Yet some queer scholars express skepticism about visibility as a primary vehicle through which LGBT activists in different contexts articulate their grievances (Butler 1991; Hennessy 1994; Manalansan 1995). The emphasis on individual visibility as a collective goal in LGBT organizing has roots in global capitalist modes of individuation that run counter to collective action frames of liberation (Chasin 2000; Duggan 2003; Richardson 2005). In fact, "commercial publicity and democratic political representation" have become conflated as interchangeable registers in LGBT organizing such that gay economic visibility is portrayed as sociopolitical progress, a faulty equation for Eric O. Clarke (2000, 30–31). Some queer theorists object to the strategic pursuit of normalcy in LGBT organizing when activists equate visibility with assimilation. According to some queer theorists, when a LGBT movement achieves a certain visibility for privileged constituents that resembles normalcy, activists will abandon other transformative political projects (Phelan 2001; Warner 1999).[14] According to this logic, attaining a certain type of visibility can depoliticize and demobilize LGBT activists (Duggan 2003). In these queer critiques, visibility is a final result of LGBT activism.

There is another way to conceptualize visibility as a social-movement process. Instead of treating visibility only as an attainable goal, accomplishment, or end result, I treat it as a strategy. Regarding visibility as a strategy prevents scholars from seeing it as a flattened attribute in the sense that social movements are either visible or invisible. As a strategy, movement visibility (or invisibility) unfolds as activists interact with target audiences (Jasper 1997). As activists anticipate changes in the sociopolitical field or certain responses from target audiences, activists modify the forms and content of movement visibility or invisibility. Such changes may elicit desired or unwelcome responses from target audiences. For example, engaging in flamboyant protest tactics can garner media coverage, but the content of the coverage may portray activists in an unflattering light, sparking a trend of negative visibility for the movement (Sobieraj 2011; Taylor and Van Dyke 2004).

I view Namibian and South African LGBT activists as desiring specific visibilities at particular times in particular contexts for their movement organizations; at times, they have chosen less visibility or invisibility for movement organizations and constituents. Similar to the child sexual abuse survivors Nancy Whittier (2009, 181) studied in the United States, gender and sexual dissidents in Namibia and South Africa wanted "visibility to occur on their own terms." LGBT activists in Namibia and South Africa sought resources and spaces that would enable them to forge and control their public visibility and invisibility. My conceptualization of visibility is not limited only to that of LGBT movement constituents. Activists cultivated visibility or invisibility for different elements of the LGBT movement, including for constituents, movement organizations, and the movement itself. Next I outline the theoretical framework guiding my inquiry into visibility strategies, and then I discuss how visibility strategies unfolded in LGBT organizing in postapartheid Namibia and South Africa.

Theoretical Framework

What do visibility and invisibility mean for social movements? Scholars usually associate visibility with effervescent social movements, whereas invisibility constitutes evidence of a movement's decline, a repressive sociopolitical field, or a movement's illegal activities (Koopmans 2004; Taylor 1989; Tilly 2004). Public visibility becomes a way to measure the sociopolitical relevance of a social movement. Unfortunately, this treatment freezes public visibility as a fixed quality, or accomplishment, that movements attain or lose. A common perception in social movement theory is that movements aspire to public visibility. Not all movements attain this elusive goal. As social movements struggle for visibility, very little social movement activity percolates into public view. In this sense, social movements "struggle to be seen" by the general public, sympathizers, potential recruits, the state, targeted social institutions, and the media (Guidry 2003, 493; emphasis removed). Movements labor to publicize their claims to influential political actors, to persuade affluent donors to make financial contributions, to convince diverse stakeholders to participate in public protests, and to sway journalists to cover their activities (Bob 2005; Gitlin 2003; Ryan 1991). In some movements, collective action goes unnoticed by the general public, even though, at the time, it might seem certain that a protest will capture the public's imagination (Koopmans 2004; Sobieraj 2011). Additionally, movements work to control how different audiences see them, not just as representing a particular constituency or advancing a certain grievance but also as supporting a specific ideology or upholding the values of a nation, ethnic group, subculture, or religious tradition (Currier 2010b). Not only are struggles for visibility multiple, but they also pull movements' resources, emotions, and energies in different directions.

My focus on visibility strategies is significant for two reasons. First, activists manage movement visibility and invisibility in complex ways that deserve their own focus. Because activists' quest for (in)visibility cuts across different elements of social movements, including resources, emotions, frames, collective identities, tactics, and strategies, I draw on different strands of social movement theorizing to understand the visibility strategies at work in Namibian and South African LGBT organizing. Second, I recognize that visibility and invisibility as movement qualities have enabled scholars to unearth and understand other social movement processes. Centering visibility strategies in social movement analysis enables scholars, for example, to trace how activists interact with journalists and to explain how internal disagreements necessitate activists' public withdrawal from other audiences. In other words, considering the roles of visibility and invisibility in social movements allows scholars to analyze other social movement processes. In this sense, visibility is a helpful movement diagnostic.

Visibility matters for social movements. This is not an abstract statement but rather one that reflects that visibility has material consequences for social movements. Activists make choices about how they want target audiences to see social movements. Even activists who appear disinterested in managing movements' public profiles may spare some energy for making decisions about their public visibility or invisibility (Haines 2006). Because activists care about how target audiences and bystanders view them and their movements, they devise strategies that synchronize actions with desired outcomes (Jasper 2004). Activists may prioritize certain aspects of a movement for visibility, or different elements of social movements may strive for public visibility (or invisibility) on their own. *Visibility items* can include leaders, a group of activists, constituents, a movement organization, grievances, campaigns, and tactics, among other items.

Visibility encompasses multiple aspects of a social movement's public profile, including its reputation, credibility with target audiences, presence in mainstream and Internet media, and sustained contact with target audiences and constituents. Invisibility involves withdrawal from public interactions, whether intentional or not. *Visibility strategies* refer to activists' efforts to control how target audiences and bystanders view movements, movement organizations, and constituents. I conceptualize "target audiences" more broadly than "targets." Target audiences include institutions, groups, and individuals that movements may not necessarily target for social change but may hope to influence; these audiences may include groups from which movements need something or groups they are trying to elude (McCarthy and Zald 1977; Williams 1995).[15] The media can constitute target audiences if activists desire favorable media coverage for the movement (Rohlinger 2006). Media visibility aids the dissemination of movement organizations' messages and affects how different audiences view movement organizations (Gamson and Wolfsfeld 1993; Gitlin 2003; Koopmans 2004; Ryan 1991; Sobieraj 2011). Yet many opportunities for media visibility are fleeting, making it difficult for groups to publicize their efforts (Koopmans 2004; Sobieraj 2011). However, movement visibility is not reducible to its media visibility.

I treat social movements' public visibility as dynamic, multidirectional, and engaged with multiple audiences, hence the focus on strategy, which shifts with changes in the sociopolitical field. Following Raka Ray (1999, 6), I understand a field as a "structured, unequal, and socially constructed environment *within* which organizations are embedded and *to* which organizations and activists constantly respond." National fields inform how movements craft strategies that reflect or contest local cultural and political norms. The sociopolitical field affects the strategic choices available to activists—what they view as possible strategic action to make themselves visible.

I also view social movements as desiring both visibility and invisibility at different times, instead of assuming that public visibility is always desirable. Regarding social movement actors as actively desiring visibility or invisibility centralizes activist agency and movement strategy (Jasper 2004; Moodie 2002). In addition, I resist positing visibility and invisibility as polar opposites and treat these concepts as complementary and simultaneously coexistent. No social movement group is completely publicly visible or invisible all of the time. In fact, organizations may be visible to one audience and invisible to another simultaneously. Organizations are more likely to maintain partial visibility with different target audiences. In other words, once LGBT movement organizations initially "come out" publicly, they may not remain out. If LGBT movement organizations retreat from public visibility, they do not necessarily withdraw into a political "closet," a concept that more accurately captures individual-level identity processes and does not necessarily reflect how organizational- or movement-level visibility and invisibility unfold. In addition, organizations' visibility and invisibility fluctuate in patterns that do not neatly reflect the coming-out model of entering greater public visibility as individuals reveal their gender or sexual identities to others. Moreover, the reasons for activists' strategic selection of movement or organizational invisibility may at times have more to do with internal crises or material necessity than with overt political hostility.

Activists' intentionality affects the contours of movement (in)visibilities (Taylor and Van Dyke 2004). To cultivate *intentional visibility*, activists work to make a particular item visible to one or more target audiences so that the audience responds in a desired manner. Not only do activists prize certain forms of visibility for their movement organizations, but occasionally, they cultivate *intentional invisibility*. Intentional invisibility can grant movement organizations temporary respite from repression, prying gazes, or unfavorable media coverage, allowing activists to assess their options (Evans and Boyte 1992).[16] Intentional invisibility may resemble *visibility disruptions* as organizations retreat temporarily from public interactions. Visibility disruptions refer to episodes during which movement organizations withdraw from interactions with different audiences, suspend campaigns, or terminate tactical operations, possibly in response to unpredictable or hostile sociopolitical conditions.[17] Invisibility can give activists the conceptual and emotional space to engage in "strategic adaptation," a process in which activists mold their tactics and rhetoric to the changing sociopolitical field (McCammon et al. 2008, 1105). Invisibility also aids in the diagnosis of a movement in distress. If public visibility signals a movement's good health, then invisibility can indicate that a movement is experiencing difficulty. Verta Taylor (1989, 762) explains how "abeyance structures" buoyed the U.S. women's movement, which withdrew from public scrutiny in the hostile sociopolitical environment of the 1950s. In her usage, "abeyance" refers to a "holding process" whereby a hibernating movement waits for more receptive sociopolitical conditions to emerge (Taylor 1989, 761). If a movement disappears from public view for a sustained time, scholars can use its invisibility to detect intramovement discord, cultural hostility to the movement and its goals, and other constraints that inhibit movement actions.

Unintentional visibility results when activists, movement organizations, or movements unwillingly become the focus of attention. Strategic blunders are a common cause of unintentional visibility for social movements (Jasper and Poulsen 1993). Unintentional visibility can acquire a disciplinary quality when target audiences or bystanders attach negative meanings and consequences to activists' actions or messages. *Unintentional invisibility* occurs when activists, movement organizations, or movements lapse into invisibility without cultivating the conditions that would allow them to sustain limited or total invisibility on their own terms. Movements may slip into invisibility if activists become preoccupied with emergencies. Repression can be a source of unintentional invisibility if it overwhelms activists' ability to formulate autonomous strategic decisions (Earl 2003).

Social movements may identify multiple social institutions as targets for their strategies and campaigns (Armstrong and Bernstein 2008). Elizabeth A. Armstrong and Mary Bernstein's multi-institutional politics model is helpful for explaining how social movements navigate multiple, interlocking systems of domination and "subjectivation"—the process whereby individuals become the subjects of institutional power (Butler 1993, 34). Multiple institutions produce multiple modes of domination and subjectivation. Because individuals and social groups regularly interact with a complex array of institutions, it makes sense that some social movements will target more than one institution at a time. In fact, the state may be one of several institutions that a movement targets. In this way, the state becomes decentered as the only institution social movements target with their grievances (Van Dyke, Soule, and Taylor 2004).[18]

Movements juggle multiple public presentations for different audiences (Koopmans 2004). Activists may present the movement or movement organization in one way for one audience and in a remarkably different way for another audience. Thus, visibility strategies result in *multiple visibilities and invisibilities*. Visibility strategies are multidirectional, moving along different vectors to reach target audiences. Activists may create multiple public presentations of their movement organization for different local audiences, resulting in local multiple visibilities for one movement organization (Reger 2002). Achille Mbembe's (2001, 145–48) concept of *simultaneous multiplicities* exemplifies the multiple visibilities movement organizations may cultivate. Movement organizations craft multiple public presentations with differing content and for different audiences, making it possible for two audiences to have divergent understandings of the same organization.[19] If activists present a radical image of a movement organization to one audience and a moderate image to another audience, this might confuse and alienate local target audiences and bystanders who are unsure how to reconcile differing presentations of the organization (Haines 1984). Activists' work controlling public presentations can generate "disagreement and controversy" among target audiences (Einwohner, Reger, and Myers 2008, 8).

Movement organizations develop strategic orientations to public visibility or invisibility. *Strategic orientation* refers to a set of "general logics or templates" that movement organizations develop regarding how they achieve their goals, which tactics they deploy, whom they recruit, which ideologies they espouse, and how they assemble and project their collective identities (Downey and Rohlinger 2008, 6). Activists involved with unpopular movements may develop insular strategic orientations and tend toward lesser visibility or invisibility because they do not want to risk a negative backlash (Simi and

Futrell 2009). Insularity may involve reducing the number of audiences to which movement groups are visible. Conversely, some activists involved with unpopular movements purposely seek attention from multiple audiences to publicize their controversial ideas, strategies, or goals (Blee 2002). Activists engaged in clandestine activities, such as extralegal tactics, may intentionally cultivate invisibility to evade state surveillance or social opprobrium (Earl 2004; Seidman 2001). Strategic orientations can also affect activists' bodily comportment, gender and sexual performativity, and personal style. Tattoos, slogans, and other bodily adornments publicize wearers' allegiance to a movement (Gilman 2009; Scott 2007; Simi and Futrell 2009). Understanding the strategic orientation of movement organizations allows scholars to predict how organizations might react in the future, particularly to matters of visibility and invisibility.

Over time, a movement's visibility and invisibility fluctuate in response to changes in the sociopolitical field. One contribution of political process theory (PPT), which examines how movements interact with the external sociopolitical environment, has been to explain movements' protest cycles (or "waves") of growth and decline (McAdam 1999; Tarrow 2011). PPT offers a way to understand patterns of movement visibility and invisibility over time. In its early stages of development, a movement attracts new adherents and acquires more resources and political clout on its uphill climb on the tracks. Eventually, the movement reaches a zenith in its visibility at the height of its trajectory. (This climb may not be sluggish; it may occur quickly.) On its descent, a movement may experience internal conflicts, adherents' exit, and the loss of resources, all of which contribute to its decline and concomitant invisibility (Ferree 1994; Ghaziani 2008; Klandermans 2004). Some movements dissolve at this point, but others may experience revitalization and begin an ascendant trajectory again (McAdam, Tarrow, and Tilly 2001).

The conditions governing public visibility vary across societies such that forms and strategies of visibility common in the global North may not be viable in the global South. This means that although lessons from LGBT organizing in the global North may be instructive, they do not dictate how visibility strategies unfold in national contexts in the global South (Alexander 2005; Bhaskaran 2004). Not all strategies translate well from one field to another. Cultural differences and political conditions can constrain the diffusion of particular strategies (Chabot and Duyvendak 2002). Transnational linkages also affect how activists manage their (in)visibility in national sociopolitical fields (Keck and Sikkink 1998; Tarrow 2005). The patronage of well-connected, influential Northern donors, nongovernmental organizations (NGOs), and diplomats might enhance the local reputation and resources available to activists in the global South (Bob 2005). Conversely, some African leaders who were active in the national liberation movement might interpret such backing as unwelcome foreign interference in national politics (Hoad 2007). In the Namibian and South African sociopolitical fields, the state constituted an important target audience for LGBT movements, but activists identified additional institutional target audiences besides the state for their visibility strategies.

Visibility Strategies in Namibian and South African LGBT Organizing

The democratic transition away from apartheid rule in Namibia and South Africa began with promise for gender and sexual minorities (Dunton and Palmberg 1996). Pledging equality for all Namibians, SWAPO and liberation hero Sam Nujoma won the postindependence election in 1989 (Bauer 1998; Forrest 1994). In 1994, the African National Congress (ANC) and Nelson Mandela emerged as electoral victors in South Africa (Seidman 1999; Younis 2000). Early in both countries' democratic transitions, lawmakers passed pro-gay legislation. The Namibian Labour Act of 1992 prohibited employers' discrimination of workers on the basis of sexual orientation (Hubbard 2007). In 1996, South African lawmakers permanently enshrined the Equality Clause (EC), a sexual-orientation nondiscrimination clause, in the nation's constitution (Cock 2003; Croucher 2002). With pro-gay legislation in place, wouldn't LGBT movement organizations in both nations have experienced control of their public visibility? Shouldn't they have been able to initiate campaigns, hold public events, and obtain media coverage with little difficulty?

Pro-gay legislation did not translate into control of public visibility for LGBT movement organizations, activists, or constituents. Political leaders' positions on LGBT rights and same-sex sexualities, in conjunction with material constraints, affected Namibian and South African LGBT movement organizations' visibility strategies. Ruling party leaders in Namibia and South Africa developed divergent public stances on LGBT rights. Whereas ANC leaders in South Africa supported LGBT rights, SWAPO leaders in Namibia publicly vilified homosexuality and LGBT rights and ignored pro-gay legislation already in place (Croucher 2002; Currier 2010a; Dirsuweit 2006; Lorway 2006, 2008a, 2008b). In sociopolitical fields characterized by complexity and contradiction, LGBT activists developed nuanced visibility strategies that reflected their historical-material conditions.

Newly Democratizing States and LGBT Organizing

Namibia and South Africa are two of many newly democratizing nations in Africa (Diamond and Plattner 2010). In both countries, decolonization, or national self-determination, provided the "necessary framework for democratization" (Melber 2004, 238).[20] After democratic elections, leaders of newly democratizing African nations experienced a "honeymoon period" (Ndegwa 2001, 2) but had to act before uncertainty undermined citizens' hopes (Przeworski 2010, 2). Postindependence African leaders faced staggering expectations, including improving the provision of social services; responding to gender inequalities, ethnic divisions, and traditional authorities; nurturing economic recovery after decades of colonial plunder and impoverishment; undertaking law reform; and negotiating development assistance from Northern donors and bilateral funding agencies (Fallon 2008; Ferguson 2006; Lynch and Crawford 2011; Sandberg 2000; Sandbrook 2000; Tripp et al. 2009; Young 2004). Although ruling parties in Namibia and South Africa have made great strides since independence, experts have expressed concerns that democratization has stalled (Melber 2003a, 2003b, 2007). Postapartheid democracy in Namibia and South Africa acquired an aura of fragility, leading some scholars to question the direction and nature of future democratic developments, in part because SWAPO and the ANC still remain in power (Bauer 2001; Lynch and Crawford 2011; Melber 2007; Salih 2007).[21] In addition, neoliberal reforms have exacerbated "inequality and marginalization" in both countries (Ferguson 2006, 11).[22]

Democratization in Namibia and South Africa constituted a political opportunity for aggrieved groups to form social movements and press for additional social change (Ballard, Habib, and Valodia 2006; Robins 2008; Susser 2009; Zuern 2011). However, the political opportunity that democratization posed influenced LGBT organizing differently in Namibia and South Africa. In South Africa, lesbian and gay activism has existed since 1966, although it has metamorphosed over time.[23] On the cusp of the democratic transition away from apartheid in the late 1980s and early 1990s, lesbian and gay activists took advantage of national liberation movement frames of equality to encourage ANC leaders to endorse lesbian and gay rights in the reimagined, inclusive South Africa (Cock 2003).[24] Lesbian and gay activists' networking with and lobbying of ANC leaders before the official transition enhanced their political standing and reputation in the postapartheid democracy.

In Namibia, LGBT activism emerged in the mid-1990s after independence. Like lesbian and gay activists in South Africa, LGBT activists in Namibia embraced national liberation movement frames of equality (Lorway 2008b). Rather than affirming that LGBT activists' demands for equality resonated culturally and politically in newly independent Namibia, SWAPO leaders perceived the movement's emergence after independence as cowardly. SWAPO leaders alleged that activists' invisibility as LGBT Namibians before independence meant that they were absent from the national liberation effort. Therefore, their claims to equality after independence were repudiated, as SWAPO leaders argued that the movement's postindependence emergence, coupled with LGBT constituents' gender and sexual nonconformity, disqualified them from national belonging (Currier 2012). Since the 1990s, the Namibian LGBT movement has had an adversarial relationship with SWAPO leaders, whereas the South African LGBT movement has enjoyed a largely receptive relationship with ANC leaders since the democratic transition away from apartheid.

LGBT Movement Visibilities

Colonial and apartheid policies racially segregated Namibia and South Africa. In both countries, authorities strictly regulated same-sex intimacy and prosecuted white men suspected of homosexuality (Botha and Cameron 1997; Jones 2008).[25] The apartheid state's criminalization of homosexuality focused largely on white men, although black, coloured,[26] and Asian Indian men who had sex with men were still vulnerable to police scrutiny (Achmat 1993). In the late 1960s, apartheid lawmakers enlarged their surveillance to include white lesbians (Gevisser 1995). In light of the state's repressive stance on same-sex sexualities, many gender and sexual minorities were forced into positions of unintentional invisibility. Despite the illegality of same-sex sexualities, black and coloured gender and sexual minorities were able to create sanctuaries within their racial communities that evaded state scrutiny (Tucker 2009). In this way, gender and sexual minorities found ways to control their public visibility by retreating into safe spaces. However, retreat did not amount to quiescence. Vibrant lesbian and gay subcultures emerged in different racial communities, nurturing racial, gender, and sexual subjectivities around which lesbian and gay activists would later mobilize (Gevisser 1995).

Inequalities engineered by years of colonial and apartheid rule in both nations created obstacles to LGBT movement organizations' visibility strategies. Most of South Africa's 48.7 million citizens and Namibia's 2.1 million citizens wrestled with poverty, joblessness, and undereducation, problems that extended to black and coloured LGBT persons (World Bank 2008).[27] Whites controlled most of the wealth, despite burgeoning black middle classes in both nations (Southall 2007). Economic inequalities exacerbated racist, sexist, and homophobic violence and discrimination. Rates of reported violent crime were on the rise in South Africa (Samara 2011). In response to perceived widespread violence, affluent whites withdrew into fortified urban enclaves (Dirsuweit 2002). LGBT communities in Namibia and South Africa remained segregated by class and race, although most LGBT movement organizations were multiracial. Reports of violence against women markedly increased (Kandirikirira 2002; Vetten 2007). Black South African lesbians lived with the constant threat of antilesbian rape and violence (Muholi 2004). Homophobic and transphobic violence, much of which was concentrated in black South African townships, increased LGBT persons' risk of contracting HIV/AIDS (Lorway 2006; Muholi 2004; Reid and Dirsuweit 2002). Activists interpreted these threats as endangering the safety of constituents and LGBT movement organizations.

Public visibility was bittersweet for LGBT persons as citizens of these newly independent nations (Lorway 2008a; Tucker 2009). Although lawmakers in each country passed pro-gay legislation early in the democratic transition away from apartheid, black and coloured LGBT persons faced structural and material obstacles preventing them from actualizing their equality. This sentiment is evident in comments made by a black South African drag queen participating in the 1994 Johannesburg Lesbian and Gay Pride March. Referring to lawmakers' approval of the EC, she expressed delight about being "in the constitution" (Gevisser 2000, 111). However, when Mark Gevisser (2000, 136) asked what "her new empowerment meant," she bluntly replied, "My darling, it means sweet motherfucking nothing at all. You can rape me, rob me, what am I going to do when you attack me? Wave the constitution in your face? I'm just a nobody black queen."

Movement organizations recognized how material deprivations rendered black and coloured LGBT persons vulnerable to positions of simultaneous invisibility and hypervisibility (Oswin 2007). To protect constituents and movement organizations in these heteronormative sociopolitical fields, activists embraced the rhetorical frame of equality in their visibility strategies (Oswin 2007; Thoreson 2008). Activists' use of the equality frame both extended and challenged how Namibian and South African liberation movements utilized them. In their challenge to apartheid rule, liberation movements in Namibia and South Africa instigated national discussions about racial and gender equality that determined who belonged in the new nation. Liberation movements' discourses of blackness, Africanness, masculinity, and femininity subsequently affected LGBT organizing.

After assuming office, SWAPO and ANC leaders emphasized racially inclusive societies, but antigay opponents within both societies, some of whom were members of SWAPO and the ANC, argued that this inclusion did not extend to gender and sexual minorities (Gevisser 2000). In their estimation, LGBT persons did not belong in the new nation. For SWAPO leaders, nationalist discourses of Africanness and citizenship depended on gender and sexual normativity; black heterosexual persons could claim Namibian citizenship, but black lesbian and gay persons could not (Currier 2012). Politicians' antigay opposition militated against Namibian gender and sexual minorities' desire "to become visible" and contributed to conditions in which they were "unable to" claim visibility and recognition as citizens (Tucker 2009, 188). In South Africa, black antigay opponents deployed similar arguments claiming that homosexuality was un-African—an undesirable vestige of colonialism (Epprecht 2004; Hoad 2007).[28]

Managing the content of visibility strategies was very important to Namibian and South African LGBT activists. Research on collective identity addresses how activists portray themselves publicly and is helpful in illuminating how activists manage the content of visibility strategies (Dugan 2008). Collective identities arise organically from activists' experiences, desires, emotions, and beliefs (Bernstein 1997; Melucci 1989; Polletta and Jasper 2001; Taylor and Whittier 1992). When individuals come together to probe whether collective action is possible, they forge group understandings of social phenomena that bind them together (Snow and McAdam 2000). Over time, activists reinforce these collective understandings of "we-ness" by delineating outsider–insider boundaries (Gamson 1997). Scholars often equate public visibility strategies with identity movements, which demand recognition from target audiences that the marginalized group's grievances are worthy of material redress and that their identities deserve cultural validation (Fraser 1997).[29] Yet identity strategies are neither reducible to nor synonymous with visibility strategies. Visibility strategies can take the form of identity strategies, but they also involve symbolic and material factors besides collective identity, such as amassing enough activists to convey widespread support for a cause or securing the safety of threatened constituents. It is important to remember that activists do not desire public visibility at all times. In addition, it is not necessarily the case that once visibility items attain visibility, they remain visible. Instead, visibility items cycle in and out of public (in)visibility (Tarrow 2011).

The racialization of discourses of sexuality necessitated that Namibian and South African LGBT movement organizations cultivate an intentional visibility strategy promoting the Africanness of the movement, movement organizations, and constituents. Visibility strategies corresponded to different structural levels of movement organizing such that different movement items acquired multiple visibilities (Stoecker 1995). Structural levels of movements include individual activists or constituents, an entire constituency, a movement organization, a movement, or a movement coalition. When tailoring strategies to different levels of movement organization or items, Namibian and South African LGBT activists anticipated and incorporated negative and positive "feedback" they might receive from target audiences (Bernstein 2008, 290).[30] By publicly presenting their constituents and goals as "African," activists created a particular kind of public visibility for their movement organizations (Guidry 2003; Tilly 2004; Sobieraj 2011). Tapping into preexisting understandings of Africanness, activists wanted organizations *to be seen as* mainstream and credible (Bob 2005; Whittier 2009). Namibian and South African LGBT activists strove to engineer a specific reputation for movement organizations that depended on generating consistent movement presentations and behavior over time (Jasper 2006).

There have been internal divisions within the South African LGBT movement about the content of movement visibility. In the 1980s, white gay and lesbian activists refused to voice their public support for antiapartheid organizing, fearing state retribution (Gevisser 1995). They worried that aligning the lesbian and gay movement with antiapartheid activism would blemish the movement's reputation indelibly. The emergence of multiracial, antiapartheid lesbian and gay South African movement organizations in the 1980s revolutionized the movements' public visibility and initiated a trend of multiracial visibility for the LGBT movement; this trend was observable in Namibia as well. With the exception of FEW, the other Namibian and South African LGBT movement organizations I studied emphasized their multiracial composition as a way to signify their inclusion of individuals from racially and class-diverse backgrounds. Emphasizing organizations' racial inclusion was especially important in light of historic racial inequalities, if activists wanted "any credibility" in the new nation (Johannes, coloured gay man and TRP member, interview with the author, July 11, 2006).

Visibility Strategies in an International Context: LGBT Organizing, the Development Industry, and the Gay International

Behind the Mask, FEW, Sister Namibia, and TRP were "professional" social movement organizations (McCarthy and Zald 1977, 1223). All received funding from Northern donors, had office space, employed full- and part-time staff, held office meetings routinely, and developed internal regulations governing organizational activities. Professionalization encouraged activists to develop *visibility routines* that affected the forms that constituent, organizational, and movement visibilities took. As movement organizations settled into predictable routines, certain strategic choices became "quotidian" and expected (Borland and Sutton 2007, 708). Such routines involved LGBT activists' monitoring of public spaces and defining who could access organizations.

Organizations constructed interior spaces that served as sanctuaries for some LGBT constituents, allowing them to socialize with other LGBT persons away from public scrutiny. These spaces responded to the "psychological needs of insecure and harassed gays and lesbians" (Palmberg 1999, 267). Safe spaces allow individuals "to learn a new self-respect, a deeper and more assertive group identity, public skills, and values of cooperation and civic virtue" (Evans and Boyte 1992, 17; see also Gamson 1996; Morris 1984). These spaces functioned as sites of intentional invisibility when constituents sought solace in the company of people with similar experiences, including experiences of victimization. These spaces also fostered oppositional consciousness and counterpublicity that contested heteronormative spaces (Stockdill 2003; Warner 2002). Organizations like FEW controlled who could access these interior spaces. Spaces of retreat did not necessarily signal LGBT activists' quiescence; these spaces permitted activists to regroup and plan their next moves. Without funding from Northern donors, these safe spaces within Behind the Mask, FEW, Sister Namibia, and TRP would not have existed. Although scholars typically regard office space only as a movement resource, office and other movement spaces confirmed movement organizations' legitimacy for Northern donors and became hubs for movement activity (Cress and Snow 1996).

Behind the Mask, FEW, Sister Namibia, and TRP cultivated Northern donors, particularly "private funding agencies," as target audiences to obtain funding (Michael 2004, 59).[31] Northern donor funding of LGBT organizing in Namibia and South Africa reflects two developments. First, LGBT activism in Namibia and South Africa entered the orbit of the "global development industry," which Amy Lind (2009, 34) defines as "including multilateral institutions, bilateral aid agencies, state agencies," and NGOs that "play a pivotal role in governing people's sexual and familial lives." Gender and sexual minorities emerged as groups "worthy" of development aid in relation to their vulnerability to HIV/AIDS and political homophobia (Mindry 2001, 1189; see also Lind 2010). Second, Northern donor funding contributed to the *NGO-ization* of LGBT organizing, which refers to the structuring of social movements in a way that favors centralized, hierarchical patterns of decision making (Alvarez 1998; de la Dehesa 2010).

LGBT activists in Namibia and South Africa worked to project technocratic competency to convince Northern donors that they could manage funding well (Britton 2006).[32] Resource-rich movement organizations with staff and volunteers could devote more resources to the management of multiple visibilities, whereas organizations with fewer resources would have to focus on their presentation with one or two audiences and suspend communication with other audiences, resulting in temporary invisibility (McCarthy and Zald 1977). Donor funding and relationships with international LGBT movement organizations facilitated Namibian and South African LGBT activists' networks with activists elsewhere in Africa, buttressing their international visibility. Thus, LGBT movement organizations were not entirely beholden to Northern donors and LGBT activists; instead, they were able to use these resources in ways that benefited a growing African LGBT movement.

In the form of knowledge and transnational advocacy, resources also flowed from Northern-based international LGBT movement organizations, such as the International Gay and Lesbian Human Rights Commission (IGLHRC), to Namibian and South African LGBT movement organizations (Keck and Sikkink 1998). IGLHRC and other organizations that promote LGBT rights throughout the world make up the "Gay International," a circuit of organizations that Joseph Massad (2002, 362) and others regard as engaged in the "missionary tasks" of bringing Western-style gay liberation to the global South (Hoad 2007; Manalansan 1995; Puar 2007). While some interrogate the accuracy of this characterization of transnational LGBT organizing, this criticism of the Gay International surprisingly dovetails with antigay suspicion in Namibia and South Africa of the international dimensions of Namibian and South African LGBT movement organizations' visibility strategies (Boellstorff 2008). Some leaders invested in African nationalism interpreted activists' receipt of Northern funding as LGBT movement organizations being in the pockets of Northern governments, donor agencies, and activists (Hoad 2007). Receiving funding from Northern donors put LGBT movement organizations in the position of pitting one target audience against another; this necessitated crafting more than one strategy for target audiences (Armstrong and Bernstein 2008). In this way, the international dimension and alleged foreignness of LGBT movement organizations' visibility threatened to undercut their credibility with state actors and unsympathetic audiences within their national sociopolitical fields.

Some scholars argue that NGO-ization is a disempowering development in the global South (Michael 2004; Nzegwu 2002). Through this process, movement organizations become less accountable to constituents and activists, eroding their democratic procedures (Eschle and Stammers 2004). For instance, donors might attach demands to funding that require movement organizations' greater visibility to them (Markowitz and Tice 2002). If donors asked to see organizations' bookkeeping records, activists had to comply or risk losing funding. Organizations' visibility with donors could acquire a disciplinary quality if donors insisted on organizational transparency. In this case, transparency amounted to organizations' total visibility with donors, rendering them quite vulnerable to donor decisions that would adversely affect their operations.

Satisfying donors' requests contributed to some LGBT movement organizations' unintentional invisibility with constituents. While organizations concentrated on their relationships with donors, they unwittingly became invisible to members, a development about which some members complained.

Jansen, a black gay man and TRP member, stated that after TRP distributed evaluation forms to members in 2000 after a workshop, "there is nothing happening" (interview with the author, May 29, 2006). Before our interview, Jansen learned that TRP was holding another workshop, an event that surprised him. He stated, "I don't know what happened. . . . Like I told you, since 2004 until now, I just heard yesterday or before yesterday that there's another workshop. What happened between 2000 and 2005?" Members who did not live in Windhoek or surrounding townships registered similar feelings about TRP's invisibility, an example of how office locations affected movement organizations' relationships with constituents. Peter, a black gay man and TRP member who lived in Swakopmund, a town in western Namibia on the Atlantic coast, explained that he and other TRP members who lived in the area did not "even know what the social events are they are doing there in Windhoek—anything. We don't know anything. We don't even know the members" (interview with the author, May 19, 2006). Peter wanted more frequent contact with TRP but opined that staff ignored members who lived outside of Windhoek because they were "concerned about the resources, I mean, about the money they have to spend" on transportation, lodging, and meals for TRP members who live outside of Windhoek. Peter maintained that many Namibians were resourceful and made it to events in the capital without financial assistance from TRP. "But it's not always that you are depending on them to pay for your transport fees. As long as they contacted you in advance so you can make plans for yourself to get there." Invisibility was not limited to intentional withdrawal from target audiences; it could include involuntary, unplanned lapses in organizational visibility.

An Overview of the Book

I analyzed Namibian and South African LGBT movement organizations' visibility strategies thematically.[33] This approach enabled me to trace similarities and differences in organizations' strategic orientations toward public visibility, invisibility in times of political opportunity, and strategies for challenging discourses alleging that homosexuality was un-African. I tracked movement organizations' public presentations, variations in these public presentations, and how different audiences, such as Northern donors and state officials, influenced activists' choices about their public (in)visibility and presentation. When analyzing activists' visibility strategies, I resist making pronouncements about organizations' public visibility, keeping in mind my criticism of theories that treat public visibility and invisibility as static positions movement organizations occupy. Thus, I make no assertions that one organization is more publicly visible than another. Such a statement would make little sense, given that visibility and invisibility remain slippery, objective measures for social movement scholars (Koopmans 2004; Vliegenthart, Oegema, and Klandermans 2005).

Chapter 1 examines the emergence of LGBT organizing first in South Africa and then in Namibia. White gay and lesbian South Africans quietly organized in the late 1960s to counter the apartheid state's repressive tactics. As antiapartheid organizing intensified in the 1970s and 1980s, the lesbian and gay movement struggled to remain politically relevant. Black lesbian and gay activists challenged white activists who were unwilling to oppose apartheid publicly or to recruit nonwhite lesbians and gay men. In conjunction with antiapartheid activism, LGBT activists recruited individuals of different races to form multiracial movement organizations to work for racial and sexual equality. Activists convinced ANC leaders to support LGBT rights in the postapartheid, democratic transition in the 1990s. The Namibian LGBT movement is much younger than the South African movement. In 1995, SWAPO leaders unleashed political homophobia for the first time, eliciting responses from LGBT activists who publicly refuted leaders' antigay remarks and proceeded cautiously with their strategies.

Chapter 2 extends my theorizing about how Namibian and South African LGBT movement organizations' strategic choices about their public visibility are not uniform. I show how FEW and Sister Namibia cultivated different strategic orientations to visibility as lesbian movement organizations, even though both confronted antilesbian hostility. Antilesbian violence haunted black South African lesbians who lived in Johannesburg and local townships. In response to violent surroundings, FEW developed an orientation to public visibility that protected black lesbians and the organization's public reputation. This chapter recounts black lesbian activists' experiences protesting at the rape trial of Jacob Zuma, the current president of South Africa, amid fiercely devoted pro-Zuma supporters. In contrast with FEW, Sister Namibia cultivated an inclusive strategic orientation. Sister Namibia became known as a controversial lesbian organization for regarding lesbian rights as women's rights and publicly countering SWAPO leaders' homophobic comments, a reputation the organization leveraged into donor funding and international recognition.

Recognizing invisibility as helpful in diagnosing missed opportunities, in chapter 3, I consider different ways in which movement organizations miss political opportunities. I show how and why South African LGBT movement organizations failed to mobilize immediately after the Constitutional Court ruled in favor of same-sex marriage late in 2005 and early in 2006. In Namibia, TRP deferred launching a public law-reform campaign because of

SWAPO leaders' homophobia and internal conflicts over the organization's strategic priorities.

In chapter 4, I look at how Namibian and South African LGBT activists negotiated "homosexuality-is-un-African" discourse. Activists responded to assertions that they were "gay for pay." Behind the Mask and TRP faced the gay-for-pay dilemma of being perceived as un-African because they received funding from Northern donors. By accepting money from Northern donors, they were seen by antigay opponents as doing the bidding of foreigners. Without funding, Behind the Mask and TRP would have had to suspend their projects and fire staff members. Activists also struggled with how to present a pan-African LGBT movement to the African Commission on Human and Peoples' Rights (ACHPR). They were concerned that unfavorable visibility at the ACHPR could result in negative consequences for local organizing and for LGBT persons in different African countries. With input from representatives from IGLHRC, activists assembled a coherent strategy for making LGBT movement claims visible and intelligible to commissioners.

In the conclusion, I reflect on how visibility and invisibility mattered to Namibian and South African LGBT activists. In particular, I revisit the meanings visibility strategies had for activists. The phrase "visibility matters" refers to the strategic priority that public visibility held for activists involved with Behind the Mask, FEW, Sister Namibia, and TRP. It also evokes the material and symbolic features of visibility strategies. Public visibility and invisibility generated both advantageous and harmful consequences for LGBT movement organizations, outcomes that activists sought to control, albeit not always successfully. I end the book by discussing how visibility and invisibility as movement strategies may matter in studies of social movements.

1

The Rise of LGBT Organizing
in Namibia and South Africa

This chapter provides a historical overview of LGBT organizing in Namibia and South Africa.[1] After examining the effects of repression on social movement visibility strategies, I consider how racial, gender, and sexual ideologies intertwined and buttressed the apartheid state's repressive policing of sexuality. My historical examination of LGBT movement visibility strategies begins in South Africa because the movement there has a much longer history than the Namibian movement.

Lesbian and gay resistance in South Africa coalesced in response to apartheid state repression in the late 1960s. White lesbians and gay men dominated the movement's early years, but activists struggled to maintain the movement's visibility in the 1970s in the face of state hostility. In the 1980s, white lesbian and gay activists experienced national and international pressure to adopt a multiracial visibility representative of South African society and to abandon an apolitical visibility in favor of supporting antiapartheid efforts. The ANC, political parties, and the state emerged as important target audiences for the movement in the democratic transition away from apartheid in the late 1980s and early 1990s. When pressing for LGBT rights, activists developed a moderate visibility strategy; activists strategically couched their demands for LGBT rights in terms of inclusion, a framework that state leaders embraced in their effort to undo apartheid-era exclusionary practices. In 1996, lawmakers enshrined the EC, a sexual-orientation nondiscrimination clause, in the South African Constitution, which removed many legal barriers to LGBT constituents' public visibility. Within this newly democratizing context, LGBT movement organizations proliferated and tackled new and lingering inequalities. The existence of multiple, specialized LGBT movement organizations enabled activists to develop their own agendas and organization-specific visibility strategies.

LGBT organizing in Namibia surfaced in response to SWAPO leaders' political homophobia. After Namibia gained independence from South Africa in 1989 in a settlement negotiated by the United Nations (UN), SWAPO assumed control of the postindependence democratic government. Gender and sexual minorities believed that SWAPO's platform of equality for all Namibians included them. However, SWAPO officials' antigay comments in 1995 indicated that the ruling party intended to render LGBT persons invisible in the newly democratizing Namibia. Instead of forcing LGBT persons into unintentional invisibility, SWAPO officials' statements fomented visible resistance to their political homophobia. Beginning in 1995, Sister Namibia demanded that SWAPO leaders retract their harmful statements, and late in 1996, TRP emerged to challenge SWAPO. Sister Namibia and TRP forged ties with national and international audiences. In Namibia, they worked with human rights NGOs and independently owned media, and they pursued international visibility to obtain funding from Northern donors and support from international LGBT movement organizations.

Apartheid Repression in South Africa

Formally implemented in 1948 when the National Party (NP) came to power, the apartheid principle of "separate development" enforced racial segregation in South Africa and South West Africa (now Namibia), a former German colony that South Africa annexed in 1915 (Posel 1987, 125). In 1950, lawmakers passed the Population Registration Act, legislation compelling individuals to register their race with the state (Posel 2001). The regime banished many black Namibians and South Africans to ethnic homelands, reducing many to extreme poverty. The regime also controlled nonwhites' mobility with pass laws and blocked nonwhites from accessing skilled jobs and better educational opportunities (Mamdani 1996). Although the apartheid regime politically excluded nonwhites through legislation, whites needed nonwhites' labor to propel South Africa's industrial development forward. The simultaneous economic exploitation and political exclusion of nonwhites nurtured a disgruntled working class from which the ANC and labor unions recruited (Seidman 1994; Younis 2000).

The apartheid regime used an array of repressive tactics to force political dissenters into involuntary invisibility. The regime detained, tortured, and killed antiapartheid activists whom the state labeled as "terrorists," unleashed indiscriminate police violence on protestors, censored the publication and distribution of material critical of the regime, and subjected suspected dissidents to state surveillance (Seidman 2001, 120; Younis 2000). These actions conform to standard understandings of state repression: "actions taken by government authorities (or other elites) to impede mobilization of social movement participants; harass and intimidate activists; divide organizations; and physically assault, arrest, imprison and kill movement members" (Stockdill 2003, 121).

Invisibility is a common outcome of state repression when the state seeks to snuff out dissent. Activists' public visibility can elicit brutal state responses, necessitating the development of mechanisms for managing movement (in)visibility. State repression can force activists to demobilize and abandon activism or to retreat into spaces of refuge (Earl 2003). Yet if repression is supposed to force movements into invisibility, why do some movements persist in seeking public visibility? Activists may insist on engaging in public action, despite the risks, if they perceive that the situation will worsen if they do not act (Almeida 2003).[2]

Soft repression sometimes accompanies hard state repression (Ferree 2004). *Hard repression* entails the use of violence to quash political organizing, whereas *soft repression* involves nonviolent means to discourage or eliminate "oppositional ideas" and mobilization (Ferree 2004, 88). The apartheid regime's deployment of "controlling images" constituted soft repression, which helped maintain white supremacy (Hill Collins 2000, 85). Controlling images denigrated blackness and Africans, elevated whites and whiteness, and vilified same-sex sexualities, which Afrikaner nationalist ideology portrayed as unnatural and abnormal (Gunkel 2010). Controlling images metamorphosed into controlling visibilities for sexual minorities of all races, constraining the strategic choices available to lesbian and gay activists in this repressive sociopolitical field. Controlling visibilities attached both to individuals and groups and limited what they could do, where they could go, and what they perceived as possible. Operating as a form of stigma, controlling visibilities were inescapable until gender and sexual dissidents developed strategies that challenged and undermined them.

How Race, Gender, and Sexuality Were Linked under Apartheid

Racial, gender, and sexual ideologies formed the basis of controlling visibilities in colonial and apartheid Namibia and South Africa. European cultural anxieties about race, gender, and sexuality found expression in scientific theories of degeneracy and eugenics, which circulated among European colonizers in Africa in the mid- to late-nineteenth century (McClintock 1995).[3] Focused on preserving racial purity, these theories prescribed that people should have sex with individuals of the opposite gender but of the same race and class.

According to Anne McClintock (1995, 47), bodily "boundaries were felt to be dangerously permeable and demanding continual purification, so that sexuality, in particular women' sexuality, was cordoned off as the central transmitter of racial and hence cultural contagion." Using "sexual ambiguity" to mark racial boundaries, scientific experts racialized normality as white and identified monogamous, procreative heterosexuality as natural sexuality (Somerville 1994, 252).[4] Nonmonogamous, nonreproductive, interracial, and same-sex sexual behavior constituted nonnormative sexual practices that the colonial state sought to eradicate. Thus, one source of homophobia in Namibia and South Africa was European ideology.

Racial, gender, and sexual ideologies underscored colonial and, subsequently, apartheid authority, which rested on colonizers' perception that their visible, racial difference from Africans translated into white racial supremacy (McClintock 1995). Belief in whites' racial superiority motivated Afrikaner nationalism.[5] In the early twentieth century, whites of British heritage controlled most sectors of the economy in South Africa, save agriculture, and many white Afrikaners lived in poverty (Thompson 2001). Afrikaners' economic hardship contributed to the consolidation of racial segregation policies, which extended colonial policies of racial separation and Christian nationalism.[6] These policies worsened economic conditions for many black Africans, most of whom "were preoccupied with day-to-day survival" (Thompson 2001, 156). "Afrikaner 'freedom' came to be understood as freedom to exercise racial hegemony. The right to be 'white' was yoked to the rightlessness of 'nonwhites'" (Steyn 2001, 32).

Afrikaner nationalism relied not only on racial distinctions but also on gender distinctions. White women served as "boundary markers" for "race and gender purity" (McClintock 1995, 377). In fact, patriarchal nationalist ideology expected white women, in their roles as mothers, to protect Afrikaner culture and youth. Afrikaner nationalism created similarly controlling visibilities for black women and men. Building on colonialist mythology that Africans were exclusively heterosexual, apartheid supporters disparaged Africans' fertility and heterosexualities (Epprecht 2008). Comparing African sexualities to European sexualities, colonialists alleged that African sexualities were aberrant and deviant (Arnfred 2004; Lewis 2011).[7] Such controlling images contributed to twentieth-century "Black Peril" sex panics that portrayed black men as sexually assaulting white women (McCulloch 2000). Whites also expressed concerns about the presence of black women in urban areas, fearing black women would seduce white men (Keegan 2001). In reality, white men were more likely to abuse or exploit black women sexually, but white men were largely invisible as culpable subjects in legal narratives (Phillips 2011). Concerns about miscegenation spurred formal injunctions on interracial sex as a way to preserve white racial purity.[8] In this context, African women and men became hypervisible sexual subjects of apartheid.

The apartheid regime's strict policing of sexuality installed heterosexuality as normative for all South Africans and continued the legacy of colonial homophobia (Gunkel 2010). Apartheid "ideology was based on keeping the white nation not only racially pure, but 'morally' pure as well" (Cage 2003, 14). Outlawing sex between men, antisodomy laws served this purpose and mandated the invisibility of same-sex sexualities (Botha and Cameron 1997). White men's same-sex sexuality worried lawmakers, who viewed it "as an alien threat to the Afrikaner domain of masculinity" (Jones 2008, 403). Beginning in the 1940s, police engaged in "low-key surveillance" of gay areas, inhibiting the visibility of gay men (Botha and Cameron 1997, 21). In contrast, white lesbians were already invisible as apartheid leaders assumed lesbians existed in "lesser numbers than homosexual men" (Retief 1995, 103). Dominant attitudes presumed that white women lacked "sexual agency," and in such settings, sex between women "is not outlawed because it is not imagined to exist" (Bacchetta 2002, 951). According to patriarchal heteronormativity in different ethnic groups in South Africa, lesbians were expected to marry as their homosexuality was not acknowledged and remained invisible (Lewis and Loots 1995).

Although the apartheid regime maintained an "obsessive interest" in policing white gay men's sexualities, authorities responded to black men's same-sex sexuality in contradictory ways (Cage 2003, 14). Antihomosexuality laws and discourses were intended to restore white men's masculinity and sexual purity, allowing the apartheid regime to develop the "strength to resist the black communist onslaught" (Retief 1995, 100). This political propensity might suggest that the regime ignored same-sex sexual practices among black and coloured men in favor of policing white men. On the contrary, authorities targeted black men who had sex with men for prosecution for sodomy (Achmat 1993). Black men "were three to four times more likely to be convicted than whites" of sodomy in the mid-twentieth century; between the mid-1970s and early 1990s, black men were almost "ten times more likely to be prosecuted for sodomy" than white men (Botha and Cameron 1997, 16, 18).

Although NP authorities prosecuted black men for sodomy, some quietly sanctioned black men's same-sex sexual practices. Some black men engaged in same-sex intimacy in single-sex housing in township hostels and mines (Elder 1995; Harries 1990). For the sake of profit margins, mine managers tolerated these relationships as long as they did not disrupt mine operations (Moodie 1988). Apartheid authorities knew about black same-sex relationships in these environs but believed that these relationships channeled black men's sexualities, "limiting the possibility of sexual activity with white women" (Tucker 2009, 110).

Controlling visibilities created by apartheid authorities limited what gender and sexual dissidents perceived as social and political possibilities. However, controlling visibilities did not extinguish dissidents' agency, even in the face of police surveillance and repressive antihomosexuality legislation. In 1957, lawmakers passed the Sexual Offences Act (No. 23 of 1957), legislation that reinforced lesbian and gay invisibility (Cage 2003). The act banned private gatherings of two or more gay men, which "meant that gay clubs and gay restaurants were theoretically operating illegally" (Reddy 1998, 69). State repression prompted gay men and lesbians to turn inward and concentrate on building gay cultural institutions, such as bars, social spaces, "health clubs,"[9] and publications; these activities allowed white gay subcultures to exist but to remain publicly invisible (Gevisser 1995).[10] There was safety in invisibility. Black and coloured communities developed indigenous spaces, such as drag shows, in which gender and sexual minorities socialized (Chetty 1995). These cultural spaces also acted as "indigenous" free spaces that nurtured the formation of sexual subjectivities that would serve as the basis for mobilizable lesbian and gay collective identities (Polletta 1999, 10–11). Although state repression appeared to drive gender and sexual dissidents underground, they could be found if one knew where to look. In this way, gender and sexual dissidents created pockets of limited visibility for themselves in different racial communities that survived state surveillance (Tucker 2009).

South African Lesbian and Gay Organizing, 1960s–1970s

White lesbians and gay men emerged from positions of invisibility in the 1960s when it appeared that apartheid leaders were on the verge of escalating state repression of gender and sexual minorities. However, the decision to pursue visibility was not easy for activists in the context of widespread hostility. In the 1960s, apartheid authorities took action against any group they viewed as sowing the seeds of revolt. Thus, apartheid leaders did not single out gender and sexual dissidents for harassment; lesbian and gay activism was part of a constellation of organized resistance groups the NP portrayed as enemies of the state. As apartheid leaders became nervous about independence movements in neighboring countries, they remained determined to uphold white supremacy (Frederickson 2002).[11] Within South Africa, covert resistance to apartheid erupted into public protest and armed conflict in both Namibia and South Africa (Leys and Saul 1995). Some antiapartheid movement leaders went into exile and pressured Western governments to take action against South Africa, while others, such as Nelson Mandela, were imprisoned for opposing the apartheid state (Younis 2000). Fearing conspiratorial plots to overthrow apartheid rule, NP leaders recommended infiltrating and spying on "black African, communist, Jewish, and English" groups; apartheid authorities added gay groups to this list (Tucker 2009, 41). Intent on eradicating same-sex sexualities among whites, police raided white gay bars, massage parlors, and clubs between the 1950s and 1970s (Gevisser 1995).

Hard state repression made white gay men and lesbians question whether they should engage in public organizing in the 1960s. Few were "prepared to 'go public' as leaders" (Gevisser 1995, 45). This reticence changed in January 1966, after police raided a private party in a Johannesburg suburb and arrested white gay men in attendance (Gevisser 1995; Isaacs and McKendrick 1992). The raid and proposed amendments to the Sexual Offences Act (No. 23 of 1957) in 1968 prompted white lesbians and gay men to organize politically, albeit from a position of protected visibility. If they did not oppose proposed repressive legislation, gender and sexual minorities' legal and social situation could worsen.

In 1968, organized lesbian and gay resistance to legislated invisibility emerged. White lesbians and gay men launched the Homosexual Law Reform Fund, known simply as "Law Reform," to oppose proposed amendments to the Sexual Offences Act that would criminalize sex between women and increase penalties for sex between men (Gevisser 1995, 32).[12] Parliamentary proceedings tasked with revising the Sexual Offences Act exposed lawmakers' obsession with policing same-sex sexual practices (Botha and Cameron 1997).[13] White lesbians were initially invisible in the movement, in keeping with gay men's exclusion of lesbians from gay venues because "in the patriarchal society of apartheid South Africa, these places were the hunting grounds of men only" (Cage 2003, 11). In this repressive field, Law Reform members developed an insular strategic orientation to visibility that guided how they publicized their meetings and whom they included in the organizing effort. Their first meeting, on April 10, 1968, constituted the "first gay public meeting ever held in South Africa" (Gevisser 1995, 32). Members advertised the meeting "by word of mouth and by very discreet pamphleteering in the bars. About 100 people attended. There was strict screening at the door—to prevent intrusion by either police or the media" (Gevisser 1995, 32). Activists favored protected visibility throughout the campaign, which lasted for several months.

This guarded visibility strategy also influenced Law Reform's cultivation of a moderate approach to lawmakers' threats of repressive legislation. Instead of mobilizing the white gay and lesbian community for a sustained campaign to change public opinion about same-sex sexuality, Law Reform members targeted only lawmakers and organized "quietly and professionally, attempting to protect themselves by carving a niche within apartheid South Africa while not disrupting the status quo" (Gevisser 1995, 35). However, the "threat of repression galvanised the gay subculture, creating community as never before" (Gevisser 1995, 33). Law Reform members persuaded lawmakers to drop some of the more severe criminal measures, although lawmakers passed amendments that prohibited the sale and distribution of dildos, raised the age of consent to sex between men from sixteen to nineteen, and criminalized the congregation of two or more men for the purpose of "sexual gratification" (Gevisser 1995, 35; see also Gunkel 2010). Thus, antisodomy laws remained intact. Law Reform quickly disintegrated, owing to the organization's single-issue orientation (Gevisser 1995).

After the disappearance of Law Reform, the lesbian and gay movement entered a period of invisibility in the 1970s. As a subculture, white lesbians and gay men concentrated on creating venues for socializing, rather than mobilizing around political goals, and intentionally cultivated invisibility (Gevisser 1995). Though several white lesbian and gay movement organizations were launched in the 1970s, most did not come into public view because they did not widely advertise their goals, or they withered under state scrutiny (Gevisser 1995). A few gay publications emerged and quickly disappeared in the late 1970s. Gay magazines were financially unsustainable, owing in part to state censorship (Botha and Cameron 1997).

Although police raids of gay clubs abated after 1969, they resumed in the late 1970s amid the social opprobrium that alleged drug and alcohol abuse brought (Gevisser 1995). Some lesbians and gay men depicted a police raid at a bar named the New Mandy's[14] as the South African equivalent of the Stonewall raid and gay protests in New York City. Gay men "were manhandled [by police], photographed, verbally abused, and kept locked up in the building until morning. There were a few black gay men present at the club, and they came in for the harshest treatment" (Gevisser 1995, 47). Police maltreatment of black gay men was not surprising, given that the state convicted black men of sodomy at a higher rate than white men (Botha and Cameron 1997). The raid, along with one the next year at the same club, led some black and white gay men to "begin talking of rights once more" (Gevisser 1995, 47). Although the New Mandy's raid did not catalyze the union of lesbian–gay and antiapartheid organizing, some whites' growing resentment of state repression positioned the movement in the mid-1980s to have more in common with the antiapartheid movement than it had in the past. However, white lesbian and gay activists still favored guarded visibility in this repressive sociopolitical field. In addition, the public face of the movement remained white, a condition that did not change until the 1980s.

South African Lesbian and Gay Organizing and Antiapartheid Activism in the 1980s

As mass antiapartheid opposition erupted publicly in the 1970s and 1980s, the South African sociopolitical field began to change. Overseas sentiment was turning against the apartheid regime as groups elsewhere expressed solidarity with the plight of nonwhite South Africans. More groups in South Africa voiced opposition to apartheid (Marx 1992). In this changing sociopolitical field, white lesbian and gay activists faced a visibility dilemma: should they publicly oppose apartheid or remain silent?

Preferring apolitical visibility, some white, middle-class gay men and lesbians did not want to provoke the state's hostility by challenging institutionalized racism. Remaining apolitical proved difficult while a mass antiapartheid movement was brewing. As antiapartheid activists expressed their discontent more vocally in the mid- and late 1970s, moderate white Afrikaner leaders, such as President P. W. Botha, claimed that Afrikaners "must adapt or die" (Welsh 2000, 479). Such a change required a corresponding transformation of Afrikaner nationalist ideals, which historically had been "synonymous with white male interests, white male aspirations and white male politics" (McClintock 1995, 369). Botha's proposed constitutional reforms included "giving Asian Indian and coloured persons the right to vote in their own separate parliamentary chambers; abolishing pass laws restricting the movement of Blacks into cities; increasing spending on Black education; and abandoning the laws prohibiting interracial sex and marriage" (Olzak, Beasley, and Olivier 2002, 28). However, Botha and his NP supporters intended these reforms "to manage conflict" and eliminate antiapartheid activism, forcing organized resistance into invisibility (Meer 1984, 84).

White lesbian and gay movement organizations distanced themselves from antiapartheid organizing in the early 1980s and forged an apolitical reputation. One reason was that some white, middle-class gay men were racist (Kraak 2005, 123). Although bars and nightclubs, such as the New Mandy's, were slowly becoming racially integrated, some white gay men worried that "people of colour [were] 'taking over,'" and they enforced racial segregation in gay venues (Isaacs and McKendrick 1992, 94). Additionally, "there was very little sense of a black gay community. So for white political activists the spheres of political and gay identities just did not come together, as they might have in a Western country" (Kraak 2005, 123).

In April 1982, white, middle-class gay men and lesbians launched the Gay Association of South Africa (GASA), the first national-level lesbian and gay movement organization, which cultivated apolitical visibility. More than twenty years after the launch of GASA, Ann Smith (2005), a white lesbian founding member of GASA, acknowledged the short-sightedness of GASA's apolitical visibility and of white activists' refusal to frame gay liberation as a larger problem of social and political oppression that sexual minorities, women, and nonwhite South Africans faced. GASA had little in common with other liberation movements, save a "kind of basic feminism. . . . Women were fighting for equality and so were we" (Smith 2005, 60).[15]

Western lesbian and gay activists pressured white South African lesbian and gay activists to embrace nonwhite constituents and to oppose apartheid publicly, generating a transnational dimension for South African sexual politics. GASA's marginalization of black members and its apolitical visibility contributed to its negative reputation internationally. In 1983, the International Lesbian and Gay Association (ILGA) discussed whether to decline GASA's application for membership after it refused to take a stand on apartheid (Croucher 2002). If ILGA was going to reject GASA's membership request for this reason, GASA's representative asserted that other ILGA members "must be scrutinised for their lack of inclusiveness towards women and racial or ethnic minorities" (Rydström 2005, 35). Fearing apartheid state repression, GASA leaders still did not oppose apartheid (Smith 2005). According to some GASA members, providing a "racially integrated space" was "not just the best we could do, it was all we could do" (Smith 2005, 61).

ILGA and black GASA members, such as Simon Nkoli (1995), disagreed that racially integrated space granted black lesbians and gay men access to GASA or resulted in a lasting multiracial visibility. In black activists' view, multiracial visibility signaled social and political inclusion. Nkoli joined GASA in 1983 and formed an internal group of black gay men that met at GASA's office, which frustrated white members who feared that the presence of black gay men in GASA spaces would elicit police scrutiny (Gevisser 1995). In 1976, Nkoli joined the Congress of South African Students, and in 1984, he was arrested and jailed with other antiapartheid activists for murdering a supposed police informant at the funeral of victims killed by police in Sebokeng (Luirink 2000). Much to the dismay of his comrades, Nkoli came out as gay while he was in prison, undermining the notion that homosexuality was un-African (Kraak 2005). Nkoli gained international visibility as a bridge between gay and antiapartheid organizing, as lesbian and gay antiapartheid activists in the global North supported him (Gevisser 1995).

GASA's silence about Nkoli's imprisonment confirmed its apolitical visibility for ILGA members, who grew concerned that no South African lesbian and gay movement organization would "[reach] out to black people" (Rydström 2005, 37). In August 1986, the formation of the Rand Gay Organisation

(RGO), a black-led lesbian and gay movement organization, partially alleviated this concern (Gevisser 1995). RGO's founder, Alfred Machela, disputed GASA's defense of its apolitical visibility and argued that "GASA does not represent the entire gay movement in South Africa. We would like to distance ourselves from GASA. And we don't wish them to represent us at any level without our mandate" (as quoted in Croucher 2002, 319). In 1987, ILGA expelled an already faltering GASA for failing to support Nkoli and for not opposing apartheid publicly (Cock 2003; Rydström 2005; see also Botha 2005a, 2005b). GASA's apolitical visibility proved unsustainable amid growing antiapartheid sentiment among gender and sexual dissidents.

In the mid-1980s, lesbian and gay activists began rejecting apolitical visibility and developed inclusive visibility strategies allied with antiapartheid organizing. In this way, activists adapted their strategies to the changing sociopolitical field. RGO soon became invisible, but any vacuum that it may have left was filled by the founding of Lesbians and Gays Against Oppression (LAGO) in 1986 in Cape Town.[16] LAGO opposed apartheid and sought to demonstrate that "gay rights [were] human rights" (Nicol 2005, 72). Yet antiapartheid activists did not necessarily welcome lesbian and gay activists' participation. LAGO members faced accusations that they were "hijacking the anti-apartheid struggle for [their] own partisan ends. The fact that both LAGO . . . had approximately 90 per cent white membership made [them] especially vulnerable to such perceptions" (Nicol 2005, 72–73). Some antiapartheid activists alleged that homosexuality was un-African, which operated as a political deterrent to render black gay men and lesbians invisible in the antiapartheid movement.

In 1987, LAGO members dissolved the organization because some members wanted to pursue gay liberation only, whereas others wanted LAGO to join the antiapartheid movement (Nicol 2005). Some former LAGO members launched the Organisation of Lesbians and Gay Activists (OLGA) to replace LAGO (Nicol 2005). The emergence of antiapartheid groups like OLGA initiated a new trend of visibility in South African lesbian and gay organizing: antiapartheid, black-led, multiracial lesbian and gay activism (Nicol 2005). In fact, OLGA joined the United Democratic Front (UDF) in 1987, which confirmed multiracial lesbian and gay activists' participation in the antiapartheid movement (Nicol 2005).[17]

Toward the end of the 1980s, as apartheid control of South Africa crumbled, multiracial lesbian and gay movement organizations targeted the ANC as an audience. Lesbian and gay antiapartheid activists in Western Europe pressured ANC leaders in exile to include gay rights in the new constitution and to address homophobia within the organization (Kraak 2005; Rydström 2005). Peter

Tatchell (2005), a gay rights activist in Great Britain, exposed homophobia within the ANC in a 1987 interview with Ruth Mompati, a women's rights activist and member of the ANC executive. Insinuating that homosexuality was un-African and a Western phenomenon that had not gained visibility in South Africa "until recently," Mompati stated, "I cannot even begin to understand why people want gay and lesbian rights. The gays have no problems. . . . I don't see them suffering. No one is persecuting them. . . . We don't have a policy on gays and lesbians. We don't have a policy on flower sellers either" (Kraak 2005, 132). Mompati viewed the sudden visibility of lesbian and gay organizing as derailing the ANC's efforts to liberate South Africa from apartheid rule. According to her logic, national and racial liberation outranked gay liberation. However, lesbian and gay activists did not hierarchize each movement's goals; instead, they emphasized the complementarity of these goals in the creation of a nonracial, nonsexist, and nonhomophobic South Africa.[18] In the new South Africa, activists hoped that constitutionally guaranteed equality would eliminate apartheid-era repression and controlling visibilities.

Mompati's remarks elicited concerned responses from lesbian and gay antiapartheid activists in the global North. The ANC publicly signaled support for gay rights (Fine and Nicol 1995). After Mompati's interview with Tatchell, Thabo Mbeki, "then Director of Information" for the ANC, explained that the "ANC had never been nor ever would be opposed to gay rights" (Fine and Nicol 1995, 271). Through Mbeki, the ANC formulated an official policy on lesbian and gay rights: "The ANC is . . . firmly committed to removing all forms of discrimination and oppression in a liberated South Africa. . . . That commitment must surely extend to the protection of gay rights" (as quoted in Fine and Nicol 1995, 271; emphasis removed). The ANC's pro-gay rights stance distinguished it from the apartheid regime's antigay platform; the more distance the ANC put between itself and the NP, the more successful its leaders hoped it would be in creating a nonracial democracy (Altman 2001). However, support for gay rights remained confined to ANC leaders; many rank-and-file members disagreed with this position (Gevisser 2000; Kraak 2005).

In the 1980s, HIV/AIDS emerged as a major concern for South Africans and LGBT persons. GASA devoted a column in its newspaper *Link/Skakel*, which later became the monthly publication *Exit*, to providing the (white) gay community information about HIV/AIDS. Mass media and the apartheid regime racialized HIV/AIDS as white in the mid-1980s. Dagmawi Woubshet (2007, 133) argues that the apartheid regime purposely associated HIV/AIDS with white gay men not to provide care or services for them but rather "to show itself and the world how much" the epidemic in South Africa resembled HIV/AIDS in Western countries. The regime also represented "African AIDS as foreign, blaming initially other African nations (mine workers from Malawi) and later" ANC militants for bringing the disease to South Africa (Woubshet 2007, 133). Eventually, "black gay men who moved between the white gay subculture and the townships" were blamed for exposing heterosexuals to HIV (Gevisser 1995, 59). Around 1985, the media stopped referring to HIV/AIDS as the "gay plague" and reracialized and degayed AIDS as the "black death" (Gevisser 1995, 59). Multiracial lesbian and gay movement organizations, such as OLGA, offered HIV/AIDS support services to black, coloured, Asian Indian, and white persons beginning in the mid-1980s. Lesbian and gay activists became known as one of the only groups willing to address the pandemic publicly (Mbali 2008).

LGBT Organizing in Postapartheid South Africa: New Options for Visibility

During and after the transition away from apartheid, South African LGBT activists seized political opportunities to pursue comprehensive rights for LGBT persons, including immigration, adoption, and marriage rights for same-sex couples.[19] In this period, they emphasized the movement's multiracial visibility. Launched in 1988 by Nkoli, Gays and Lesbians of the Witwatersrand (GLOW), a black-led, multiracial lesbian and gay movement organization, emerged as a visible force (Jara and Lapinsky 1998). According to Sipho, a black gay man and former member of GLOW, black LGBT persons

> never had a movement that they could go to and feel at home. There was GASA, and there were other white movements. But a lot of black people didn't feel welcomed, or they didn't feel safe to go to those organizations. When GLOW was started in 1988, we found that a lot of black people, especially within the LGBT community, came out, and then they joined the movement. (Sipho, interview with the author, November 4, 2005)

For many black LGBT persons in Johannesburg, GLOW was the first group to recruit and show them that the lesbian and gay movement was not restricted to whites (McLean and Ngcobo 1995). Beginning in 1990, GLOW sponsored the yearly Lesbian and Gay Pride March in Johannesburg and championed "gay rights as human rights" (Gevisser 1995, 63). In the early 1990s, white LGBT persons dominated the march, although more black LGBT persons participated each year (Gevisser and Reid 1995).

Until its demise in the mid-1990s, GLOW struggled to balance the tension between pursuing LGBT rights and providing social spaces and services for constituents, a dilemma that surfaced for TRP in Namibia (Gevisser 1995; Gevisser and Reid 1995). This dilemma took the form of public visibility: should GLOW prioritize visibility strategies geared toward the state and social institutions or strategies that strengthened nonwhite LGBT communities? In part, this tension corresponded to leaders' and constituents' divergent interests. Privileged leaders wanted to challenge homophobia and obtain gay rights, and members were interested in less visible strategies: "anything that generates income and provides a safe social space" (McLean and Ngcobo 1995, 182). Movement leaders developed a dichotomous understanding of how visibility worked in the movement. Visibility strategies were those that lobbied for rights on behalf of LGBT constituents, whereas strategies intended to respond to constituents' material needs were insular and did little to generate public visibility for the movement.

Owing to internal conflicts and its sponsorship of Pride, GLOW experienced trouble maintaining a public presence in Johannesburg and surrounding townships, a difficulty that contemporary LGBT movement organizations in Namibia and South Africa also faced. Although GLOW's annual Lesbian and Gay Pride March generated "an annual moment of public visibility" for LGBT persons and organizing, it did not contribute to movement building in townships (Gevisser and Reid 1995, 280).[20] To critics, Pride was an expensive event that siphoned time and resources that organizers could have spent on organizing "township chapters of GLOW" that could "march under their own banners.... The march would then present to South Africa a more representative spectacle of gay life," reflecting the movement's multiracial composition (Gevisser and Reid 1995, 208). Although some activists criticized GLOW's investment in Pride, they did not object to the event's purpose. Many LGBT activists and constituents viewed the march as an opportunity to draw public attention to the movement's demands for equality.

Managing the visibility of Pride marchers was a matter of contention in the LGBT movement. At Pride, some LGBT activists wanted to portray the movement and constituents in a nonthreatening way that would communicate to the public and politicians that the movement operated within the sociopolitical mainstream (Currier 2010b). For these activists, visibility management involved minimizing the public visibility of gender dissidence (Currier 2011). The playful, publicly visible protest embodied by drag queens alienated activists who preferred conventional protest tactics that evoked antiapartheid protests (Gevisser and Reid 1995). These activists complained about "half-naked leather dykes and drag queens and people being crass and outrageous" at Pride, fearing that these images would generate uncontrollable hypervisibility for the movement (Somerville 2006, 137). To these critics, the visibility of gender-diverse persons deflected attention away from "serious" politics, an example of the racial, gender, sexual, and political hierarchies within the movement (Stobbs 2006).

Concerns about public spectacles overwhelming Pride's political message about equality emerged at the 1996 Johannesburg Pride March. Steven Cohen and Vasili Kapetanakis carried a provocative and sarcastic banner that read, "Give us your children. What we can't fuck, we eat," a confrontational style similar to North American queer direct-action tactics (de Waal and Manion 2006, 98). Cohen and Kapetanakis mocked antigay claims that gay men molested children, which made same-sex sexualities visible in a way the movement could not control. Noted gay activist Zackie Achmat (1996) observed that only white, middle-class gay carriers could, according to his logic, afford to engage in similar public transgression. Achmat suggested that although black LGBT persons were more visible in the movement than they had been in the past, race continued to affect the visibility of the LGBT movement and individual constituents. He insinuated that it would have been difficult for black lesbian and gay activists to engage in this confrontational tactic in part because the banner appealed more to those familiar with queer "European and North American slogans than with South Africa's" antiapartheid protest tactics; black activists were more likely to use protest tactics and imagery associated with antiapartheid activism (Achmat 1996, 10). This debate about public visibility revealed a strategic propensity for LGBT activists to hew to the precedents set by the antiapartheid struggle.

Early in 1990, President F. W. de Klerk authorized the release of Nelson Mandela from prison and unbanned the ANC as a political party (Welsh 2000). LGBT movement organizations took advantage of this democratic transformation. According to Sipho,

> that was the time of the revolution and things changing for South Africa because people like Nelson Mandela were released from prison. We were looking into our future; we were looking into having our first elections. So many things were happening at once at that time, and I think our [Pride] march also made that stand to say, "We are there. Gay people exist."

With the nation's first democratic elections approaching, LGBT activists continued to press the ANC about LGBT rights. However, the movement faced homophobic opposition within the ANC and other political parties that threatened to stifle the movement's growing public visibility.

Between 1991 and 1993, Winnie Madikizela-Mandela, the former wife of acclaimed ANC and antiapartheid leader Nelson Mandela, scandalized LGBT activists with her antigay defense at her trial for her role in the 1988 death of teenager Stompie Moeketsi Seipei and the assault of three other black youths (Holmes 1995, 1997). Her defense alleged that she and members of the football (soccer) club she led rescued four black youths from the sexual advances of a white gay Methodist minister, who were cloistered together in cramped sleeping quarters "familiar to many subjects of apartheid residential conditions, such as in industrial compounds and hostels" (Holmes 1995, 289). Not only did her defense team claim that Madikizela-Mandela saved the four young black men from homosexuality, which they painted as a perversion, but they also insinuated that homosexuality was a product of colonialism and apartheid—"a white contamination of black culture" (Holmes 1995, 289). Staging protests at the trial, GLOW members contested this controlling visibility and demanded that the ANC reject her antigay defense that homosexuality was un-African (Gevisser 1995; Holmes 1995). However, Madikizela-Mandela's political clout within antiapartheid activist circles seemed to paralyze the ANC executive (Holmes 1997). Ultimately, ANC officials did not act on the homophobia that the trial perpetuated in part to concentrate on securing the party's victory in the democratic election. Their inaction also revealed "an executive-level inability to deal with real public differences within the ranks of the liberation movement" (Holmes 1995, 291).[21] The nationalist association of homosexuality with European colonialism and apartheid continued to affect Namibian and South African LGBT activists' visibility strategies in the late 1990s and 2000s.

Despite ANC leaders' uneven record of addressing homophobia within the party, LGBT activists worked closely with officials from the ANC and other political parties to develop a constitution that would protect gender and sexual minorities from discrimination. Activists hoped this would grant constituents unfettered visibility, freedom, and mobility. An important step in this process was OLGA's creation of a Charter of Lesbian and Gay Rights in 1990, which OLGA revised in 1992 after consulting with Xhosa-, English-, and Afrikaans-speaking LGBT persons (Fine and Nicol 1995). Based on the ANC Freedom Charter, which emphasized nonracialism and inclusive politics, the Charter of Lesbian and Gay Rights would "serve as a judicially-recognised guideline" for the constitutional protection of LGBT rights (Fine and Nicol 1995, 275). The ANC included LGBT rights in its bill of rights late in 1992, as did the Democratic Party and Inkatha Freedom Party (Croucher 2002). Most opposition political parties followed suit because politicians did not want to be seen perpetuating apartheid-era injustices (Massoud 2003).

In December 1994, more than sixty movement organizations formed a "single-issue" umbrella organization, the National Coalition for Gay and Lesbian Equality (NCGLE) (Cock 2003, 37). Led mostly by men, the NCGLE was tasked with managing the "lobbying effort to retain the sexual orientation clause [EC] in the draft South African Constitution" (37). An "atmosphere of inclusivity" typified the constitutional drafting and ratification (Croucher 2002, 322). The ANC ushered in this open atmosphere by soliciting public input on both its bill of rights and constitutional amendments enacted between 1990 and 1993 (Croucher 2002).

The NCGLE "presented a moderate and disciplined image" of respectable LGBT activism to targeted political parties and state leaders (Stychin 1996, 466). This normalized visibility meant that LGBT movement organizations did not ask for too much of the state; instead, they worked within rules of postapartheid institutional politics (Currier 2010c). For instance, this moderate visibility strategy resulted in official recognition from President Nelson Mandela, who met with NCGLE leaders and Sir Ian McKellen in 1995 and affirmed his support for gay rights (Holmes 1997). Working with different political parties, the NCGLE participated fully in drafting the EC and responded to party statements supporting, modifying, or opposing the clause.[22] Instead of couching LGBT rights as "minority rights," the NCGLE used a frame of equality and nondiscrimination consistent with the ANC's platform (Croucher 2002, 324). In May 1996, after the EC was permanently enshrined in the constitution, the NCGLE sought additional rights for LGBT persons. The group also prioritized "the continued development of the lesbian, gay, bisexual, and transgender movement throughout Southern Africa" and would later help TRP in Namibia formulate a strategy for challenging antisodomy legislation (National Coalition for Gay and Lesbian Equality 1995).[23]

The NCGLE favored decriminalizing sodomy and changing public attitudes toward gender and sexual diversity (Massoud 2003). The NCGLE's Equal Rights Project focused on educating the public to minimize the discrepancy between South Africans' antigay attitudes and the nation's pro-gay constitution ("The Coalition's" 1996).[24] Building on the success of the EC, the NCGLE, which later became the Lesbian and Gay Equality Project, filed successful lawsuits that decriminalized sodomy (1998), permitted same-sex couples to access pension benefits jointly (1999), granted immigration rights to foreign same-sex partners of South African citizens (1999), allowed same-sex couples to adopt children (2002), and obtained the right for same-sex couples to marry (2005–6) (Cock 2003; Dirsuweit 2006; Epprecht 2004; Goodman 2001; Reddy 2006).[25]

These legal gains largely benefited LGBT persons. Advocacy for transgender persons was spotty in postapartheid South Africa (Swarr 2003). Under apartheid, transgender persons of different races were able to undergo medicalized gender transitions and to change their identity documents to reflect their altered gender (Swarr 2003). Legislation introduced in 1992 no longer permitted the state "to change the legal documents [transgender persons] need to function in society" (Swarr 2003, 65). However, the passage of the Alteration of Sex Description and Sex Status Act 49 in May 2003 allowed transgender and intersex persons to "apply for legal adjustment of [their] sex description without genital surgery" (Klein 2008, 5). This legislation enabled transgender persons to bypass medical pathways for changing their gender officially. There are reports that the Department of Home Affairs has changed identity documents only for those who have undergone gender reassignment surgery and have presented "letters from the surgeons who carried them out" (Klein 2008, 5). Before the legalization of same-sex marriage in 2006, married people who underwent a gender transition had to divorce their spouses and remarry under gender-specific marriage laws (Delport and Delport 2008). The law did not accommodate married, transgender persons, so transgender persons had to accommodate the law. Marriage-equality legislation removed legal barriers related to the state's recognition of transgender persons' relationships.

Postapartheid LGBT movement organizations, especially the NCGLE, have been criticized by scholars and activists for the contradictions between their public presentations and behind-the-scenes practices. The NCGLE forged a public image that promised to represent the needs of LGBT constituents from different racial, ethnic, class, and religious backgrounds. This image diverged from its "elitist," "undemocratic" practices (Oswin 2007, 653).[26] The movement's social conservatism and largely male leadership excluded women and black persons (Cock 2003). The NCGLE's selection of campaigns promoted "not only gendered interests but class ones, too, focusing, as it did, on such middle-class issues as pensions and immigration rights for foreign same-sex partners" (Bullington and Swarr 2010, 97). Channeling resources into legal and lobbying strategies meant that some of the NCGLE's goals went unmet. In particular, leaders claimed that the NCGLE would serve a "poor and black" LGBT constituency, a public image of constituents they created in the 1990s (Oswin 2007, 654). Critics within the movement stated that the NCGLE's strategies did little to improve black LGBT constituents' lives; in fact, LGBT rights remained intangible to many black constituents (Cock 2003; Gevisser 2000).

The NCGLE also projected a public image of a large LGBT movement, a strategy that struck some activists as misguided. Some activists believed this focus kept the NCGLE from supporting black LGBT movement organizations. Ditsie asserts that few of the sixty (or eighty, depending on the source) member organizations were active in the NCGLE (Gunkel 2010). She also claims that the NCGLE channeled resources toward dormant, invisible organizations, instead of supporting, for example, a growing black LGBT movement "organization in Kwa-Thema," a Johannesburg township (Gunkel 2010, 71). The NCGLE's size resulted from an unsustainable form of inclusion and contributed to its demise (Dirsuweit 2006). The NCGLE could not cope with multiple organizations' requests for funding and bureaucratic support (Dirsuweit 2006). Activists dismantled the NCGLE and launched the Lesbian and Gay Equality Project in 1999 (*Outright* 2000; Dirsuweit 2006).

As the Equality Project concentrated on legal issues, other LGBT movement organizations engaged in "niche activism" in urban areas by specializing in different issues such as providing mental and physical health services to LGBT persons, monitoring media portrayals of LGBT persons, and caring for the specific needs of HIV-positive LGBT persons (Levitsky 2007, 271). Movement organizations, including Behind the Mask and FEW, worked together as a loose coalition named the Joint Working Group (JWG), which met twice a year.[27] Movement organizations selectively worked together on campaigns that benefited them and their constituents, as in the case of joint research projects that movement organizations used to lobby local and regional state officials about anti-LGBT violence and discrimination. Movement organizations also confronted anti-LGBT hostility and lack of a concerted state response to HIV/AIDS (Mbali 2008).[28] Niche activism allowed LGBT movement organizations to tailor their visibility strategies to their particular interests, enabling FEW to develop an insular strategic orientation to visibility centered on protecting black lesbians and Behind the Mask to monitor the continental visibility of LGBT persons, rights, and activism throughout Africa.

LGBT Organizing in Postapartheid Namibia

In 1995, LGBT activists in Namibia began organizing publicly to oppose SWAPO leaders' soft repression. SWAPO leaders' political homophobia surprised some LGBT activists who believed that the national liberation movement's promise to institute equality for all Namibians included gender and sexual minorities. The state and SWAPO were primary targets of LGBT activists' visibility strategies.

From 1915 to 1989, South Africa ruled Namibia. Although South African authorities did not extend all apartheid laws to Namibia, such as the Group Areas Act, which codified racial segregation in rural and urban areas, they implemented the spirit of apartheid policies by racially dividing towns into black, coloured, and white areas (Simon 1986). In Namibia, state "oppression occurred not so much by terror per se as by the routinization of terror in day-to-day interaction" (Gordon 2002, 77). During the occupation, apartheid military forces brutalized Namibian civilians, especially those who lived in northern Namibia (du Pisani 2004).

In 1960, Namibians, mostly from the Ovambo ethnic group, formed SWAPO as a successor to the Ovamboland People's Congress to challenge South African apartheid rule (Dobell 1998).[29] Decolonization via national liberation was SWAPO's primary goal (Melber 2003b). Beginning in 1966, SWAPO's armed wing, the People's Liberation Army of Namibia (PLAN), mobilized against South African forces (Leys and Saul 1994). SWAPO also petitioned the UN to order South Africa to surrender control of Namibia, an official order that the apartheid regime disobeyed (Dobell 1998).[30] While in exile, SWAPO leaders developed a reputation for suppressing internal dissent harshly. They detained and allegedly tortured those involved in a supposed plot in the mid-1970s to dethrone SWAPO leaders, "the first signs of crystallisation of an authoritarian political ethos" within SWAPO (Leys and Saul 1994, 126). In the late 1970s and 1980s, South African authorities in Namibia began eliminating apartheid laws, such as antimiscegenation laws, anticipating Namibia's eventual independence (Simon 1996). In 1989, South Africa relinquished Namibia in a "negotiated settlement," and in March 1990, Namibia's independence became official (Melber 2007, 61). SWAPO's formal takeover of power was unusual in that it "had the privilege of being the only internationally recognised representative of the Namibian people," making it the UN-designated victor in the postindependence democratic transition (Melber 2003b, 15).

The new democratic government held great promise for Namibians. SWAPO "made a remarkable transformation from being an authoritarian liberation movement into being a relatively open and tolerant electoral party" (Lindeke 1995, 16–17). The new constitution upheld equality for all Namibians, regardless of their race, gender, or class (Diescho 1994). Many gender and sexual minorities believed that this included them. However, SWAPO leaders interpreted equality in a way that excluded LGBT persons, rendering them invisible in the national imaginary.

In the early years of independence, SWAPO adopted a "paternalist[ic]" approach to democracy, evidenced in SWAPO leaders' reminder that without their sacrifices, independence would never have been realized (Fosse 1997, 428). Since independence, SWAPO has managed to consolidate its control over local, regional, and national politics by winning and retaining seats at all levels of government (Melber 2007).[31] SWAPO's consolidation of political power emboldened leaders to stifle dissent. State repression did not disappear when a democratic government replaced the authoritarian regime. Newly democratizing states like postindependence Namibia sometimes use soft repression to discourage dissent (Almeida 2003; Fallon 2008). Taking the form of discursive threats, soft repression prompts activists to question whether they should engage in or abstain from public action. Even when state actors do not employ violence, arrest, detention, or property destruction to deter political organizing, their use of discursive threats can render sociopolitical fields inhospitable to activists. SWAPO leaders' deployment of political homophobia constituted soft repression, causing Namibian LGBT activists to question whether they should engage in visible action.

The Emergence of Namibian LGBT Organizing

LGBT organizing became visible in the early 1990s after independence. Johannes, a coloured gay man and TRP member, remembered this time as a period of "postindependence euphoria," when "Namibia was heaven"; he and his partner could show their affection in public without attracting undue attention. In 1992, lawmakers passed Labour Act 6, which included a clause prohibiting employment discrimination on the basis of sexual orientation (Hubbard 2007).[32] Johannes believed that "things were going to be okay" for LGBT Namibians and that SWAPO leaders would honor their promise to institute and practice equality in the new democracy.

In the early 1990s, the Social Committee of Gays and Lesbians (SCOG) brought white and coloured lesbians and gay men together for social activities.[33] According to Rina, a white lesbian and Sister Namibia member, SCOG organizers threw "a good party every two months" and used party admission fees to sponsor the next party (interview with the author, May 23, 2006). SCOG organizers launched the Gay and Lesbian Organisation of Namibia (GLON) with a political agenda. In its first public action in 1995, GLON voiced opposition to the Lutheran Church's attempt to block lesbians and gay men from becoming ordained ministers and announced plans to form a Christian church for sexual minorities (Frank and |Khaxas 1996; Munamava 1995). Rina recalled that GLON organizers adopted a diffident strategic orientation to public visibility, disappointing those who wanted to press for LGBT rights. Mimicking GLON organizers' ambivalent attitude to activism, Rina stated, "'Let's first get registered with the Ministry of Health and Social Services as a welfare organization, and then, maybe, we'll dare to come out of the closet and do something.' So that was sort of the GLON strategy, which we hadn't realized. . . . And I think that was part of the frustration."

GLON's reputation as a white group also prevented it from effecting social change for LGBT constituents. Johannes stated that many "black people . . . didn't feel that they could identify with GLON" (interview with the author, July 11, 2006). Echoing Johannes's sentiment, Christopher, a black gay man and TRP member, asserted that GLON garnered a reputation for being "very racially skewed and exclusive," which alienated black LGBT persons (interview with the author, July 18, 2006). GLON eventually dissolved because of internal conflicts over the organization's direction. "Some members wanted to participate in formal legal action while others wanted to focus their activities on establishing LGBT social spaces" (Lorway 2008a, 31).

In 1995, SWAPO leaders' antigay attacks commenced. This initial outburst followed Zimbabwean President Robert Mugabe's antigay statements in August 1995 denouncing the Gays and Lesbians of Zimbabwe's presence at the Zimbabwe International Book Fair (Aarmo 1999; Hoad 2007; Spurlin 2006). Like Mugabe, SWAPO leaders characterized same-sex sexualities as un-African, statements that Sister Namibia refuted publicly (Currier 2010b).[34] Instead of forcing gender and sexual dissidents into invisibility, SWAPO officials' soft repression was in effect a catalyst for LGBT activism in the mid-1990s (Dunton and Palmberg 1996; Palmberg 1999; LaFont 2007). In this sense, "Mugabe and Nujoma [were] indeed 'promoters' of 'homosexuality' in their societies" (Human Rights Watch and the International Gay and Lesbian Rights Commission 2003, 8). By attacking LGBT persons publicly, SWAPO leaders handed them politicized collective identities around which they could organize.

After a year of official silence about same-sex sexualities, Nujoma used the SWAPO Women's Council Congress in Gobabis in December 1996 as an opportunity to denigrate lesbians and gay men (Günzel 1996). Human rights NGOs in Namibia and elsewhere responded to and condemned Nujoma's attack "as an indication of emerging authoritarianism in Namibia" (Human Rights Watch and the International Gay and Lesbian Rights Commission 2003, 5–6). Sister Namibia and the newly formed TRP responded to Nujoma's aggression by insisting that he stop making "statements regarding issues with which he is not familiar and which could have a detrimental impact on part of the Namibian population" (Rainbow Project 1996, 11). Secretary for Information and Publicity Alpheus !Naruseb articulated SWAPO's official position on homosexuality, which eventually became a familiar anti-Western, antigay, and xenophobic refrain: "Most of the ardent supporters of this [sic] perverts are Europeans who imagine themselves to be the bulwark of civilisation and enlightenment. They not only appropriating foreign ideas in our society but also destroying the local culture by hiding behind the façade of the very democracy and human rights we have created" (Namibian 1997a, 3).

Foreign onlookers became unnerved by SWAPO officials' homophobia, signaling to LGBT activists that they had allies elsewhere in Africa and in the global North. Diplomats, including ambassadors from European Union (EU) nations and LGBT movement organizations in South Africa, Zimbabwe, and the global North, voiced their concern about SWAPO's antigay position (Namibian 1997b). Attempting to quell foreign diplomats' and activists' concerns, Prime Minister Hage Geingob reminded the public that "no homosexuals or lesbians [had] ever been prosecuted, intimidated, arrested or denied employment" in Namibia (Namibian 1997d, 2). His comment suggested that the state would not take action against gender and sexual dissidents and force them into invisibility, which contradicted other SWAPO officials' positions. Evidently, there was some disagreement within SWAPO about how to treat gender and sexual diversity.[35] To dispel misconceptions about same-sex sexualities, in 1997, Sister Namibia and TRP organized a panel of speakers featuring Namibian and South African LGBT activists and human rights experts, the first public LGBT movement event in Namibia (Maffeis 1997). Rina remembered this as the movement's "coming out" into public visibility, a surfacing that activists sought to sustain. According to Rina, the event organizers "decided, 'Let's have a panel discussion at the Polytechnic [a local college]. You know, we're in town; we're targeting young people. But let's not do it alone; let's get someone from South Africa on the panel, you know, to sort of strengthen our forces and show we're not alone here in Namibia.'" Close ties with South African LGBT activists helped Namibian activists secure their footing in the hostile sociopolitical field; this relationship became especially important as activists with TRP considered initiating a public law-reform campaign.

Nujoma used SWAPO venues to call on Namibians loyal to the party to persecute gays and lesbians on the basis that homosexuality was foreign to Namibian and African cultures. Nujoma claimed that lesbians and gay men were unpatriotic and therefore did not deserve citizenship rights (Currier 2010b, 2012). "Where were they [gays and lesbians] when we sacrificed our lives during the bitter liberation struggle?" (*Namibian* 1997e, 1). An indication of a growing authoritarian streak, Nujoma also insulted "independent media, political opposition leaders, women's rights activists, and foreigners," believing they would derail SWAPO's political agenda (Human Rights Watch and the International Gay and Lesbian Rights Commission 2003, 5–6).

Antigay political attacks ceased for more than a year, until late in 1998, when Minister of Home Affairs Jerry Ekandjo threatened to increase penalties for individuals convicted of sodomy, an offense that pertained only to men who have sex with men (Weidlich 1998).[36] TRP and other human rights NGOs asked Ekandjo to retract his statement and asserted that such legislation would contravene the constitution. Activists with TRP speculated that political homophobia might be a ruse to deflect attention away from problems like corruption and poverty. For example, in 1999, when discussing the national budget in the National Assembly (NA), an unlikely forum for debating LGBT rights, Ekandjo's deputy, Jeremiah Nambinga, renewed Ekandjo's promise to increase penalties for sodomy (Maletsky 1999). Playing a conciliatory role, Geingob assured LGBT persons that this would not happen.[37]

Some SWAPO officials seemed bent on rendering LGBT persons entirely invisible in Namibia, whereas some opposition party lawmakers defended gender and sexual minorities. Resuming his antigay attacks in 2000, Ekandjo exhorted police officers to "eliminate" gays and lesbians, which elicited demands from TRP and other human rights NGOs that he apologize for and retract his statement (*Namibian* 2000). Congress of Democrats (CoD) lawmaker Rosa Namises, a respected women's rights activist, called on Ekandjo to clarify whether he advocated that "gay and lesbian people should be murdered" (Angula 2000). At a subsequent NA meeting, Ekandjo stated that "elimination does not only mean to kill. According to the dictionary meaning, elimination also means to ignore, to put aside, and [get] rid of" (Hamata 2000), a clarification that was by no means mollifying or nonviolent. Katuutire Kaura, the leader of the Democratic Turnhalle Alliance, threatened to call for a vote of no confidence in Ekandjo because of his "incompetence" and "total disregard for and ignorance of the Namibian Constitution in his recent attacks on . . . gays and lesbians" (Angula 2000). Ultimately, Ekandjo stated that his call for eliminating gays and lesbians was not an incitement to violence, but he still maintained an antigay position: "We never had moffies in mind when Swapo drafted the Namibian Constitution 10 years ago" (Hamata 2000).[38] According to Ekandjo and other SWAPO leaders, LGBT persons' invisibility prior to independence should continue in the present.

Human rights NGOs and opposition party lawmakers joined LGBT activists in demanding that SWAPO leaders recant their homophobic statements. In March 2001, when addressing University of Namibia students, whom Nujoma regarded as youths vulnerable to the supposedly predatory appetites of gays and lesbians, he encouraged police to "arrest, imprison, and deport homosexuals and lesbians found in Namibia" (*Namibian* 2001b). Along with TRP, leaders of the National Society for Human Rights (NSHR) and the Legal Assistance Centre (LAC) condemned Nujoma's antigay remarks; the leader of NSHR stated that Nujoma's "homophobic attack" could "lead to violence against innocent citizens" (Menges 2001a). These fears were realized when members of the Special Field Forces (SFF) singled out men in Katutura, a township outside of Windhoek:

> wearing earrings and, in some cases, ripped them off the surprised victims' ears. . . . One of the SFF members . . . said the order had come from the President. "Where did you see men wearing earrings in our Oshiwambo culture? These things never happened before Independence. Why are they [men wearing earrings] only happening now after Independence?" (Hamata 2001)

Men's visible gender nonconformity signaled to SFF unit members that they might be gay and served as the basis for their antigay harassment of gender-diverse men.

Nujoma's remarks became internationally visible and drew criticism from varied sources: the Black Radical Congress in the United States, the South

African Durban Lesbian and Gay Community and Health Centre, and the EU (*Namibian* 2001a; Council of the European Union 2001; Mkhize 2001). Attributing Nujoma's antigay attacks to authoritarian tendencies, Sister Namibia denounced soft repression: "Creating enemy images diverts attention from the failure to stem poverty, unemployment, violence against women and children and HIV/AIDS, and makes it easier to fiddle with the constitution while no-one is looking," a reference to SWAPO's success in amending the constitution to allow Nujoma to run for a third term as president (Sister Namibia 2001, 2). SWAPO leaders' homophobia also affected how Namibians perceived the HIV/AIDS epidemic. Such rhetoric portrayed HIV/AIDS as only affecting heterosexual persons, except when black gay and bisexual men were blamed for spreading HIV (Epprecht 2008; Lorway 2006).

Although Nujoma abstained from issuing antigay remarks in 2002, he resumed making them in September 2003 when he addressed a "hastily-organised gathering of University of Namibia and Polytechnic students" and maligned "whites, homosexuals, and journalists," whom he accused of openly opposing the state (Kuteeue 2003). SWAPO leaders declared any political dissent as unpatriotic and undemocratic, an example of SWAPO's claim to legitimacy as the democratizing and decolonizing authority in Namibia (Melber 2006a, 2006b). In 2004, as SWAPO officials continued harassing human rights NGOs, journalists, and LGBT persons, TRP bemoaned the "slow erosion of good governance practices," as evidenced in the difficulties that many sexual dissidents experienced in being open about their sexualities (Shigwedha 2004). For instance, in September 2005, Deputy Minister of Home Affairs and Immigration Theopolina Mushelenga blamed sexual minorities for HIV/AIDS, which Sister Namibia and TRP condemned as "hate speech" and a "direct attack against the civil rights" of LGBT persons in Namibia (Graig 2005). Since assuming office in March 2005, President Hifikepunye Pohamba and his cabinet have refrained from ridiculing LGBT persons, with the exception of Mushelenga's unexpected comments. Henno, a coloured gay man and TRP member, thought that "with the new president, there is a much more open, accepting kind of atmosphere" that LGBT activists could exploit (interview with the author, June 30, 2006). The absence of hate speech has given hope to LGBT activists that they might be able to negotiate with Pohamba's administration in the future.

Namibian LGBT activists recognized the double-edged visibility that political homophobia brought the movement. On one hand, political homophobia perpetuated controlling visibilities of gender and sexual minorities that LGBT activists fought; controlling visibilities were linked to violence against LGBT persons. For example, after Nujoma's antigay comments in June 2000, LGBT activists claimed that "three gay men were beaten up by people in Rescue 911 vehicles" (Amupadhi 2000). On the other hand, political homophobia created a political opportunity for LGBT movement visibility. Daniel, a black gay man and TRP member, admitted that when Nujoma "was high in arms with the gays and lesbians and saying that they should be deported . . . a lot of people came out and talked about it. It was not a silent thing. And now people are aware that there are gays around" (interview with the author, June 26, 2006). SWAPO leaders' political homophobia in the late 1990s and early 2000s provided LGBT activists with the opportunity to generate basic visibility for constituents, even if they had to work to correct the content of this visibility. Political hostility toward gender and sexual diversity also prompted Sister Namibia and TRP to look beyond the Namibian sociopolitical field and develop international visibility with Northern donors, other African LGBT movement organizations, and international LGBT movement organizations.

Advancing Visibilities?

The regime of controlling visibilities affected LGBT movement organizations in Namibia and South Africa. The myth that same-sex sexualities were un-African persisted, generating conditions inimical to LGBT organizing. In South Africa, this discourse sanctioned black men's use of antilesbian violence to police African culture and women's bodies, despite the constitutional protection prohibiting hostility toward LGBT persons. Black lesbian activists affiliated with FEW struggled with the specter of antilesbian violence in Johannesburg and surrounding townships. It may have been tempting for some activists to retreat and develop survival strategies that solely favored invisibility. However, adopting a strategy of strict invisibility would have done little to transform the circumstances giving rise to antilesbian violence. What could FEW do in this context? What visibility strategies would empower black lesbian women without publicly revictimizing them in campaigns to eliminate antilesbian violence?

Discourses claiming that same-sex sexualities were un-African took a political form in Namibia. President Nujoma and his peers within SWAPO deployed scathing rhetoric intended to render political opponents, including LGBT activists, invisible (Currier 2010b). Activists with Sister Namibia, a feminist movement organization, challenged SWAPO leaders' political homophobia and framed lesbian rights as women's rights instead of distancing the organization from lesbian issues. Elsewhere in Africa, feminist activists had declined to include or mobilize on behalf of lesbians (McFadden 1996; Tamale 2007). Eschewing lesbian rights would likely have yielded material rewards for Sister Namibia in the form of symbolic and financial support from the state. What led Sister Namibia to develop a visibility strategy that defended lesbian rights as women's human rights in this hostile field? What were the consequences of these strategic choices for Sister Namibia?

2

"This Lesbian Issue":
Navigating Public Visibility as Lesbian Movement Organizations

In many newly democratizing African nations, sexuality is a publicly contentious matter (Posel 2005). Citing a need to preserve cultural sovereignty, some political leaders use sexuality to mandate a return to an African heteropatriarchy that predates European colonialist interference.[1] When African women activists, especially those affiliated with autonomous women's movements, disagreed with political leaders on questions of sexuality (or other political issues), they risked "being treated as non-African, uprooted, bourgeois, or worse...lesbian" (Sow 1997, 33).[2] In such circumstances, political leaders deployed the term *lesbian* to disparage women's movement campaigns and to discourage them from challenging the ruling party's authority (Rothschild 2005). In heteronormative sociopolitical fields, sexuality can become a vehicle for disciplining the visibility of social movements, and movements advocating for sexual diversity rights particularly risk unfavorable, unintentional visibility. In Namibia, SWAPO leaders used political homophobia not only to drive LGBT persons underground but also to deter public LGBT activism, including the activities Sister Namibia sponsored.

Soft repression is not the only factor affecting movement organizations' strategic orientations to visibility. Quotidian hostilities inform activist orientations to visibility. When hostilities take the form of anti-LGBT abuse, violence, or verbal threats, gender and sexual minorities may begin to anticipate and incorporate these incursions into their quotidian routines by taking different routes to work and avoiding certain places or individuals (Reid and Dirsuweit 2002). Violence and harassment can continue to surprise persecuted minorities, even when they are aware of the possibility of harm. In this way, violence haunts the quotidian, never disappearing completely as a horizon of possibility. In South Africa, black lesbians living in Johannesburg townships navigated the quotidian possibility of antilesbian violence,[3] a material reality that influenced FEW's strategic orientation to visibility.

It might be tempting to assume that soft repression in Namibia and antilesbian violence in South Africa forced Sister Namibia and FEW, respectively, into default positions of invisibility. However, this presumption would overestimate the effect of sociopolitical deterrence on LGBT activism and overlook the strategic possibilities that temporary, intentional invisibility offers movements. In this chapter, I show how activists with FEW and Sister Namibia managed lesbian movement organizations' visibility. Activists internalized and responded to salient features of the sociopolitical field, namely, antilesbian violence in the case of FEW and soft repression in the case of Sister Namibia, when fashioning a strategic orientation to visibility.

Depending on the sociopolitical field and movement's focus, organizations may develop particular strategic orientations to public visibility and invisibility (Downey and Rohlinger 2008).[4] Activists may craft a strategic orientation that tends toward invisibility, screening the organization from unwanted attention or hostility. An approach to lessened public visibility or invisibility can shield an organization and constituents from harm and scrutiny in a hostile sociopolitical field and cement a homogeneous and insular collective identity. Invisibility or guarded visibility can resemble exclusion in that activists refuse membership status to individuals or groups or reject advances from certain prospective audiences (Bernstein 1997; Zald and Ash 1966). Organizations with strategic orientations favoring public visibility may forge relationships with multiple audiences. Openness to working with different audiences may garner a movement organization a reputation for inclusivity. A hospitable sociopolitical field is not a necessary condition for strategic orientations that favor public visibility; in fact, activists may intentionally cultivate inclusion and openness in a hostile field to rally allies to their cause.

I show how FEW and Sister Namibia cultivated different strategic orientations to visibility specific to the nature of anti-LGBT hostility in their respective sociopolitical fields. Using interviews and ethnographic observation, I illustrate how FEW fashioned an orientation that favored lessened visibility in the context of black South African lesbians' experiences of violence, harassment, and discrimination. FEW provided safe spaces for black lesbians away from everyday hostilities. Targeting "this lesbian issue" in Namibia, SWAPO leaders mobilized against same-sex sexualities, which sought to undermine the public standing of LGBT movement organizations (New Era 1997, 8). With interviews, ethnographic observation, and newspaper articles, I document how Sister Namibia adopted a strategic orientation with an inclination toward public visibility in response to SWAPO leaders' antagonism. Sister Namibia staff presented the organization as a visible ally with LGBT persons and activism, included lesbian women and rights in its mandate, and forged ties with human rights NGOs, Namibian newspapers, and Northern donors.

Owing to differences in the form and content of anti-LGBT hostility in South Africa and Namibia, activists with FEW approached public visibility in distinct ways.[5] Antilesbian violence in South Africa targeted individual black lesbian women for bodily injury and humiliation. This form of violence took a material form that black lesbian activists dreaded. Despite taking a specific form, the threat of antilesbian violence was diffuse; many black lesbians feared that strangers, acquaintances, or even family members would harass, rape, or abuse them. This specter of violence necessitated an orientation to decreased visibility, resulting in a default position of invisibility that FEW used to protect constituents and the organization. In Namibia, SWAPO leaders deployed soft repression in the form of political homophobia. Although activists with Sister Namibia could not predict exactly when SWAPO leaders would issue homophobic remarks, these discursive threats differed in substance from bodily injury. Certainly, Sister Namibia faced penalties for challenging SWAPO leaders, in the form of a sullied reputation and lack of access to state funding, but these consequences did not approximate the brutality of some black lesbians' experiences. The severity of antilesbian hostility affected organizations' strategic orientations to visibility.

Despite their differing strategic orientations, both FEW and Sister Namibia fostered safe spaces for women to congregate and learn more about sexual diversity. In addition, organizations' strategic orientations did not mean that FEW tended entirely toward invisibility and Sister Namibia toward visibility. FEW charted a pathway from a protected position of less visibility toward greater public visibility as the organization joined a feminist, antiviolence coalition in 2006. In 2005 and 2006, Sister Namibia's tendency to be publicly visible could not prevent the organization from lapsing into a period of invisibility with constituents when it experienced an interruption in funding from Northern donors.

FEW: A Protected Visibility

African radical feminism informed FEW's strategic orientation toward decreased visibility.[6] Establishing safe spaces for black lesbians to meet and organize was consistent with a radical feminist position that prioritized "exclusively female organizations that would offer a safe organizational space for women, one characterized by the values of teamwork, nurturing, and mutual support"

(Hassim 2005, 33). FEW's strategy evoked predecessor black lesbian activist groups (Ditsie 2006, 20).[7] According to black lesbian activists, a black lesbian women's organization was not "a separatist move"; it was meant to empower black lesbians. Before black lesbians could discuss "violence with black gay men, white women and men," they "needed an opportunity" to disclose their experiences in a safe space. "In this sense, we do not apologise for excluding others" (Kwesi and Webster 1997, 90). As a strategy of visibility, insularity nurtured constituents' exploration of their identities, which they would deploy later publicly under controlled circumstances.

Antilesbian violence constitutes part of a larger landscape of violence against women in postapartheid South Africa (Gqola 2007; Gunkel 2010; Jewkes and Abrahams 2002; Mkhize et al. 2010; Moffett 2009; Sanger 2010; Wood 2005).[8] High rates of violence against women have roots in apartheid structures. Apartheid authorities used controlling visibilities linking African masculinities to violence to justify constraints they placed on African men's mobility (Morrell 1998; Ratele 2008). Apartheid policies impeded African men's "ability to attain the signifiers of social manhood. This emasculation occurred both as a result of economic change and of ideologies which infantilised or pathologised African men and their sexuality" (Epprecht 1998, 641). African nationalist discourses and images of armed black men challenged harmful constructions of African masculinities, generating "hyper-heterosexism" (Epprecht 2004, 208).

Violence has become a salient feature in black women's and men's postapartheid renegotiation of intimate, heterosexual relationships (Walker 2005). Violence is a mechanism through which some black men reassert their patriarchal dominance over black women and register their dissatisfaction with their lack of economic opportunities and cultural displacement, structural inequalities the postapartheid state has not sufficiently redressed (Gqola 2007; Moffett 2009). Rape has received much popular, political, and academic attention in the last fifteen years, and an oft-heard refrain is that South Africa has one of the highest rates of sexual violence in the world (Posel 2005). The "rate of reported rape is 194 per 100,000" South African women, which is "at least three times higher than . . . the rate in the United States" (Jewkes et al. 2006, 2950). There are an estimated 2,070 incidents of rape or attempted rape per 100,000 women between 17 and 48 years of age each year (Jewkes and Abrahams 2002, 1231). This specter of violence overshadows the EC, which guarantees gender and sexual equality. This includes the right for women to "be free from all forms of violence from either public or private sources," rendering "sexual violence . . . an avowedly public matter" (Posel 2005, 129). However, no law currently recognizes hate-motivated crimes, including antilesbian rape

(Anguita 2011; Nel and Judge 2008).[9] Despite the lack of anti–hate crimes legislation, the transformation of private issues of intimacy and violence into public gender and sexual politics has heightened the visibility of not only feminist activism but also LGBT activism.

Practicing strategic invisibility, FEW staff created a sanctuary for black lesbians from the threat of homophobic violence, specifically from antilesbian violence. Some FEW staff and members had survived the brutality of antilesbian violence evident in the February 2006 murder of Zoliswa Nkonyana, a young black lesbian woman who was killed by a group of men in Khayelitsha, a Cape Town township, because of her sexuality (Huisman 2006; Thamm 2006).[10] The circumstances of Nkonyana's murder mirrored the psychological and physical insecurity that many black lesbians faced daily.[11] A black woman's masculine dress and behavior might lead perpetrators to target black lesbians for punishment, according to Duduzile, a black lesbian and FEW member:[12]

> If you are femme, it doesn't really show that you are a lesbian. . . . But when you are butch, it's when you dress like a man and you act like a man in a way, and that's when you become maybe a target, I would say. . . . That's when they [men] see that you are born with the breasts and all that, but you are acting differently. You dress differently because you dress like a man. That's when they want to prove a point to you that actually you are a woman, you know; that's when they start raping you. . . . [We're] trying to be like them, and they [men] want to see how strong you are and all that. . . . Are you really, you know, can you stand for it or whatever? And [they] prove it to you that actually you are a woman, and they rape you. (interview with the author, February 17, 2006)

The incongruence of women's sexed bodies and gender presentations rendered black butch lesbians visible as "lesbians."[13] To male perpetrators of violence, black lesbians' visible gender and sexual nonconformity threatened to upend the heteropatriarchal order; for perpetrators, antilesbian violence restored the public normalcy of this order. The public visibility of gender and sexual variance on individual bodies was a basic concern for black lesbians and FEW staff. Invisibility was an attractive cloak to some black lesbians who survived or feared being the targets of antilesbian violence.[14]

Within a sociopolitical field that generated insecurity for black lesbians, FEW worked from a default position of invisibility and insularity to target local audiences and recruit black lesbians.[15] FEW's strategic orientation favoring decreased visibility involved movement from a default position of invisibility and insularity to one of gradual public visibility, as FEW engaged with other audiences such as feminist and HIV/AIDS activists. FEW prioritized fostering a black lesbian collective identity among members by creating and maintaining safe spaces for members. Staff monitored the safety of its spaces in all services and activities that FEW offered. Services and activities included, but were not limited to, a gender and sexuality resource center; computer, communication, life, and photography skills training; a theatrical troupe (SAfrodykes); a women-only soccer team (the Chosen FEW); self-defense training; gender and sexual identity workshops; and counseling (Naidoo and Muholi 2010). These services and activities reinforced the collective identity FEW crafted around empowering black lesbian women who would visibly challenge sexist and homophobic violence. To maintain identity cohesiveness and organizational insularity, FEW staff made a series of strategic decisions about organizational spaces.

Who Belonged to FEW?

To create uniform spaces that protected and insulated constituents from prying visibility, FEW staff homogenized constituents' identities. Managing and reducing identity ambiguity was an important feature of FEW's "identity work" (Einwohner, Reger, and Myers 2008; Snow and McAdam 2000). Through identity work, FEW staff controlled who could access the organization, yet many potential members did not necessarily identify as either "women" or "lesbians," requiring staff to consider how they recognized and interpreted gender and sexual nonconformity.

FEW framed its goal of stopping antilesbian violence within a larger framework of redressing inequalities that stemmed from apartheid—an example of how apartheid-era exclusionary practices continued to structure the choices available to LGBT activists. Poor, working-class, and jobless black lesbians constituted a marginalized group in a nation in which black Africans had historically been denied access to decent education and jobs and subjected to state violence (Mamdani 1996; Swarr and Nagar 2003). Gendered and sexualized aggression was marked by frustration and an uncertain sense of the future. Poor, undereducated, and unemployed black lesbians who could not escape unpredictable township life sometimes became victims of violence (Moothoo-Padayachie 2004; Muholi 2004). FEW worked exclusively with poor or working-class black lesbian women who had survived antilesbian violence in Johannesburg and the surrounding townships, in part because the LGBT movement had not addressed their needs specifically (Oswin 2007). FEW staff tried to insulate them from additional hardships and to allow black lesbians to develop individual strengths that would accumulate into collective black lesbian visibility.

Community representatives enforced most membership exclusions because they were best suited to do so. FEW's leaders earned a decent income because of their paid positions at the organization and did not live in townships. Although, as black lesbians, they felt at risk for violence, their experiences did not mirror those of prospective members as closely as those of community representatives. Community representatives hailed from townships and identified as black lesbians, and before joining FEW, they had little prior job experience, if any. Some community representatives had survived antilesbian violence and could empathize with prospective members in similar situations, making them ideal for recruiting members.

To ensure membership exclusivity, prospective members completed questionnaires that community representatives brought on their recruitment trips to townships. Prospective members answered questions about their sexuality, gender, class, race, and antilesbian-violence survivor status. To make constituents feel safe in organizational spaces, FEW excluded biological males, regardless of their sexual orientation. Staff allowed only women without jobs or a secondary school diploma to enroll in skills training courses they offered; however, women with diplomas and jobs could still participate in events and use FEW's library. Women who had survived violence had the greatest access to all of FEW's services and spaces.

FEW intentionally recruited black lesbians only, but defining who a "black lesbian" was became a concern when constituents did not already use these identity categories.[16] During a visit I made to Tembisa, a township east of Johannesburg, with a community representative in December 2005, a prospective member hesitated in naming her gender and sexuality. She asked the representative, "Am I a man or a lesbian?" Such gender and sexual identity "confusion" was not uncommon among black lesbians whom FEW recruited. Those who recognized themselves as gay or lesbian might be pejoratively referred to as *istabane,* an intersex person whose body was "not strictly male or female" (Swarr 2003, 196).[17] Because sexual desire, anatomical sex, and socially constructed sex, gender, and sexual identity categories did not map neatly on to one another, such slippages sometimes erupted as identity incongruence, an unsettling idea for some black South Africans and a potential dilemma for an organization built on stable notions of gender and sexuality (Swarr 2009). Fixing sex, gender, and sexuality in place emerged as necessary for FEW's identity work.

Duduzile described how, before coming into contact with FEW, some black lesbians identified themselves as heterosexual men:

> Some . . . will think that they are straight [men] at this point. They don't really know. Maybe they've got this feeling to gravitate to another woman, but they don't know what to do with that. I mean, according to the community that

we are around . . . it's wrong to feel like that and because of culture, because of the religion . . . I mean, they don't know what to do with how they feel.

Duduzile's depiction illustrates the existence of alternative, indigenous ways for black lesbians to understand their gender and sexuality, modes of identification that did not map directly onto Western models of gender and sexuality.

Owing to the cultural saturation of heteronormativity, the conflation of visible gender and sexual nonconformity caused some black South Africans to assume that women who dressed like men and were in relationships with women identified as men. Mandisa explained,

> The public has a perception that lesbians are trying to change themselves to be men. . . . The only difference between me and a straight person is that I love women; they love the opposite sex. At the end of the day, behind this lesbian is a woman. I wouldn't change to be a man for anything. They need to understand that we're lesbians because we love other women, not because I look butch that I'm trying to be a man.

Some female-bodied persons unfamiliar with the terminology used by black lesbian activists referred to themselves as "men." Staff extended membership to these recruits and encouraged them to enroll in sexual and gender identity workshops in which they learned "about lesbianism" (Thandiswa) and "what to do with how they feel" (Duduzile). According to Thandiswa, before joining FEW, "I didn't know anything [about being a lesbian]. I just thought I was just a tomboy. . . . I didn't know the basics of being lesbian, but yes, they [FEW] told me" about what it meant to be a lesbian and how to protect herself (see also Kheswa 2005).[18] Strategically including prospective members who initially identified as men instead of as lesbian women allowed FEW staff to mold and supervise the homogeneity of members' gender and sexual identities and to apply these identity categories to constituents; it did not disrupt FEW's strategic orientation toward lessened visibility. FEW staff still viewed female-bodied persons who identified as "men," by virtue of their being in a relationship with a woman or attracted to women, as constituents. Such recruits had not yet been exposed to categories about gender and sexual identities.[19] This decision enabled FEW to cast a wider membership net than if the organization had restricted itself to recruiting only women who were sure they were lesbians and were familiar with lesbian identity terminology.

FEW strategically recruited women from similar backgrounds to create a distinctive, mobilizable, and homogeneous collective identity that addressed disadvantage, which contributed to the organization's default position of invisibility. For FEW, race, gender, class, sexuality, and antilesbian-violence survivor status were signifiers of disadvantage against which it worked to empower black lesbians to become women who could overcome oppression. Activists with FEW did not politicize a black racial identity when constructing a lesbian collective identity, though blackness had been a mobilizable force within South African townships, a legacy from the Black Consciousness movement (Bozzoli 2004; Magaziner 2010). Instead, they coded race (black) and class (working poor) to signify disadvantage, much as the NCGLE and Equality Project had done (Oswin 2007). The conflation of these indicators of disadvantage insulated FEW's safe spaces and members.[20]

Despite FEW's success in achieving homogeneity in members' class, gender, sexual, and antilesbian-violence survivor status, membership exclusions around race and ethnicity proved discordant for some members.[21] When I observed the organization, FEW excluded white, Asian Indian, and coloured South Africans as members and staff, a decision that alienated some members. Celia, a FEW member, explained how the director refused to hire her because she was coloured, even though she was qualified for the job:[22]

> When they took me in at FEW, they knew I was coloured. . . . When I went to apply for a job at FEW, a lot of people said to me, "You've got a lot of potential." . . . And then she [FEW's director] said to me, "I'm first going to give preference to black people because it's a black organization." And then I said, "Well, I'm black; my skin is black." And then she said to me, "No, but you're coloured; that is the race that you come from." And she said she was going to give coloureds last preference. . . . I see myself, identify myself as a black woman. . . . I'm also from a poverty-stricken community and family. . . . I also come from a disadvantaged community. (interview with the author, February 9, 2006)

Celia's disgruntlement stemmed from the director's narrow interpretation of her racial identity within an apartheid-era racial framework. To rectify the injustices that poor black South African lesbians suffered, the director discounted Celia's self-identification as black and the rape she had survived. The director also assumed that coloured lesbians did not experience the same racial and class inequalities as black lesbians because coloured South Africans benefited from some apartheid practices and laws that disadvantaged black South Africans.[23] The visibility of racial classification mattered to the director, as it helped to cement and promote black lesbian constituents as a unified group to South Africans. The director's promulgation of a narrow collective identity did not accommodate Celia, who was surprised that an organization that represented her political and social interests would pass her over for a paid staff position. Except for her heritage, Celia met all FEW's membership requirements for employment. She understood her exclusion from employment within FEW as another form of discrimination.

Some staff and members remained unaware of FEW's membership exclusions. FEW's positive messages of feminist empowerment strategically promoted a homogeneity that masked its exclusionary strategic choices. According to Lindiwe,

> At FEW, they don't look at who you are. They don't look at the face or your appearance or anything. They just like the soul behind the appearance, and at FEW, there's no discrimination. There's no black or white. There's no better or bad; there's no ugly or beautiful. It's all about sisterhood and womanhood. And whenever you are sitting in that room, you look at the person sitting next to you, [and] you feel that you're all the same because in a different way you've been through the same experiences. So looking at the person next to you, you see the reflection of yourself.

The exclusionary principle guiding recruitment produced inclusion for Lindiwe. She claimed that members' appearances or self-identifications were not important because their experiences produced sameness within FEW. It was just the opposite. FEW carefully engineered constituents' collective sameness. The processes that inculcated organizational homogeneity were invisible to constituents. Staff enacted exclusionary strategic choices swiftly when new individuals accessed FEW; members did not witness these choices in the open because community representatives and staff made them as embedded bureaucratic decisions, such as when staff decided at meetings which members to enroll in communication, computer, and photography skills courses based on the answers members provided on membership questionnaires.

The omission of difference helped produce FEW's default position of insularity and invisibility, which anchored the organization's homogeneous black lesbian collective identity. Insularity held black lesbians together. In turn, this cohesiveness served as the material foundation for constituents seeking the solace of invisibility in FEW's safe spaces.

Cultivating Organizational Spaces

In 2005, staff had to decide where to locate FEW's office. In 2003, the Johannesburg Development Authority (JDA) invited organizations representing groups marginalized under apartheid, such as LGBT persons, to apply for office space. Behind the Mask obtained office space there. As two Behind the Mask staff members became more interested in the needs of black South

African lesbians, they launched FEW. After receiving funding from Northern donors, in 2005, primarily because of safety concerns, FEW leased office space in the Constitution Hill complex, which housed the Constitutional Court, instead of in one of the townships, where most members lived.[24]

Despite Constitution Hill's new, halcyon image, it was located in "decaying" Hillbrow (Murray 2008, 30). From the 1950s until the 1970s, the neighborhood was known for its white gay community (Conway 2009). In the 1980s, as state authorities repressed antiapartheid protest, the nation experienced an economic downturn, disrupting the provision of social services to inner-city Johannesburg. Residents of Johannesburg regarded Hillbrow as a dangerous, inner-city neighborhood, despite the city's "political, social and economic transformation . . . [which] had moved the city away from its racialised past by 1999" (Dykes 2004, 175). As in other South African cities, the signs of security are visible in central Johannesburg (Samara 2011). Armed security guards stand outside businesses. Homes, businesses, and schools resemble impenetrable fortresses with high walls topped with barbed and/or razor wire and electric gates designed to keep strangers away. Johannesburg's fortified enclaves facilitated the flight of black, coloured, Asian Indian, and white middle classes (Murray 2011). The threat of generalized violence in Hillbrow and Johannesburg townships underscored the antilesbian violence against which FEW organized.

A culture of security engulfed FEW, undergirding its default invisibility. When visitors entered the office area, housed in the Women's Gaol, they passed through security.[25] A few footsteps took visitors past a well-tended garden, through a courtyard filled with apartheid memories, and into FEW's buzzing office. Noise from the office confirmed the presence of staff and members and reinforced a sense of belonging for young black lesbians, some of whom had been thrown out of their homes because of their sexuality. That FEW had an office in the former Women's Gaol was of historic significance, which members like Lindiwe recognized. She stated,

> Looking at this place, it makes you think and realize that everything is possible to be changed. As long as there's wrong, a right can be done. . . . And through the process of corrections, I see the brighter future. . . . And it makes you as a lesbian—because we always think and feel we are always oppressed in so many ways—I feel that for the first time we are given a fair platform to [be] mainstream, to be part of the normal society.

The former prison, a site of hidden human rights violations, had become a safe space for black lesbians seeking safety. Embossed testimony from former women prisoners on the windows reminded visitors, members, and staff of the prison's role in sustaining apartheid. It would have been unthinkable thirty years ago for young black lesbians to congregate visibly in the courtyard at the Women's Gaol, unless they were prisoners being escorted to their cells.

FEW worked to create safe spaces for black lesbians. As a result, many members described FEW as a "home," a home that some constituents lacked:

> It's a home in a sense that you get empowered mentally. You get informa-
> tion, you get informed . . . you get skills . . . and you grow as an individual
> personality. You get to identify yourself, you get to assert, to learn more about
> yourself. And you get to deal with your issues in a right way, in a good way,
> positive way. And it's . . . a safe space for everyone. (Lindiwe, black lesbian
> and FEW member, interview with the author, February 14, 2006)

FEW structured its spaces as welcoming and nurturing to members to enable them to become more assertive so that they could protect themselves from violence when they left the confines of the organization. Homogeneity doubled as insularity. Members and staff prized the security that came from associating with other black lesbians, which both created homogeneity among members and staff, reinforcing their individual and collective identities as black lesbians, and insulated them from cultivating relationships with South Africans who differed from them.

FEW's decision to locate its office in central Johannesburg frustrated some members who had to travel long distances to reach the main office.[26] Satellite offices in townships could have enabled members to "access all of these resources near them instead of them coming all the way to town" (Mandisa, black lesbian and FEW member, interview with the author, March 16, 2006). Nomsa, a black lesbian and FEW member, echoed this sentiment (interview with the author, March 17, 2006):

> If they [FEW] had offices down there, it would be easier for them [members]
> because they'd [members] know that the office is just within walking distance,
> you know, instead of having to catch a taxi. And it's quite a long drive. And
> they still have to walk up the steep hill [from the Park Station taxi rank in
> downtown Johannesburg to the office]. So, yes, it's quite a distance. If they
> had offices [in the townships], they [members] wouldn't have to walk the
> distance and worry about transport fare because sometimes they don't even
> have that money to go there. You [members] want to speak to someone. You're
> dying to speak to someone. You're dying to be heard. You can't even make a
> call because you can't afford it at that time. So if they [FEW] had offices in
> the townships, it would be easier for them [members] because they'd know,
> "I'm just walking there, and I know I'm going to find someone to talk to."

Members sacrificed materially to make the trip into central Johannesburg by forgoing cell phone calls. FEW was not the first LGBT movement organization to confront the dilemma of balancing constituents' material needs with professionalization. In the 1990s, GLOW experienced problems "related to transport, communication, distance, dispersion, and lack of money," which prevented constituents' "real and consistent involvement" in the organization (McLean and Ngcobo 1995, 182). FEW's decision to locate the office in central Johannesburg trumped individual members' needs, demonstrating the organizational and ethical tension that existed between providing social services directly to black lesbians and creating a visible black lesbian activist presence in South Africa.

FEW combated members' concerns about its invisibility in townships by hiring community representatives to recruit black lesbians and meet with current and prospective members. Staff claimed that FEW was one of the few South African LGBT movement organizations to bring activism directly to constituents. Community representatives traveled to one familiar township and one new township on a monthly basis. They met with women individually or in small groups, often in their homes. By meeting lesbians where they lived, community representatives circumvented the problem of requiring current and prospective members to travel to inner Johannesburg because it was expensive for many constituents (Swarr and Nagar 2003).[27]

FEW's office location facilitated its physical access to the Constitutional Court. In turn, this location enhanced FEW's gradual visibility with political institutions and other organizations. For several days in May 2005, FEW provided transportation for dozens of black lesbian members from townships to the office so that they could participate in protests pressuring the Constitutional Court to legalize same-sex marriage. FEW became known among South African LGBT and feminist movement organizations for being able to mobilize large numbers of black lesbians.[28] During Zuma's rape trial, feminist movement organizations approached FEW about mobilizing black lesbians for protests at the Johannesburg High Court. Access to meeting spaces in the Constitutional Court complex enabled FEW to host or cohost (with Behind the Mask) LGBT movement activities, such as JWG meetings, allowing FEW to demonstrate its ability to handle logistical concerns, and possibly portending the allocation of more LGBT movement-related responsibilities to FEW.

FEW's office generated both advantages and disadvantages for the organization's visibility management. The security features of FEW's office constituted material sanctuary for black lesbian constituents seeking intentional invisibility, which, in turn, bolstered staff and members' efforts to reinforce the gradual visibility of black lesbian activists. However, the location of FEW's office in central Johannesburg was an obstacle for some constituents. The physical distance between FEW's office and Johannesburg townships may have contributed to the organization's invisibility with black lesbian members. Yet FEW's proximity to the Constitutional Court and downtown served to enhance the organization's reputation with the state, other LGBT movement organizations, and feminist groups.

Who Could Access Organizational Spaces?

FEW staff also made decisions about who was permitted in FEW's office and workshop spaces. Such exclusionary strategic choices worked well within the space of the office but posed difficulties when staff hosted events beyond FEW's office. Spatial exclusions at FEW were inflexible, as evidenced in the office's physical safety. Visitors had to pass through and sign in with security before entering the office complex. Men were not allowed to step into FEW's office space. The receptionist was able to see if men were approaching the office from across the courtyard. Instead of allowing men in the office, staff met with them in the courtyard to preserve the office's gendered integrity.[29] FEW's rules did not allow individual staff or members to be alone with men. This strategic choice helped members feel safe within the organization. The absence of men gave survivors of antilesbian violence the space to mend in a nonthreatening environment.

FEW staff had to figure out how to enforce spatial exclusions based on gender and sexuality at events held outside the organization's office. Each year, FEW staged a community intervention in a township. FEW staff and constituents met with local authorities, such as the police, educators, and health care providers, to discuss how they could better serve black lesbians. At a community intervention in April 2006 in Mohlakeng, a township one hour southwest of Johannesburg, FEW staff held an antiviolence training workshop for constituents. Before the workshop began, FEW's director asked several feminine black gay men, who helped staff clean and set up the facility, to leave. These men identified as gay, not as transgender, according to a FEW staff member.[30] Even though black gay men might suffer the similar stigmatization that black lesbians did, FEW excluded black gay men from its events. Thandiswa, a black lesbian and FEW member, attributed the decision to exclude gay men from events to the director, who "for one doesn't like gay men. Every time we have an event and gay men are here, she just tells them, you know, 'This is a lesbian organization.' . . . But we work with the LGBTI [community], but mainly it's the 'L' that we're interested in" (interview with the author, March 8, 2006). The director worried that the presence of men, no matter what their sexual orientation was, would undermine an ethos of honesty and disclosure she hoped to instill at the workshop. The director also stated, "I don't know what their [gay men's] issues are," suggesting that a gulf separated black lesbians' issues from those of black gay men.

Even though black gay men experienced violence and discrimination because of their perceived gender and sexual transgression, as many black lesbian women did, creating a women-only space trumped black LGBT persons' common experience of violence. In this way, staff actively emphasized the bonds of gender within FEW. Including gay men in events might have alienated black lesbian members because they might have perceived black gay men as men before they viewed them as similarly vulnerable based on their gender and sexual nonconformity.[31] FEW's approach diverged from that of a Pretoria-based movement organization, OUT LGBT Well-Being (OUT), which addressed the vulnerability of both black lesbians and gay men "in under-resourced contexts" to sexual violence in its booklet explaining how LGBT persons could survive rape (International Lesbian and Gay Association 2006b, 14). In contrast, FEW staff treated black lesbians' vulnerability in a gender-specific manner by encouraging constituents to identify how South African cultures required women to be passive and to challenge this cultural norm by becoming assertive. Under the rubric of "empowerment," FEW offered services specifically to help black lesbians to become more assertive, particularly by articulating their needs and desires. FEW's communication, computer training, and photography classes and counseling services and the director's professionalization of staff members all boosted members' self-esteem in women-only spaces. The presence of gay men may have dampened the camaraderie and support I witnessed during a self-defense training workshop for staff. As staff practiced self-defense moves, some hesitated to engage in a show of force. To energize those reluctant to practice self-defense tactics on the instructor, a white man who wore full-body padding, some shouted encouraging phrases such as "Kick him hard in the groin!"

Sponsoring self-defense training workshops and distributing pamphlets on safety precautions were also ways in which FEW staff tried to instill spatial monitoring of visibility in members. Spatial monitoring allowed black lesbians to manage the unpredictability of new, mixed-gender environments. For instance, community representatives were careful about their personal safety when visiting unfamiliar townships, opting for invisibility. They normally made appointments with gatekeepers and did not wear T-shirts that identified them as being with FEW. Several current and prospective members usually met the community representative when she arrived in the township. FEW staff also encouraged members to engage in similar practices and precautions. As FEW staff intended the antiviolence training workshop to result in participants duplicating safe spaces outside the workshop, FEW staff recommended that members monitor their behavior and surroundings. Advocating sexual invisibility, one staff member stated, "We can't expect to be lovey-dovey in a heterosexual tavern" because men might think "they're on each other, and we can't put our thing there," a depiction of men's aggression toward lesbians. FEW's director reminded members that even though LGBT persons had the same constitutionally guaranteed rights as heterosexuals, public same-sex sexual behavior was not tolerated: "We can do this in a safe space, not in a taxi or at the Bree or Noord taxi rank [a hub for taxis to townships]."

FEW staff urged members to be aware of the gendered composition of space. In a disturbing tale of violence, a member's account of how a heterosexual woman acquaintance participated in setting up her rape reminded constituents to be aware of their context.[32] A FEW staff member stressed that unless constituents knew exactly with whom they were socializing, it might be better to socialize only with black lesbians, further reinforcing the safety of homogeneous spaces and lowering the visibility of individual women. Although internal homogeneity only suspended the insecurity black lesbians experienced outside the confines of FEW's organizational spaces temporarily, it provided FEW with a way to model managing uncertainty for constituents.

Visibility strategies unfolded at both the organizational and individual levels within FEW. Not only did staff foster safe space within FEW's office but this visibility strategy also extended to spaces outside the office. Excluding men from FEW spaces and events upheld the organization's commitment to security, cloaking the organization in lessened visibility. Promoting spatial monitoring as an individual-level visibility strategy, FEW indirectly patrolled the spaces constituents inhabited and traversed when they left the confines of FEW's office. In this way, FEW staff transmitted visibility strategies to individuals. Constituents' safety and invisibility were strategic priorities for FEW; spatial monitoring composed a short-term strategy that empowered black lesbians, while the organization pursued a long-term strategy of eradicating antilesbian violence, which would remove obstacles to black lesbians' visibility. These visibility priorities were complementary. In fact, spatial monitoring became crucial for activists with FEW when they probed the possibility of protesting at Jacob Zuma's rape trial in central Johannesburg in February 2006.

Visibility as Vulnerability: Should FEW Protest Publicly?

The postapartheid specter of violence influenced FEW's decision to participate in public protest. At the antiviolence training workshop, FEW's director aptly depicted how violence had become routinized in the lives of many South Africans. She remarked that all South Africans "should be in therapy [because of apartheid]. We've grown accustomed to violence, and we do nothing about it.

We should have a problem with violence being perpetrated against us." Since FEW had a goal of eradicating violence against lesbians, staff and constituents tried to avoid it, which was evident in two public protests in which FEW participated. In September 2005, FEW mobilized 150 black LGBT persons to march in the first black LGBT Pride March in Soweto. Mandisa felt safe participating in the march. "Nothing would have happened because it was a whole lot of people. . . . Anything was possible, but I felt, you know, when we're together, that's your safe space, when you're with lesbians in the same spot. That's our safe space. I felt safe simply because it was a group of us, and nothing would have happened." Mandisa thought that the presence of many black LGBT attendees likely quelled any potential countermovement activity or violence. In this instance, the public visibility of black LGBT activists did not produce hostility in Soweto, despite individual black lesbian women's experiences to the contrary.

A larger number of multiracial LGBT persons and supporters could not prevent an isolated violent episode a few days later at the Johannesburg LGBT Pride March. A black lesbian woman on FEW's float was wounded when a broken bottle volleyed from the crowd struck and lacerated her neck (Ayanda 2006). A nurse practitioner, the partner of a FEW staff member, rushed to the woman's aid; the member survived this act of violence, which FEW staff interpreted as an attack against black lesbians. For Thandi, a black lesbian and FEW member, the violence "spoiled" Pride for her. She explained, "I was in the truck as well. It could have been me [who was injured]. It could have been my partner. It could have been anybody" (interview with the author, March 16, 2006). Within the span of a few days, FEW staff and members experienced exhilaration when marching unimpeded through Soweto for the first time as part of a black LGBT activist contingent and then disquiet when one of their own was injured. These varied experiences exemplify how FEW negotiated tumultuous public spaces. The salience of violence influenced how, when, and why FEW engaged in public protest.

FEW staff and members marshaled their intolerance for violence into selective visibility at public protests. In May 2005, FEW mobilized dozens of black lesbians to attend protests supporting marriage equality at the Constitutional Court, which was on FEW's turf. Venturing outside of their routinized insularity and into greater public visibility required activists' careful deliberation. In February 2006, a group of FEW staff and members decided to participate in protests outside the Johannesburg High Court at former Deputy President Jacob Zuma's rape trial. Dubbed "Khwezi" ("star") in media accounts, a black, HIV-positive female activist and family friend of Zuma in her thirties accused him of raping her while she was staying at his Johannesburg home in November 2005 (Hassim 2009b, 58). Just a few months before his arrest for rape, Zuma had been dismissed from his executive post amid a corruption scandal (Russell 2009).[33] Zuma's defense claimed that the sex was consensual, an assertion with which prosecutors disagreed. Khwezi, a Zulu woman, regarded Zuma as a father figure and not as a potential sexual partner. Khwezi even identified herself as a lesbian to demonstrate that she would not have chosen Zuma as a sexual partner (*Mail & Guardian* 2006b).[34] Testifying in spoken isiZulu, Zuma claimed that the garment Khwezi was wearing at the time constituted a request to have sex; not to honor her unspoken request to have sex would have amounted to rape, according to Zuma's interpretation of Zulu customs.[35] In other words, Zuma alleged that Khwezi's clothing provoked his attack. The prosecution stated that Zuma entered the bedroom where Khwezi was sleeping with the intention of raping her. The defense refuted the prosecution's version of events and tried to discredit Khwezi by casting her as someone who, in the past, had falsely accused other men of rape in her effort to gain attention. During and after the trial, Zuma maintained that the rape trial was part of a political conspiracy that his enemies within the ANC had hatched to derail his presidential campaign (Evans and Wolmarans 2006).

Zuma's rape trial served as a rallying call for LGBT, feminist, and HIV/AIDS activists to fight violence against women (Hassim 2009b). On the first day of the trial in February 2006, several dozen feminist and HIV/AIDS activists protested the high rates of violence against women in South Africa and demanded justice for all female survivors of violence. Hundreds of pro-Zuma activists demonized Khwezi and feminist activists with chants and signs, some of which read "Burn the Bitch," and lit pictures of her on fire (Hassim 2009b; Robins 2008, 152).[36] Discussing her experience protesting on the trial's first day, Carrie Shelver, the spokesperson for People Opposing Woman Abuse (POWA), suggested that Zuma's "inappropriate" performance of the liberation movement song "My Machine Gun" ("Umshini Wami"), incited the crowd to perpetrate violence against women (Jasson da Costa 2006). Shelver also stated, "Zuma supporters broke through the barriers and came very close to us and made signs that our throats would be slit" (Jasson da Costa 2006, 3). Although Zuma supporters' performances of violent misogyny set feminist activists on edge, these tactics of intimidation did not subdue feminists.

Invited by feminist activists to join them for protests demanding an end to violence against women, FEW activists walked from their office to the High Court on the second day of Zuma's trial, which fell on Valentine's Day. As a group, FEW members cautiously approached the group of pro-Zuma protestors, who were surrounded by armed police officers, at the Johannesburg High

Court. FEW activists could not easily identify the feminist activist contingent they intended to join. Zuma supporters were shouting hostile, antifeminist slogans and demanding Zuma's acquittal. Some Zuma supporters carried provocative signs that indicated they would resort to violence if he was not acquitted. One sign read, "SANDF [South African National Defence Force] and SAPS [South African Police Service] Be Prepared for Civil War If Zuma Is Convicted!" Anyone perceived to be critical of Zuma, including black lesbian activists, would not have been welcomed by the crowd of Zuma supporters and could have faced physical violence. FEW activists faced a dilemma: should they enter the crowd to find feminist activists and register their visible presence as opposing violence against women, or should they pursue invisibility and withdraw from the protest to preserve their safety?

Engaging in spatial monitoring of their unpredictable surroundings, FEW staff and members made their way through the crowd, trying to locate the feminist activist contingent. The atmosphere outside the Johannesburg High Court, which is situated in the downtown business district, was tense. After consulting with FEW's public relations and outreach officer, who had attended the protest on the previous day, they decided to carry a folded banner with FEW's logo in a bag. Drawing public visibility to their sexual identities on this well-trafficked route was undesirable for FEW activists. Underneath plain T-shirts and jackets, they wore FEW T-shirts with catchy slogans such as "Hate Won't Make Me Straight," "Get It Straight, I Can't Be Fixed," and "The Rose Has Thorns," the slogan from FEW's antilesbian-violence campaign; staff and members planned on shedding their outerwear once they reached the feminist activist contingent. FEW activists walked about ten blocks from FEW's Hillbrow office to the High Court, a route that took them past the Park Station bus and train terminal and through a throng of street hawkers. Once they arrived in front of the courthouse, FEW staff and members ducked under police cordons and melted into the crowd of black pro-Zuma supporters who were *toyi-toyi*-ing.[37] FEW activists looked no different than pro-Zuma supporters, apart from their lack of Zulu nationalist symbols, such as the T-shirt "100% Zulu Boy," a reference to Zuma's adherence to Zulu customs (Moya 2006). Black lesbian activists wondered if they should sacrifice their invisibility and stage a counterprotest.

FEW activists risked snaking through the multitude of opponents on the assumption that other feminist activists were on the other side of the crowd. FEW activists spent fifteen minutes wandering through the crowd with no luck; they located no feminist or HIV/AIDS activists. For an additional twenty minutes, they discussed finding a place at the edge of the crowd to set up a protest, but all admitted to feeling uncomfortable and unsafe among pro-Zuma supporters. Jackie, a black lesbian and FEW member, described her discomfort being outside the court amid Zuma's supporters:

> It was very scary for us because the Zulu men and women were busy swearing at us, and we were so scared that if we just decided to leave that place, they would follow us. . . . They were busy swearing at us, and they had the *sjambok* [nightstick used by the South African Police Service] in their hands and everything, and we got so scared. Anything could have happened in that space. (interview with the author, March 8, 2006)

Jackie described her nervousness at the protest's unpredictability and the likelihood that the Zulu pro-Zuma protestors would have harassed them as black lesbian activists. That Zuma supporters and the police had *sjamboks,* a symbol of apartheid violence sometimes wielded indiscriminately by South African police, made FEW activists nervous. FEW activists' careful public self-presentations kept them safe in this politically charged environment.

FEW staff and members did not want to provoke the animated crowd. As Njabulo, a black LGBT student activist, explained,

> Zulu culture is very masculine oriented, very patriarchal with very strict and clear definitions of what makes a man. Anything that deviates from that, which would include issues around sexual orientation, would then be taboo. . . . In terms of culture, you'd get arguments coming up like . . . if the family starts taking different forms, our culture will lose its vibrancy or . . . its moral fiber. (interview with the author, December 5, 2005)

Zulu pro-Zuma activists could have used black lesbian activists' racial and sexual identities to declare them racial and cultural traitors and viewed their violation of African patriarchal gender norms as worthy of punishment (Robins 2008). Thus, the visibility of black lesbian activism in this venue could have threatened men's masculinities.

After calling the FEW media and outreach officer who was not in attendance, staff and members decided against publicly protesting that day because they feared that their presence as black lesbian activists would aggravate protestors.[38] They opted not to identify themselves visibly as being with FEW or as lesbians. FEW staff and members believed that choosing invisibility kept them safe. Activists' choices affected what they perceived as strategic possibilities later. FEW staff lacked accurate information about the protest and did not understand how politically charged the protest was. Although FEW staff and members opted to remain publicly invisible on that day, a strategic decision that ensured their safety, they protested alongside feminist and HIV/AIDS activists on subsequent days.

FEW could have used the rape trial to advance the organization's goals by framing the rape of Khwezi, a self-identified lesbian, as part of the spectrum of antilesbian violence (News24 2006). Such a framing could have drawn public attention to antilesbian violence. However, activists with FEW declined to frame the case solely in terms of antilesbian violence. Jackie interpreted FEW's participation in protests at the rape trial as requiring black lesbian activists "to be invisible" in favor of fighting the more general problem of violence against women. According to Jackie, activists with FEW were "not saying just black lesbians" faced gender-based violence; FEW joined the protests "to support" female rape survivors "because each and every day a woman gets raped."

Black lesbian activists' regular participation in protests at the rape trial widened FEW's vision to accommodate larger campaigns focused on eradicating violence against all women, instead of concentrating only on violence against black lesbians. Their participation facilitated FEW's greater visibility within feminist antiviolence initiatives. FEW recruited members to attend and participate in the protests at the Zuma rape trial between February and May 2006. This did not conflict with community representatives' ongoing recruitment of members because they simultaneously recruited new members while publicizing the protests. A feminist, antiviolence movement organization even paid for some FEW constituents' public transportation from Johannesburg townships. Outside the Johannesburg High Court, feminist, HIV/AIDS, and black lesbian activists linked the antifeminist discourse espoused by pro-Zuma activists to institutionalized misogyny (Govender 2006; Swart 2006). Some Zuma supporters "threatened and attempted to intimidate" feminist activists on subsequent protest days, but this did not deter feminist, HIV/AIDS, and black lesbian activists (Haffajee 2006, 26).

Participating in the protests led FEW to join a larger national feminist antiviolence coalition, the One in Nine Campaign, whose name referred to a statistic that only one in nine South African women filed rape charges with police.[39] Staff envisioned FEW's participation in the campaign as a way to educate the general public about and protray the rape of black lesbians as a South African social problem. In this way, FEW's protected visibility, which, in some cases, amounted to invisibility, led the group eventually to a wider public visibility.

Material necessity motivated staff to forge a strategic orientation favoring decreased visibility that not only kept staff and constituents safe but also protected FEW's public reputation. Staff limited the organization's public visibility in several ways. First, a strict membership policy allowed only black lesbian survivors of antilesbian violence to access FEW's full range of services and employment. Such insularity reinforced constituents' homogeneous collective identity but alienated some members whose identities did not conform to these membership criteria. Second, FEW located its office in central Johannesburg in a former prison. Although some members struggled to travel from townships to the city center, those who visited FEW's office found a safe space within the fortified Constitutional Court complex. This choice of office location also benefited FEW politically. The organization's close proximity to the Constitutional Court enabled FEW to mobilize black lesbians to protest at the court in support of marriage equality, enhancing FEW's political clout within the LGBT movement. Third, FEW monitored the gendered composition of its spaces. Staff refusal to allow men, even black gay men, in FEW's spaces confirmed FEW's public profile as an organization that served and represented black lesbian women. Staff encouraged constituents to emulate FEW's policies by monitoring the spaces they frequented as a way to keep themselves safe. Fourth, FEW staff and members improvised their choice to delay joining feminist protestors at Zuma's rape trial. Worried that the boisterous crowd of Zuma supporters might react to the presence of black lesbian activists negatively, FEW staff and members withdrew from the crowd and joined the protest on later days. This microlevel choice reflected FEW's strategic orientation to guarded visibility; the personal safety of FEW's staff and members came first.

Sister Namibia: Strategically Disposed to Visibility

Launched in 1989 on the eve of independence by a small group of women, Sister Namibia was poised to take advantage of the political opportunities that a newly democratizing country could offer (Frank and |Khaxas 1996; Nghidinwa 2008). Sister Namibia nurtured a strategic orientation favoring public visibility. This strategic orientation emerged in Sister Namibia's framing of all Namibian women as the organization's constituency, treatment of lesbian rights as women's rights, and public challenges to SWAPO leaders' antigay statements. Lindsey, a white heterosexual woman and Sister Namibia member, explained that Sister Namibia was "a woman's organization" that fought for "equal rights for women and [tried] to change bad cultural practices that are dangerous for women" (interview with the author, April 25, 2006). Sister Namibia embraced its radical feminist position and sought to eradicate the inequalities that many Namibian women experienced (Hubbard and Solomon 1995).

By framing lesbian rights as women's rights, Sister Namibia garnered a public reputation as a "lesbian" organization. Rina explained,

> Sister is a cutting-edge controversial organization that will say things other
> people will not say. . . . Whatever we say, somewhere the word "lesbian" will

be in it. [Rina laughs.] But they just expect that from us now and that what we say is challenging of the status quo. So I think once you have that kind of image . . . of being a cutting-edge, controversial, sometimes off-the-map human rights organization that will speak things that nobody else will speak, but that need to be spoken, that will break silences. And I think Sister has the same kind of reputation. When Sister speaks, then the journalists will listen, and people will come. They want to know. They want to find out what's up. (interview with the author, May 23, 2006)

Sister Namibia's controversial identity generated positive national and international visibility for the organization but yielded negative consequences for Sister Namibia's feminist projects when SWAPO officials directed their antipathy toward Sister Namibia. Rina's comments also show how different audiences structure social movement organizations' (SMOs) public presentations. "It isn't just the SMO that has a stake in defining the group's collective identity. So too do movement organizations, rival SMOs, law enforcement officials, and the media" (Friedman and McAdam 1992, 166). This sentiment is evident in the director's framing of Sister Namibia as an LGBT movement organization. Expressing surprise at a Northern donor's assumption that TRP was the only LGBT movement organization in Namibia in July 2006, Sister Namibia's director claimed in a staff meeting, "Sister Namibia is an LGBT organization in our own right." She cited Sister's work in mainstreaming lesbian rights with women's rights, the stories on lesbian issues in the magazine over the years, and the videos and books in the library.[40] The director was not maligning TRP's public profile; in fact, since helping to launch TRP in 1996–97, Sister Namibia has maintained close ties with TRP. Instead, the director was affirming Sister Namibia's public reputation as advocating for LGBT persons and rights, particularly for lesbian rights.

Inclusion as a Pathway to Visibility

Whereas FEW strictly monitored membership and recruitment along the axes of race, sexuality, gender, class, and antilesbian-violence survivor status, Sister Namibia framed its constituency broadly and inclusively as consisting of all Namibian women. As a feminist organization in a newly independent nation, Sister Namibia could have aligned itself with SWAPO and recruited women along party lines, actions that would likely have facilitated Sister Namibia's access to state officials and resources (Becker 1995; Geisler 2004). However, SWAPO was one of several audiences Sister Namibia targeted in its effort to transform cultural attitudes toward women, gender, and sexuality and to achieve gender equality. This effort involved the development of a strategic orientation favoring visibility that would sustain targeting different audiences.

In the 1990s, Sister Namibia concentrated on publishing an eponymously named magazine that introduced readers to feminist concepts and issues. Stories often included glossaries that defined terms unfamiliar to readers, such as *feminism, bisexuality,* and *discrimination,* and translated stories originally written in English into Afrikaans and Oshivambo, the most widely spoken indigenous Namibian language. These publication choices facilitated the organization's outreach to ordinary Namibian women. Feminist ideas in *Sister Namibia* resonated with Ellen, a black heterosexual woman and Sister Namibia member, who described her initial acquaintance with the organization through the magazine as one of discovering answers to questions she had about gender in African cultures:

> I started reading the *Sister Namibia* magazine because I always questioned gender roles, and I always questioned the role of women in my culture, in my life, in my family. And it never made sense to me. And so I came across this magazine that explained all of these things that I had questions about, and nobody could answer me. (interview with the author, June 21, 2006)

Sister Namibia staff wanted to reach as many Namibian women as possible and adopted a relaxed understanding of its constituency, enabling as many women as possible to identify with the organization and its demand for gender and sexual equality. This open definition reinforced the image of Sister Namibia as representing Namibian women of all races, classes, and sexualities, outfitting the organization with a strategic orientation favoring public visibility.

In the mid-1990s, staff and members began exploring the issues lesbian and bisexual women faced. Sister Namibia already had a structure in place—staff, office space, and magazine—to facilitate its public profile as a lesbian organization. Two members depicted Sister Namibia's decision to work on lesbian rights:

> The SISTER collective and the magazine provide an important space in which we can develop our identity and creativity. Working together with other lesbians and supportive heterosexual women has brought us out of our social isolation and strengthened our sense of community. This has heightened our awareness of the need for political action on lesbian issues. Through the magazine we can share all this with our readers, and contribute towards the building of a new society based on new values. (Frank and |Khaxas 1996, 116)

In 1996, Sister Namibia hired an educational officer whose responsibilities included researching "issues that are not covered by the mainstream [media] such as backstreet abortions, women in the sex trade, and homosexuality in . . . various ethnic groups" (Sister Namibia meeting minutes, February 19–21, 1996). Incorporating same-sex sexuality as a feminist concern affected how the general public viewed Sister Namibia. Martha, a black lesbian and Sister Namibia member, stated, "Whenever there's an article on homosexuality or lesbianism or gay people, it's kind of like it's a rumor that's going on in the surroundings [townships] that Sister Namibia is a 'homosexual' organization. . . . It's only for gay and lesbian people" (interview with the author, May 29, 2006). Although outsiders may have viewed Sister Namibia exclusively as a lesbian organization, this characterization did not hamper activists' visibility strategies.

In the 1990s and 2000s, Sister Namibia offered gender and sexual minorities a safe space to meet. Karla, a coloured lesbian woman and Sister Namibia member, described how the organization welcomed lesbians:

> Sister [was] providing a safe space for lesbians. . . . I felt very good for the first time when I go in there, and the coordinator at that time, she really made me feel welcome, and I felt that this is just the right place that I was looking for. And I have to say that through Sister, I am growing stronger and stronger to come out and to live my life [as a lesbian]. (interview with the author, May 15, 2006)

Much like FEW, Sister Namibia provided Namibian lesbian and bisexual women with a space in which to meet and to discuss their sexuality safely, away from public scrutiny. In such "free spaces," Namibian women were able to explore cultural and political aspects of their personal identities (Evans and Boyte 1992).

Sister Namibia's safe atmosphere extended to workshops and the resource center. Martha explained that Sister Namibia did not "exclude anyone" from workshops. "These workshops that Sister is having [are] for, like, all the women in general; they invite all the women. They talk about sexuality issues, about sexual rights." Martha stated that Sister Namibia provided

> materials in the resource center for lesbian women like books. You . . . can go and borrow [books], like, free of charge because here we don't charge a fee for borrowing. You can just come and become a member of Sister, and then you can borrow the books. And Sister is a very friendly organization. You come here; nobody will judge you. Either you're a homosexual or you're a heterosexual, and that's what basically I mean about the safe space. It's kind of like a lot of like gay people they are scared because a lot are not

even so out in public, but here they can walk in free and then you can take the book and nobody will ask you, "What are you going to do with this book?" Not like you're going into a public library. And everyone will stare at you just the moment that you walk in through that door. But that's not how it is with Sister.

Martha's description of Sister Namibia's safe space is almost identical to accounts from black lesbian activists about FEW's safe space. However, Sister Namibia's inclusion of all women differed from FEW's exclusionary practices.

Although lesbians might flock to Sister Namibia for sanctuary, the organization remained open to all, including men. Ellen recalled bringing a gay friend to Sister Namibia:

> He also liked it a lot, him being gay and everything. And so I told him about Sister and how it's open about lesbian issues and issues of homosexuality. So he came here with me a couple of months after I came to Sister Namibia, and he spoke to somebody here as well because, at that time, he wanted to know a little bit more about this gay thing. He only came out a few years later when he went to university, but, you know, I know that he came here just to find out a little bit more about this homosexuality issue.

In addition to working on ending gender inequality, Sister Namibia's commitment to sexual-minority equality included gay and bisexual men.

Sister Namibia maintained an open, welcoming office in Windhoek. Ellen recounted her initial experience with Sister Namibia as quite memorable. "I swear to God, I'll never forget it. I walked in here; I was alone. I think I was still in my school uniform. . . . But it was after school, and I walked in. And it was quiet. And there were all of these books. And I just felt, I don't know; it was like this peaceful serene type of feeling that I got. I don't know how to explain it." The inviting atmosphere kept Ellen "coming back." Although the office was located in northwest Windhoek, far from the city's bustling transportation hub, visitors went out of their way to frequent the office. Visitors walked up the steep driveway past the Sister Namibia sign and rang the bell. After the receptionist buzzed them in through the security gate, staff encouraged visitors to converse, read feminist theory or literature written by women, or conduct research for school projects or personal interest. Whenever Ellen visited the office, she mingled with "people here in the resource center, whatever, and I would sit around and talk to them and ask them what they are doing." Ellen never felt like an interloper at Sister Namibia. She felt comfortable talking with women whose names she recognized from the magazine, who, in turn, would ask Ellen, "'So, who are you?" Although Sister Namibia's campaigns had changed over the years, Ellen believed that "the office hasn't changed; it's still the same vibe, . . . the vibe that I felt when I walked in here years ago." Sister Namibia's inclusive atmosphere enabled women from different ethnic groups to collaborate on gender-equality campaigns, enhancing the organization's public profile as working on behalf of all women. In turn, this atmosphere cemented a strategic orientation for Sister Namibia that privileged public visibility.

Lesbians Do Exist in Namibia: Responding to Antigay Antagonists

Configurations of gender and sexuality differed among Namibia's ethnic groups (Kandirikirira 2002). The Ovambo ethnic group, comprising almost 50 percent of the Namibian population, enforced heteronormative gender roles (Isaacks 2005). A common perception of Ovambo social structures was that men held "all the power" (Isaacks 2005, 79). The imposition of indirect rule first under German and then under South African colonial occupation buttressed patriarchal authority in Ovambo society (Becker 2007). Christian and colonial "construction[s] of gender further led to essentialist ideas of gender" (Becker 2007, 29). As many Ovambo Namibians converted to Christianity under German colonialism, Ovambo gender and sexual norms narrowed, and women and men developed a new cultural lexicon for interpreting gender and sexuality (Becker 2006, 2007).[41] Mary, a black lesbian woman and TRP member, described Ovambos as "very reserved and conservative" and opposed to gender and sexual diversity (interview with the author, July 6, 2006).

Afrikaner attitudes also emphasized gender and sexual normativity. Afrikaner social formations historically promoted heteropatriarchy, and heterosexual Afrikaner men defined masculinity in terms of repudiating "gayness" (Wise 2007, 335). Other ethnic groups adopted more tempered stances on same-sex sexualities. Himba and Herero societies recognized the existence of same-sex sexual behavior but did not nurture the open expression of same-sex sexual desire (Talavera 2002). In contemporary Damara culture, gender norms were "not strictly enforced," which, in some ways, facilitated same-sex sexualities (|Khaxas 2005, 127). This did not mean, however, that Damara sexual minorities had "an easy time" (|Khaxas 2005, 130).[42]

Ethnic groups' attitudes toward gender and sexual diversity influenced politicians' policies and public statements. In Namibia, SWAPO officials' political homophobia activated and, in some cases, aggravated ethnic-group opposition toward sexual dissidence. In turn, political homophobia generated increased visibility for LGBT persons and movement organizations in Namibia. Damara gender and sexual minorities experienced harassment primarily in relation to SWAPO political homophobia, while Herero and Ovambo LGBT persons "encountered more intense negative feedback in their communities" (Lorway 2007, 279). Claudia, a black lesbian woman and TRP member, discussed the heightened resentment Ovambo gender and sexual minorities faced as severe and violent:

> The Ovambo people [are] . . . the biggest ethnic group in Namibia. . . . They would go to an extent that they would kill you [LGBT persons]; people have tried doing that, . . . [Ovambo] parents trying to kill their own kids because their kids are gay and lesbian. And the thing is, like back then, we had very few Ovambo people that were out of the closet, you know. But now, we've known they exist, but it's just because of the way the Ovambo people are that people are scared to come out, you know. It's like you get disowned; you get thrown out of [your house]. It's really, really bad. (interview with the author, May 11, 2006)

Daniel, a black gay man and TRP member, compared Damara tolerance of same-sex sexuality with the antagonism some Ovambo gender and sexual minorities experienced. In Damara culture,

> we're very liberal. We're open-minded; we talk about everything. And, yes, it's acceptable to be gay as long as your parents know. Everybody knows; it's okay. They will accept whichever name you want them to refer you to; they'll call you by that name. They'll respect you in all aspects of that. But when it comes to other tribes like within Ovambo [culture], it's something that you don't even put on the table and say, "I am gay." You just don't put it [out] there.

Because Ovambo Namibians dominated SWAPO, Ovambo men had much "political capital" (Dobell 1998; Wise 2007, 334). Given Ovambo cultural prohibitions on gender and sexual transgression, it is not surprising that SWAPO officials expressed intolerance for same-sex sexualities. Not all SWAPO leaders publicly endorsed political homophobia. Former Prime Minister Hage Geingob, a member of the Damara ethnic group, asserted that the state would not prosecute sexual minorities for sodomy (Forrest 2000, 101; *Namibian* 1997d). While Geingob's statement fell short of dissenting with prevailing views within SWAPO about LGBT rights, nevertheless, it highlighted some politicians' disinterest in policing same-sex sexualities.

Against this backdrop, Sister Namibia confronted hostile attitudes toward same-sex sexualities. Not only did Sister Namibia directly challenge SWAPO leaders' political homophobia but the organization also contested ethnic-group attitudes, becoming a "lesbian" organization in the process (*New Era* 1997). In 1995, Sister Namibia demanded that Deputy Lands, Resettlement, and

Rehabilitation Minister Hadino Hishongwa and Finance Minister Helmut Angula apologize for antigay remarks the state-funded newspaper *New Era* solicited from them. Asserting cultural sovereignty, Hishongwa stated that "homosexuality is western, evil and destructive—and should be fought by an emerging society like Namibia" (Mwilima 1995, 2). Hishongwa also rejected the idea that freedom fighters liberated Namibia so that lesbians and gay men could demand equal rights in the new democracy (Mwilima 1995).

Sister Namibia strove to undo the negative visibility ministers' statements produced for LGBT Namibians. Setting in motion Sister Namibia's strategy for responding decisively to SWAPO leaders' homophobic remarks, staff sent a letter to all newspapers in Windhoek. Motivated by the principle of inclusion, in the letter, Sister Namibia disputed the imputation that same-sex sexuality was a disease with a cure and instead valorized same-sex sexual relationships as "alternative, life-affirming physical, emotional and spiritual forms of love" (Sister Namibia 1995). The letter refuted the claim that same-sex sexuality was un-African and cited German anthropologist Kurt Falk's (1998) findings that same-sex sexual relationships existed among Namibian ethnic groups.[43] Asserting that lesbians and gay men were a permanent part of the Namibian sociopolitical landscape, staff concluded the letter by wittily stating, "Fortunately for our two Ministers, homophobia (unlike lesbianism) can be cured!" (Sister Namibia 1995).[44]

Sister Namibia became a fierce critic of SWAPO's soft repression. Sister Namibia's public identity as a lesbian organization solidified when the organization demanded that Nujoma apologize for antigay remarks he made at the SWAPO Women's Council Congress in Gobabis in December 1996. In a press release, Sister Namibia highlighted Namibia's "firmly entrenched democracy" and argued that SWAPO could not arbitrate morality. Fighting "hate speech," Sister Namibia warned,

> Today it is homosexuals and foreigners who are being labeled and threatened, tomorrow it may be trade unionists, unemployed PLAN fighters, women, members of specific ethnic groups or political parties, people with disabilities, religious groups or others.
>
> We . . . urge him [Nujoma] to follow the example set by President Nelson Mandela of South Africa, who strongly supported the inclusion of gay and lesbian rights to freedom from harassment in the South African constitution which he signed into power last week. (Sister Namibia press release, December 17, 1996)

Sister Namibia called for tolerance based on the principle of democratic inclusion. Heralding Mandela's embrace of LGBT rights in South Africa allowed

Sister Namibia to question SWAPO's commitment to democratization and decolonization, particularly to eradicating apartheid injustices. According to Sister Namibia, SWAPO's version of democratization and decolonization differed from that favored by Mandela in South Africa, who had championed LGBT rights before and during his presidency (1994–99) (Epprecht 2001a). Using Mandela as an example, Sister Namibia interrogated SWAPO's authority and commitment to democratic change. If Mandela could magnanimously endorse LGBT rights as part of the ANC's platform to correct historic social injustices, why couldn't SWAPO as the national liberation movement?

SWAPO's understanding of national liberation differed from Mandela's postapartheid vision for the ANC. SWAPO's legitimacy rested "on the claim of the liberation [movement] being representative of the majority of the people" (Melber 2003a, 144). Because SWAPO liberated the nation, it controlled the country's democratic development. Under the aegis of political homophobia, SWAPO leaders sought to advance cultural sovereignty in conjunction with democratization (Melber 2003a). Other explanations for political homophobia also emerged. Sister Namibia, TRP, the NSHR, and the LAC cast SWAPO leaders' homophobic statements as a growing authoritarian streak in Nujoma's administration. These groups demanded that Nujoma and his peers apologize for and retract their remarks. Sister Namibia's visibility with these groups buttressed its position in civil society and reinforced its strategic orientation toward public visibility.

In 1999, SWAPO officials used Sister Namibia's controversial reputation to discredit an ambitious campaign to empower Namibian women politically (Rothschild 2005). Sister Namibia helped launch the Namibian Women's Manifesto and 50/50 Campaign, which aimed to encourage voters to consider children's and women's issues when voting, to "mobilize women as 51 per cent of the electorate to actively participate in all aspects of the forthcoming elections," to demand that more women be appointed to cabinet positions, and to ask political parties to create zebra lists that alternated women's and men's names on electoral rosters (Sister Namibia 1999). Sister Namibia worked with other women's and human rights organizations to persuade political parties to support the 50/50 Campaign (Bauer 2004; Geisler 2004). Targeting political parties as primary audiences enabled Sister Namibia to enhance its public profile.

The Namibian Women's Manifesto framed lesbian rights as "women's rights," which alienated SWAPO and other women's rights organizations (Rothschild 2005).[45] Netumbo Ndaitwah, the SWAPO-affiliated Minister of Women's Affairs, the SWAPO Women's Council, and the University of Namibia's Multidisciplinary Research Centre were all initial signatories to the manifesto, but they objected to the inclusion of lesbian rights in it (Geisler 2004). The passage in the manifesto referring to lesbian rights read, "The human rights of all women, as guaranteed in the Namibian Constitution, need to be ensured, including the rights of the girl child, women living under customary law, women in marginalised ethnic groups, sex workers, disabled women, old women and lesbian women" (Sister Namibia 1999). Taking issue with the lesbian rights passage and another calling for comprehensive sex education in public schools, Ndaitwah alleged that the manifesto would teach children "how to become gays and lesbians" (*Windhoek Observer* 1999, 12). According to Rina, Ndaitwah claimed that Sister Namibia's leaders were lesbian opportunists who were using the manifesto to legalize same-sex marriage so that they could "get married." In an informal conversation in June 2006, a Sister Namibia staff member shared that one member's "legal battle to obtain permanent residency as part of a 'black and white lesbian couple' who took the government [SWAPO] to court over holding their family together" fueled criticisms of the manifesto.[46] For some Namibians, the public commotion over lesbian rights confirmed that Sister Namibia was a lesbian organization. The organization's visibility in relation to one controversial issue skewed public perception of Sister Namibia as a whole.

Karla recalled the clamor that ensued after objectors withdrew their support for the manifesto. She expressed her disappointment that groups interested in advancing women's political representation and empowerment could not work together

> to give women training on becoming decision makers, to train them on politics, to train them on their rights . . . all of a sudden, the Minister of Women's Affairs . . . withdraw[s] just because of one sentence [about lesbian rights]. . . . They just think outside that Sister is a lesbian organization, and they look away from the other good work that Sister is actually doing as a women's organization. . . . I think they really don't look at . . . the good work that Sister is doing.

Karla attributed naysayers' objection to the classification of lesbian rights as women's rights to homophobia and a narrow understanding of Sister Namibia's work, which led to its public portrayal as a controversial lesbian organization. Karla also explained that this exchange prompted some women to "keep their distance from" Sister Namibia. Some women left workshops connected to the 50/50 Campaign and manifesto because they thought Sister Namibia was going to brainwash them by "train[ing] them to become lesbians," according to Karla.

Sister Namibia's strained relationships with state agencies generated different consequences for the group's public visibility. In an informal conversation in April 2006, Rina explained that after the manifesto's unveiling, whenever Sister Namibia submitted a petition to parliament about women's or children's rights, the minister of gender equality and child welfare—formerly, the minister of women's affairs—quashed it simply because it came from Sister Namibia. However, it was hard for the minister to ignore Sister Namibia because "we're too good at networking" with other NGOs, Rina revealed. Despite the flak Sister Namibia received, activists did not budge from the position that lesbian rights were women's rights.

Despite SWAPO-affiliated actors' rejection of the manifesto, opposition parties endorsed increasing women's political participation and representation (Bauer 2004; Geisler 2004). Privately owned newspapers also wooed Sister Namibia, a situation that was unusual for many movement organizations around the world, which often pursued media attention with few results (Sobieraj 2011). The media initiated contact with Sister Namibia about the manifesto and related events: "We stopped calling them; they started calling us" (Rina, interview with the author, May 23, 2006). Not only did SWAPO leaders have criticisms of Sister Namibia, but they also held negative views of independent newspapers such as the *Namibian*.[47] According to Martha, if "the *Namibian* [was] publishing something in the interest of Sister," SWAPO leaders felt that the "media is siding together with Sister Namibia" (interview with the author, May 29, 2006). SWAPO leaders may have perceived Sister Namibia's close ties to independent newspapers as further evidence of the organization's status as a member of the political opposition.

Sister Namibia did not have to adopt a strategy that engaged SWAPO so directly and, in doing so, expose itself to political vulnerability. However, ignoring SWAPO leaders' antigay rhetoric threatened to grant them carte blanche to harass and scapegoat LGBT persons. SWAPO leaders might have interpreted widespread silence on their antigay position as validation. Not responding would have dishonored lesbians who belonged to Sister Namibia and undermined the organization's feminist commitment to "work[ing] toward a society liberated from patriarchal domination in which all people have equal rights and opportunities and live in peace, prosperity and dignity" (Sister Namibia 2003, 2). Reaching out to different audiences, such as opposition political parties, independent media, and human rights organizations, allowed Sister Namibia to bypass the few strategic choices available to it in the Namibian sociopolitical field, which SWAPO dominated.

SWAPO officials framed Sister Namibia as a traitor because the party maintained "a highly unreceptive attitude towards criticism, especially when it is articulated within a public discourse. Non-conformity is associated with disloyalty if not betrayal" (Melber 2003a, 144). Instead of forcing Sister

Namibia into invisibility, SWAPO officials' antigay hostility augmented Sister Namibia's media visibility within Namibia and internationally, a countermovement dynamic that resembles U.S. lesbian and gay activists' and religious right activists' public sparring (Fetner 2008). Sister Namibia also tailored the content of its visibility strategies to ensure that SWAPO leaders did not interpret the organization as completely Western, which could have provided SWAPO "with a legitimate pretext to crack down" on the organization (Snow and Benford 1999, 32).

Visibility Disruptions: Northern Donors, Financial Necessity, and Strategic Priorities

Although cultivating additional audiences, including opposition parties, human rights organizations, and independently owned media, enabled Sister Namibia to bypass SWAPO, these new audiences lacked the resources that would help the organization fund its daily operations. With its public reputation as a lesbian organization and opposition to SWAPO leaders' political homophobia, Sister Namibia was unable to obtain state funding for its projects. Hence, staff had to figure out how to obtain financial support for the organization. Sister Namibia could have turned the magazine into a profitable enterprise, but this goal would have distracted staff from the 50/50 Campaign. Driven by financial necessity, Sister Namibia decided to look beyond the Namibian sociopolitical field to Northern donors for financial support. The organization's national visibility depended on staff's ability to raise funds outside of Africa.

While responding to homophobic statements earned Sister Namibia a national reputation as a controversial lesbian organization, this visibility strategy garnered Sister Namibia an international reputation as a respected LGBT movement organization and human rights defender. For publicly challenging SWAPO leaders' homophobia, Sister Namibia received IGLHRC'S 1997 Felipa de Souza Award, which "recognizes the courage and effectiveness of groups or leaders dedicated to improving the human rights of lesbian, gay, bisexual, transgender, intersex (LGBTI) and other individuals stigmatized because of their sexuality or HIV status" (International Gay and Lesbian Human Rights Commission 1997, 2009). According to Rina, Sister Namibia leveraged its national visibility into international acclaim and funding from Northern donors.

Unable to obtain funding from Namibian or southern African sources, Sister Namibia was increasingly reliant on Northern donors. Losing donor funding would incapacitate the organization. In a meeting with Norwegian and Tanzanian researchers in April 2006, the director explained how Sister Namibia had recently lost funding from two donors. One donor had ceased funding development initiatives in Namibia altogether because the donor had been involved in Namibia for many years and because the World Bank had reworked Namibia's income classification (Melber 2005).[48] Although Northern donors continued to earmark funds for HIV/AIDS campaigns, they expected that Namibia as a country was becoming more self-sufficient. This set in motion for Sister Namibia a self-reinforcing cycle of prioritizing Northern donors as the organization's primary target audience, forcing the organization to assign lesser priority to constituents: Namibian women and magazine readers. Thus, becoming visible to one target audience resulted in Sister Namibia's decreased visibility with constituents. In 2005 and 2006, Sister Namibia published the magazine irregularly and stopped maintaining its relationship with vendors and distributors, shrinking the magazine's readership and paid subscriptions. Sister Namibia slipped into invisibility with readers and members, leading some readers, including female members of parliament, to contact the organization and inquire why they had not received their magazines. The longer the organization remained invisible with a target audience, the more difficult it would be to renew or recuperate its prior relationships.

Northern donors favored funding consultants to work on short-term projects for southern African NGOs (Britton 2006). This prevented the director from hiring additional staff to handle tasks related to Sister Namibia's visibility with the media, government, human rights NGOs, and other target audiences, which would have allowed the director to concentrate on ensuring the organization's longevity. This was a "weird time" for Sister Namibia, according to Lindsey, as the director struggled "to get funding." As with many development projects, donors expected that these projects would quickly become sustainable, permitting donors to direct funding to new organizations and projects (Britton 2006; Michael 2004). Frustrated by navigating bureaucratic entanglements with donors, the director claimed on several occasions· that she had no time to find ways to make Sister Namibia sustainable. As donors reduced or withdrew funding, the director had to scramble to locate new donors or to beg donors to reconsider their decisions, eking out Sister Namibia's existence month by month. The organization was on the verge of financial collapse and unintentional invisibility. Sister Namibia had little cash on hand to meet its financial obligations, including paying staff salaries. The director was waiting for a donor that had agreed to fund staff salaries to deposit funds in Sister Namibia's bank account.

Another reason for Sister Namibia's financial woes stemmed from the director's choice to work on and solicit funding for extraorganizational initiatives. She temporarily shifted her strategic focus away from Sister Namibia to strengthen the pan-African visibility of African lesbian movement organizations.

In 2005 and 2006, Sister Namibia's director spent time writing funding proposals to launch the Coalition of African Lesbians (CAL), to support CAL's second annual meeting in Johannesburg, and to restart Katutura Community Radio (KCR), the first community radio station in Namibia, which was suspended in 2004 because of financial mismanagement. Sister Namibia suffered financially because the director's attention was not focused on soliciting new and sustained funding for the organization. Citing how time intensive the organizing and fund-raising for CAL was, Sister Namibia's board of trustees made the director promise that "she would not start a new organization for at least three years," the director related; trustees needed her to focus only on producing the magazine and locating funding for Sister Namibia, which proved to be difficult. The director did not apologize for her efforts. She almost single-handedly resurrected KCR, and she also believed it was important to establish a pan-African lesbian organization that could support lesbian movement organizations and publicize the situation of lesbians in different African countries. Launching CAL, in her view, would enhance the visibility of other African organizations working on lesbian rights. However, working on launching CAL and KCR kept the director from raising funds to sustain Sister Namibia, which could have resulted in the organization's collapse and unintentional invisibility.

Sister Namibia's sexual-rights campaign suffered and experienced a visibility disruption while the director struggled to raise funds. At an April 2006 staff meeting, the director characterized the campaign as directed at increasing the agency, particularly the sexual agency, of Namibian women. She claimed that the "ABC" HIV-prevention campaign—"abstain, be faithful, and use condoms" (Thornton 2008)—was not working in Namibia. She maintained that "horrific cultural practices" rendered women vulnerable to HIV/AIDS. The director stated, "There won't be any women left" because many women were unable to exercise sexual agency and insist that their male sexual partners use condoms when having sex. According to the director, some men physically abused female sexual partners who insisted on using condoms or contraception. The director interpreted some men's resistance to using condoms, in particular, as evidence of their commitment to patriarchal behaviors and attitudes. In a presentation to a group of international educators visiting the office, Ellen elucidated that the sexual-rights campaign involved contesting practices that undermined girls' and women's agency. She explained that some Namibian men pressured women to have sex because men had paid *lobola,* or bride-price, to marry them; some men believed that paying *lobola* amounted to unrestricted access to their wives' bodies (Talavera 2007). Challenging and making these cultural practices visible was part of the sexual-rights campaign, which would again garner Sister Namibia a reputation for being "seen as controversial and taboo" (Ellen, interview with the author, June 21, 2006). However, work on the campaign had "come to a halt in a lot of ways because [we] need money to do things," money that was unavailable, as Lindsey explained.

Guided by feminist principles, Sister Namibia staff and members framed all Namibian women as the organization's constituency and advocated women's political empowerment and the inclusion of lesbian rights as women's rights in the magazine, the Namibian Women's Manifesto, and the 50/50 Campaign. Sister Namibia also cultivated multiple audiences, including opposition political parties, privately owned newspapers, the general public, and human rights organizations, for its messages. Sister Namibia's opposition to SWAPO leaders' homophobia and public support for lesbian rights evinced the organization's inclusionary orientation. Sister Namibia's profile as a lesbian movement organization generated controversy. SWAPO-affiliated state actors shunned the Namibian Women's Manifesto because of its inclusion of lesbian rights. SWAPO leaders' hostility to Sister Namibia resulted in the organization's inability to obtain state funds. Out of financial need, Sister Namibia sought funding from Northern donors. Donors' reorganization of funding priorities negatively impacted Sister Namibia. Sister Namibia's visibility difficulties forced staff to suspend work on several projects, including the magazine. Moreover, the director's extraorganizational obligations inhibited her ability to locate additional sources of Northern funding for Sister Namibia. Although this visibility disruption negatively affected Sister Namibia's work on the magazine and sexual-rights campaign, it did not wholly derail the organization's strategic priorities.

Seeing Strategic Orientations

Perceiving a movement organization's strategic orientation is not easy. A movement organization's strategic frame, or orientation, becomes observable as a pattern in the constellation of choices activists make. Barely perceptible at a movement organization's beginning, a strategic orientation takes shape over time and can change subtly or considerably as activists respond to shifts in the sociopolitical field. Antilesbian hostility in South Africa provoked activists with FEW to develop a strategic orientation that privileged guarded visibility shielding constituents from harm. FEW's protected visibility resembled exclusion. Tending toward public visibility, Sister Namibia defended LGBT rights from soft repression and included lesbian rights in campaigns for women's rights. In contrast with FEW, Sister Namibia became associated with inclusion.

In societies characterized by inequalities, social movements may promote inclusion as a strategic goal; over time, a movement organization may develop a strategic orientation favoring visibility and inclusion that reflects this goal. In postapartheid South Africa, inclusion was a buzzword (Stychin 1996). Social institutions, the state, and social movements worked to undo racial, class, gender, and sexual inequalities created and intensified by apartheid practices and policies. Many movements had inclusionary strategic orientations; in fact, other South African LGBT movement organizations developed inclusionary orientations (Currier 2010b). In contexts where inclusion is common, it can be difficult to see inclusionary strategic orientations because they blend into the scenery.

How was I able to see the strategic orientations of FEW and Sister Namibia? I perceived both organizations' strategic orientations because their orientations were dissimilar from the surrounding environment. Exclusionary strategic orientations that tend toward decreased visibility become visible in fields that prize social inclusion, and in fields in which elites wield discourses of exclusion, inclusionary strategic orientations that emphasize public visibility garner notice. In South Africa, FEW's exclusionary strategic orientation diverged markedly from orientations of inclusive LGBT movement organizations. Sister Namibia's inclusionary strategic orientation noticeably differed from SWAPO leaders' exclusionary rhetoric about same-sex sexualities. In light of these differences, what do movement organizations' strategic orientations to visibility mean politically? Were FEW and Sister Namibia anomalies in need of synchronization with local sociopolitical realities? Might their strategic orientations toward public visibility be possible future sources of friction with other social and political actors? My sense is no. FEW and Sister Namibia might not seem strategically commensurate with major actors in their respective sociopolitical fields, but their orientations resembled those of similar organizations in other contexts. Niche activism in the South African LGBT movement meant that other organizations were working on legal campaigns and social-service provision issues of importance to LGBT constituents, allowing FEW to work with a smaller constituency in a protectionist fashion. Sister Namibia's inclusionary orientation complemented that of Namibian human rights NGOs, groups with which Sister Namibia forged partnerships; this organization was not out of step politically.

The nature of hostility in South Africa and Namibia affected the strategic orientations toward visibility that activists with FEW and Sister Namibia forged. Whereas FEW cultivated a protectionist orientation favoring decreased visibility in the context of antilesbian violence in Johannesburg, in Namibia, Sister Namibia fashioned an inclusionary orientation favoring public visibility evident in the organization's defense of lesbian rights and denunciation of SWAPO leaders' political homophobia. Strategic orientations do not totally determine when or if movement organizations will surface when opportunities for mobilization arise. Likewise, extraordinary events may interfere with and even undermine movement organizations' strategic orientations, causing organizations to lapse unintentionally into invisibility. LGBT movement organizations in Namibia and South Africa struggled with these facets of invisibility, dilemmas that I examine in the next chapter.

3

Disappearing Acts:
Organizational Invisibility in Times of Opportunity

Are movement organizations that cultivate public visibility more likely to remain visible to target audiences than organizations that tend toward less visibility or invisibility? How might scholars interpret invisibility in these circumstances? Sister Namibia, an organization with a strategic orientation that tended toward visibility, experienced invisibility with constituents when the organization stopped publishing the magazine and suspended the sexual-rights campaign. This unintentional invisibility resulted from a combination of factors. Staff could not locate dedicated funding from Northern donors who were withdrawing from Namibia, and the director devoted some of her time and energy to other activist projects. In Sister Namibia's case, unintentional invisibility stemmed partially from the loss of resources, causing staff to suspend their projects.

How might scholars construe a movement organization's invisibility in a time of political opportunity, when sociopolitical conditions are conducive to organized action? Is invisibility a temporary, one-off occurrence, or is this condition more permanent? These questions arose when I considered Namibian and South African LGBT movement invisibility with respect to two public law-reform campaigns. Namibian and South African lawmakers passed gay rights legislation shortly after Namibia gained independence in 1989 and after the negotiated end of South African apartheid rule in 1993. The Namibian Labour Act of 1992 prohibited discrimination against workers because of their sexual orientation (Hubbard 2007). South Africa's constitutional EC protected individuals from discrimination because of their sexual orientation (Croucher 2002). Other legal changes pursued by South African

LGBT movement organizations resulted in adoption and immigration rights for same-sex couples and the decriminalization of sodomy. In December 2005, the Constitutional Court, the highest court in South Africa, ruled in favor of same-sex marriage but stopped short of making it legal immediately (de Vos 2008). With pro-LGBT rights legislation in place in Namibia and South Africa, why would LGBT movement organizations become publicly invisible in these times of political opportunity?

Legal mobilization in Namibia did not materialize in the 1990s and 2000s, despite activists' plans to initiate a public law-reform campaign. After the South African Constitutional Court extended the right to marry to same-sex couples on December 1, 2005, but gave parliament until December 1, 2006, to revise existing marriage laws to accommodate the ruling, LGBT movement organizations seemed to abandon the marriage-equality campaign for several months. How might scholars interpret South African and Namibian LGBT movement organizations' invisibility during these times of political opportunity, when organizations otherwise seemed able and poised to seize them? Political process theory tends to interpret long periods of organizational or movement invisibility at a time of political opportunity to movement distress or decline. Movement organizations seem quite robust when they are publicly visible in the media or on the street protesting, but invisibility denotes movement weakness (Sawyers and Meyer 1999). Is invisibility always linked to movement difficulty, or might there be other explanations? What is the relationship between organizational invisibility and political opportunity?

How and Why Social Movement Organizations Miss Political Opportunities

What does it mean for a movement organization to miss a political opportunity? Traci M. Sawyers and David S. Meyer (1999) theorize missed opportunities as arising from the choices activists make when they enter abeyance; this approach connects invisibility to movement decline (Taylor 1989). While internal distress may explain why movement organizations are invisible in times of political opportunity, it remains unclear how organizations miss opportunities that result in their invisibility. Organizations can make *operational* or *strategic choices* that prevent them from seizing political opportunities (Minkoff and McCarthy 2005). Strategic choices involve "long-range goals and the organizational repertoires chosen to pursue them" (Minkoff and McCarthy 2005, 298). For instance, a movement organization with a mandate to focus only on local electoral politics may bypass the opportunity to exploit a national election (Blee and Currier 2006). Operational choices are "shorter-term ... decisions about how to deploy the elements of the chosen repertoire" (Minkoff and McCarthy 2005, 298). Operational choices can generate cascading consequences. A mixture of operational and strategic choices can result in activists forgoing, postponing, or ignoring opportunities.

Internal conflicts can impel activists to develop an inward focus and withdraw from public visibility and external opportunities. Internal conflicts over movement focus, strategic priorities, tactics, and resources can siphon attention from external opportunities, especially if these conflicts threaten a movement organization's existence (Ghaziani 2008). *External crises* that jeopardize a movement organization's public standing or accomplishments can necessitate immediate reactions from activists so that they can neutralize the resulting damage. Responding to external crises may take time, energy, and resources away from other campaigns. Internal conflicts and external crises can also produce *visibility disruptions,* as evidenced in the case of Sister Namibia.

Activists and movement organizations may miss discrete, smaller opportunities in several ways. Activists may intentionally *forgo* opportunities. There may be many reasons: pressing campaigns may compete for activists' attention, or movement organizations may not have enough volunteers to take advantage of an opportunity. Some activists may not believe that they are ready or in a position to make the best use of an opportunity; their organization may be struggling financially, or they may perceive that it is premature for a fledgling organization to step into the limelight so soon. If activists feel that the organization is at a turning point, they may restructure the organization's activities and priorities. If activists negatively perceive the opportunity and worry that failure is likely, they may choose to forgo the opportunity altogether (Sawyers and Meyer 1999). Activists might also realize that their rhetoric might become distorted if they seize a particular opportunity, as in the case of a U.S. animal rights group that risked being cast as an antiwar group when activists joined an antiwar demonstration (Blee and Currier 2006). It may not be common for activists to forgo opportunities, but for activists who have recently experienced failure or been the target of threats, seizing an opportunity may be unappealing at that time. Activists may also *ignore* political opportunities because of strategic or operational choices they made in the past. Such choices limit what activists are able to see as opportunities (Blee and Currier 2005). In other words, activists may not frame opportunities as such and let them disappear altogether (Kowalchuk 2005; Kurzman 1996; Meyer and Minkoff 2004). Activists may not recognize an opportunity in time; if an opportunity is invisible to activists, then a movement organization is likely to be invisible at a time of opportunity.

Activists may *postpone* (or *defer*) seizing an opportunity if they are not ready to take advantage of it, hoping that it will come around again. For instance, national elections constitute a periodic political opportunity that activists can defer until they are ready to take advantage of it (Sobieraj 2011). Activists in nascent groups may delay opportunities until they settle into a routine, agree on tactics and goals, and develop strategic priorities (Blee and Currier 2005). They may also misframe opportunities, by exaggerating their potential negative or positive consequences (Suh 2001). Internal disagreements about how to frame an opportunity can also paralyze activists such that debates "slow the process so long that the opportunity" disappears, forcing activists to forgo or postpone the opportunity (Gamson and Meyer 1996, 284). Demobilization may constitute an example of a missed opportunity if activists "define a situation as so hopeful or favorable that additional collective action is seen as unnecessary," but future developments may prove that mobilization would have garnered additional gains for a movement organization (Raeburn 2004, 62).

In this chapter, I examine how internal conflicts and external crises affect LGBT movement organizations' ability to take advantage of what appear to be political opportunities. South African LGBT movement organizations' invisibility in the weeks after the pro-same-sex-marriage ruling puzzled me. I draw on interviews, ethnographic observation, and newspaper articles to explore the dynamics of this strategic deferral. Often, scholars only detect missed opportunities in hindsight, after some time has elapsed. This occurred when I realized that TRP had not initiated a legal campaign, even though activists had identified it as a strategic priority. Reconstructing how TRP postponed this campaign required the use of multiple data sources, including interviews, newspaper articles, and historical organizational documents. Movement invisibility is a possible sign of a missed opportunity. However, diagnosing a "missed" opportunity is never straightforward, as my analysis shows.

South African Same-Sex-Marriage Mobilization

As LGBT movement organizations put gay rights on the national agenda during the transition from apartheid to democratic rule in the early 1990s, they faced opposition within the ANC and opposition political parties (Phillips 2006). Activists sought to dispel the assumption that gay rights "must take a back seat to national liberation" (Croucher 2002, 320). They argued that not only had nonwhite South Africans suffered discrimination but gender and sexual minorities had also experienced social, political, and economic exclusion. Through lobbying, activists persuaded ANC leaders to include sexual-minority rights in the ANC's 1992 Bill of Rights and pushed for the inclusion of the EC in the interim constitution (Croucher 2002).

Marriage equality became a movement priority in the mid-1990s (Reddy 2009). In 1994, at the First National Gay and Lesbian Legal and Human Rights Conference, at which the NCGLE was formed, same-sex marriage, the decriminalization of sodomy, the enshrinement of the EC in the constitution, and the cultivation of lesbian and gay movement leadership emerged as strategic priorities (Dirsuweit 2006; Reddy 2001; Stychin 1996). The Equality Project did not initiate a legal case challenging marriage inequality until 2002 because activists worried that conservative South Africans who had cautiously "voted the ANC in without really coming to terms with the radical implications of its social agenda" would oppose the campaign (Gevisser 2000, 124). A public same-sex-marriage campaign "could have caused the backlash" that the NCGLE feared (Gevisser 2000, 135).[1] In fact, LGBT activists persuaded a South African woman and her French partner not to sue for the right to marry in the late 1990s because it was "very risky litigation at the time" (Berger 2008, 24). Carl F. Stychin (1996, 465) describes this nonconfrontational strategy as "incrementalism (the tackling of issues in their order of contentiousness)," which the NCGLE used to "avoid backlash in a conservative society where it is important to avoid the appearance of a single issue agenda [such as same-sex marriage] that might detract from the pressing problems of national reconstruction" after the dismantling of apartheid. The NCGLE's incremental strategy secured marriage-related rights, such as adoption and immigration rights for same-sex couples, in the late 1990s to lay the groundwork for the marriage-equality campaign. Kevan Botha, a South African LGBT movement legal strategist, explained that thanks to the incremental strategy, same-sex marriage would be "de facto part of South African life, even if it isn't called that. Then, when we lobby for marriage itself, we can avoid the backlash by saying, 'Look, it's already there! What's the fuss?'" (Gevisser 2000, 135).

In 2002, a white lesbian couple, Marié Fourie and Cecelia Bonthuys, asked the High Court to grant their petition to marry (Judge, Manion, and de Waal 2008a). The Lesbian and Gay Equality Project, the NCGLE's successor, filed a legal brief as amicus curiae—a friend of the court—to support their case (Judge et al. 2008a). In October 2002, the High Court threw out the suit because lawyers had not contested the constitutionality of existing marriage laws and ordered the Equality Project to "pay [court] costs" (Berger 2008, 24). In July 2004, the *Fourie* case reached the Supreme Court of Appeals, which ruled existing marriage laws to be unconstitutional, enabling the Constitutional Court to hear the case (Berger 2008; Judge et al. 2008a). In May 2005, the Constitutional Court heard arguments in the *Fourie* case and in the Equality Project's separate filing "for direct access to the Constitutional Court" to demand marriage equality (Judge et al. 2008a, 2).

In May 2005, FEW mobilized black lesbians to make mass-based support for the marriage-equality campaign visible to the court, media, and South African public. FEW bused black lesbians from Johannesburg townships to participate in marches and rallies at Constitution Hill. This mobilization furthered FEW's goal of enhancing black lesbian visibility. The presence of dozens of black lesbians along with other LGBT activists outside of the Constitutional Court challenged the homogeneous visibility of the beneficiaries of same-sex marriage: white, "neatly couple-ist, 'almost normal' domesticated gays and lesbians" (Cock 2003, 40). By manifesting their support publicly for the right to marry, FEW staff wanted the public to "see that the rest of the [black LGBT] community supports this campaign, that it's not just a couple of people. And it's not just the organizations [that] want to legalize marriage, but it's the actual community," according to Sisonke, a black lesbian woman and FEW member (interview with the author, March 17, 2006). FEW's activism publicly challenged a narrow, normalized image of LGBT movement constituents and same-sex marriage supporters as white, middle-class women and men. Poor black women who identified as lesbians wanted to marry their partners; they also sought individual visibility as black lesbians and South Africans. LGBT movement organizations like FEW also wanted to correct the perception that only white lesbian and gay couples wanted to marry. By reaching out to and pursuing visibility with black constituents, staff hoped to change constituents' perceptions about LGBT movement organizations' work. Many black LGBT persons thought that movement organizations, such as the Equality Project, "catered disproportionately to the white sector of the gay and lesbian community," an indication of persisting racial divisions within the movement (Oswin 2007, 660).

Despite support from FEW and other LGBT movement organizations for the marriage-equality campaign, the Equality Project closed its doors in July 2005, just two months after its lawyers presented arguments in support of same-sex marriage to the Constitutional Court. Financial mismanagement and personality conflicts among staff and board members contributed to the Equality Project's demise (Oswin 2007). On November 30, 2005, the Constitutional Court announced that it would read its ruling the following day, giving LGBT movement organizations little time to organize a unified movement response. Even Behind the Mask, with its close proximity to the Constitutional Court and its media contacts, had little warning.

Owing to this short notice, FEW staff members were unable to arrange transportation for black lesbians to come from townships to participate in a rally supporting same-sex marriage, as they had done in the past. FEW and Behind the Mask staff and members able to attend the ruling's announcement wore T-shirts with slogans supporting same-sex marriage or identifying them with FEW. Inside the Constitutional Court, LGBT activists listened eagerly to the ruling, which granted marriage equality to same-sex couples (de Vos 2008). The court gave lawmakers one year to amend existing marriage laws to accommodate same-sex couples; if lawmakers took no action, the ruling provided for the addition of gender-neutral language in the Marriage Act (Reddy 2009). The ruling disappointed some activists because marriage was not immediately available to same-sex couples (Gqola and Isaack 2006). As Pierre de Vos (2008, 37) notes, the court's judgment did use the word "marriage"; some activists feared "Parliament would try to avoid its responsibility by providing a 'separate but equal' regime of legal protection" that would afford same-sex couples fewer rights and benefits than those that heterosexual couples enjoyed. After the hearing, approximately two dozen activists celebrated the ruling outside the court. Reporters from mainstream newspapers and radio and TV stations descended on the crowd to obtain comments about the ruling.

LGBT South Africans expressed varied views about marriage equality as a movement priority, a source of conflict within the movement. Skeptics were not united in their opposition to the primacy of same-sex marriage as a movement goal. Some decried marriage as a heteronormative institution that discriminated against those in nonheterosexual, nonmonogamous relationships (de Vos 2004). Others worried that the marriage-equality campaign would divert resources from other campaigns, such as fighting violence against LGBT persons or racism within LGBT communities. At a press conference after the Constitutional Court ruling's announcement on December 1, 2005, Sibongile, a black lesbian woman affiliated with Behind the Mask, praised the ruling but asserted that lawmakers had not protected LGBT persons with anti–hate crime legislation or prevented black lesbians from being targeted for rape. Still other LGBT activists and constituents doubted that same-sex marriage would help "people living in poverty. . . . The logic of poverty alleviation that underpinned the marriage campaign [was] clearly problematic" (Oswin 2007, 664). At the press conference, Sibongile noted that although political recognition of same-sex relationships might ignite the gradual social acceptance of LGBT persons, it would not suddenly ameliorate the poverty or unpredictability in which many black LGBT persons lived (Matebeni 2008).

Many LGBT South Africans endorsed the campaign for marriage equality (van Zyl 2011). Despite the lack of access to state-sanctioned marriage, South African same-sex couples have held their own weddings and celebrations for some time, evidence of indigenous tolerance for and recognition of some same-sex relationships (Bonthuys 2008; Louw 2001; Reid 2005). LGBT South Africans of all races demanded that the state recognize their relationships (McLean and Ngcobo 1995; Stychin 1996; Vilakazi and Chetty 2006). Some LGBT persons were impatient with lawmakers' reluctance to legalize same-sex marriage. Sisonke emphasized that "being told that you can't" marry angered many LGBT persons who "want to get married." Sisonke stated that "it's now time for South Africa to give us the right to marry." Politicians were also "starting to talk about it in . . . Parliament. A few years back, you [would] never [think] people would even sit around a table" discussing same-sex relationships because same-sex sexuality was a "disgrace or something very wrong." Sisonke construed the public visibility of same-sex marriage as progress. Her optimism typified much of the emotional energy that buoyed the marriage-equality campaign. Although LGBT activists continued to hold divergent opinions about same-sex marriage, these debates did not spill over into the public sphere. Overall, the LGBT movement was publicly seen as supporting same-sex marriage.

However, if observers used the turnout for the ruling as a barometer of LGBT movement support for same-sex marriage, they might have interpreted activists' invisibility as a sign of internal disagreement about the meaning of same-sex marriage for LGBT South Africans. In comparison with the May 2005 rallies in support of same-sex marriage, the turnout was much smaller. Unlike previous court cases, activists had little time to prepare for the December 2005 ruling. In fact, some activists with Behind the Mask and FEW were unsure about how court justices would rule. In light of the short notice about the ruling's announcements, activists could not organize a public rally celebrating the ruling or demanding immediate access to marriage. The form of LGBT activists' visibility at the court was linked to how little time there was between the initial notification that justices had arrived at a decision in the case and the reading of the ruling.

Immediately after the court read the ruling, leaders of LGBT movement organizations that belonged to the JWG discussed how to proceed with the campaign away from public scrutiny at the Constitutional Hill café. Their meeting was by no means secretive; leaders wanted to meet quickly to develop a unified response to the ruling. Leaders hoped that a press conference at Behind the Mask's office later in the day would jump-start movement publicity related to the marriage-equality campaign. Only one reporter from a local radio station attended the press conference. News coverage soon lagged, auguring the LGBT movement's eventual invisibility in relation to the campaign (Lewis 2007). Several days after the ruling, local and national newspapers stopped carrying stories about same-sex marriage. This makes sense since LGBT activists did not hold public discussions about pressing lawmakers to amend marriage laws, although at the press conference, movement leaders indicated that they would urge lawmakers to implement the court's directive swiftly. There was still work for LGBT movement organizations to do, meaning that there were additional opportunities for them to advocate for same-sex marriage publicly. The court's judgment put marriage equality in the hands of lawmakers, who in the past had opposed LGBT rights campaigns, evidenced in Minister of Justice Omar's initial opposition to the campaign to decriminalize sodomy (Goodman 2001). Was it possible that lawmakers would try to engender a separate-but-equal scheme that would differentiate same-sex marriages from heterosexual marriages (de Vos 2008)? Such a scheme could result in differential sociopolitical visibilities for and recognition of same-sex and opposite-sex marriages.

LGBT movement organizations remained invisible with respect to the marriage-equality campaign between December 2005 and April 2006.[2] Two factors contributed to organizations' invisibility. First, the strategic and operational choices made by member organizations of the JWG, a loose coalition of mainstream LGBT movement organizations, prevented individual organizations from immediately working on the campaign. Second, an external crisis involving a rogue LGBT movement organization necessitated decisive action from movement organizations, temporarily siphoning some organizations' resources and attention. Although organizations were invisible for several months, their inaction did not mean that movement leaders had forgotten about the marriage-equality campaign.

Organizational Delays Contribute to Campaign Invisibility: Deliberation within the JWG

Deliberation about how to proceed with the marriage-equality campaign in the wake of the Equality Project's closure delayed the JWG's visible mobilization around same-sex marriage. In the months before the ruling's announcement, the marriage-equality campaign disappeared from the JWG's radar as activists waited for the Constitutional Court's ruling. At the group's October 2005 meeting, representatives from current and prospective member movement organizations identified pressing movement concerns and how to approach them.[3] Movement-level issues included organizational leadership, funding, and program development; racial, ethnic, sexual, and gender diversity in the LGBT movement's leadership and goals; the need for specialized LGBT movement organizations; and the importance of lobbying and legal advocacy. Discussing movement-level issues, JWG meeting attendees bypassed single issues such as the marriage-equality campaign. The only mention of the campaign occurred when a representative from a LGBT student group urged JWG member organizations to work outside their comfort zones and make claims and ideas, such as same-sex marriage, accessible to constituencies and organizations unfamiliar with LGBT issues. This kind of visibility work would require LGBT movement organizations "to think outside of [them]selves," according to the black LGBT student activist. One way to foster dialogue, he imagined, might be to invent words in African languages, such as isiZulu, to explain LGBT concerns in an effort to counteract homophobia. According to the student activist, there was no word in isiZulu for "same-sex marriage." Despite this brief mention, the campaign vanished from the JWG's agenda. Although activists awaited the Constitutional Court's ruling, which would determine their next steps on the campaign, they could have drawn contingency plans in the event that justices ruled against same-sex marriage. Marriage equality remained invisible to LGBT activists as a strategic priority.

After the favorable Constitutional Court ruling, the marriage-equality campaign became visible within the movement as a top concern at the JWG's March 2006 meeting. A white woman representative from OUT, a Pretoria-based LGBT movement organization, noted that although Parliament had until December 1, 2006, to act, "we need to be ready to act in April or in May." She cited the importance of the JWG and member organizations approaching the media with a coherent message because activists witnessed "in December how the media went berserk" and covered the ruling extensively for a few days. Uniform movement visibility in favor of same-sex marriage was a priority. Representatives encouraged movement organizations to prepare press releases about their endorsement of same-sex marriage. Toward the beginning of the meeting, representatives introduced their movement organizations to others considering joining the JWG, yet few identified same-sex marriage, legal advocacy, and lobbying as part of their organization's current campaigns. The only organization that had such a focus, the Equality Project, was defunct and invisible at that time. Two organizations had staff members who were working on the marriage-equality campaign as part of their assigned duties, but few could afford to assign a paid staff member to work on it full time.

Meeting attendees discussed the Equality Project's revival. When it was operational, the Equality Project had devoted itself to legal lobbying and advocacy around LGBT rights, strategies that other LGBT movement organizations generally left alone (Oswin 2007), owing to the LGBT movement's niche activism (Levitsky 2007). Because movement organizations' leaders and staff regarded the NCGLE as leading early LGBT legal campaigns, they treated its successor similarly, allowing the Equality Project to spearhead legal battles for LGBT rights (Stychin 1996). Niche activism permitted movement organizations to develop their own programs. As such, organizations' leaders were used to making operational choices, not strategic choices, about extraorganizational campaigns (Minkoff and McCarthy 2005). Some activists supported the Equality Project's reopening. Isaac, a black gay man and Behind the Mask member, advocated for the Equality Project's existence (interview with the author, December 12, 2005): "there needs to be an organization like the Equality Project that [can] legally take up" LGBT rights. Isaac envisioned the Equality Project as a movement watchdog monitoring LGBT rights in South Africa, although he resisted the notion that the organization "should be a policeman, but they should guide organizations legally. . . . And you need such an organization that can take up the legal issues within the community and outside of the community."

Leaders had to contend with the power vacuum left by the Equality Project's invisibility and make operational choices about how to go ahead with the marriage-equality campaign. Consultants hired by Northern donors that financed several LGBT movement organizations' projects unveiled their recommendations for the Equality Project's resuscitation. Recognizing that the Equality Project's "public image [had] been dented but not destroyed" after its collapse (Nell and Shapiro 2006), the consultants stressed that JWG members would have to decide how to proceed with the marriage-equality campaign because the Equality Project would not be operational until mid-2006 at the earliest. The consultants suggested that the Equality Project should scale back its public and legal work once it reopened. A revived Equality Project would not have the resources to manage the movement's response to the Constitutional Court's ruling and would still have to flesh out its new mandate, ultimately leaving the JWG's member organizations in charge of the campaign. Even after reopening, the Equality Project would be invisible in the marriage-equality campaign.

Movement leaders brainstormed strategic options that would allow them to restart the marriage-equality campaign. FEW's director claimed that she would incorporate the campaign into FEW's existing agenda and poll staff and members about how to proceed with the campaign. A black lesbian woman and staff member at OUT revealed that OUT had recently begun examining strategies around marriage equality, which culminated in the organization's hiring of her. OUT's leader, a white gay man, did not want OUT to manage the marriage-equality campaign because he did not know in which direction the campaign should develop. This worry surfaced in a query from another OUT white female staff member, who asked, "Who are we representing?" Not only did she question whether OUT would represent the LGBT movement on the marriage issue, but she also interrogated which constituency OUT and the JWG claimed to represent.

JWG members were careful not to rush ahead without considering the LGBT movement as a whole and individual organizations' involvement in the marriage-equality campaign. The JWG itself was a new body, having only come into existence in 2005, and leaders and activists did not want to mismanage the campaign. They agreed that the JWG should remain invisible temporarily until they had sorted out a manageable, consistent strategy and message about the marriage-equality campaign. They also acknowledged the importance of sustaining the marriage-equality campaign, but some movement organizations could not commit resources to media or advocacy work because they were overstretched. At the end of the March 2006 JWG meeting, support for continuing joint media visibility around the campaign emerged, suggesting that the movement would resume publicizing the campaign for marriage equality. Eventually, the JWG developed a four-pronged approach to the marriage-equality campaign, consisting of lobbying lawmakers, mobilizing LGBT persons to voice their opinions about same-sex marriage and to participate in rallies and protests, collaborating with non-LGBT organizations that supported LGBT rights, and publicizing their efforts (Vilakazi 2008).

Temporary Invisibility: The Gay Blood-Donation Scandal Causes a Visibility Disruption

A scandal created by a rogue LGBT movement organization, the Gay and Lesbian Alliance (GLA), also deflected activists' attention away from same-sex marriage, contributing to organizations' invisibility with respect to the campaign (Currier 2010b). This invisibility took the form of a temporary visibility disruption. In a press release dated January 10, 2006, the GLA claimed that dozens of gay men who did not know their HIV status donated blood at South African National Blood Service (SANBS) centers, in defiance of a ban prohibiting men who have sex with men; the press release stated that the men did not disclose their sexual identities to staff and that many did not know if they were HIV negative or positive (Gallagher 2006).[4] JWG member movement organizations faced a strategic dilemma regarding whether and how to respond to this crisis.[5] Not responding to the GLA's claim could suggest to antigay opponents and the general public that LGBT movement organizations sanctioned this action, possibly giving opponents fodder for a countermovement campaign. Becoming involved meant that movement organizations would have to divert some attention and resources away from their current projects, including the marriage-equality campaign.

The GLA's claim generated unwelcome visibility for the movement as a whole and implicated all South African LGBT activists, an urgent situation that they felt demanded their attention. At stake was the credibility of the LGBT movement and constituents. The notion that renegade gay men would jeopardize the national blood supply threatened to delegitimize LGBT activists' demands for full, inclusive citizenship, including the right to marry. HIV/AIDS threatened many South Africans, and a tainted national blood supply was an unwanted crisis. For LGBT activists, the legal gains the move-ment had made would be compromised if antigay sentiments transformed into homophobic violence and rhetoric. While activists diverted visibility strategizing in the direction of the GLA, they became temporarily invisible in the marriage-equality campaign.

Flamboyant tactics and divisive claims garnered negative media coverage for the GLA, and also for the movement, just after the scandal broke. Fearing the "negative radical flank effect," leaders of JWG member organizations acted to ensure that the GLA did not discredit the movement's reputation or goals; thus, they became involved in the gay blood-donation imbroglio (Haines 1984, 32). Although LGBT activists knew that the GLA was a front for one man and not an actual organization, mainstream media treated the GLA as a legitimate LGBT movement organization (Currier 2010b). Condemning the GLA's tactics and distancing themselves from the organization, LGBT movement organizations' leaders sought to control the situation before the GLA damaged the movement's reputation. This move generated a mainstream, moderate public profile for the JWG, in contrast with the extremist GLA (Currier 2010b).

Leaders dedicated some resources between January and March 2006 to working on this issue. The JWG issued press releases deploring the GLA's action and criticizing the media for treating the GLA as a credible organiza-tion without validating its spokesperson's claims. Several days after the GLA distributed the press release, SANBS centers reported that dozens of gay men had not donated blood to protest the ban. LGBT movement leaders lodged a complaint with the press ombudsman, who in turn reprimanded *The Star*, a Johannesburg newspaper, for not thoroughly investigating the GLA's claims (Linington 2006). LGBT activists regarded journalists' lack of fact-checking as "anti-LGBT prejudice" (van der Westhuizen 2006, 1).

Circumventing the GLA, LGBT movement organizations' leaders directly approached and met with leaders of SANBS and the South African Blood Transfusion Service (SABTS) in mid-February 2006 about rescinding the ban on blood donations from men who have sex with men. FEW staff participated in these negotiations, which coincided with Jacob Zuma's rape trial; FEW's involvement with both signaled the organization's gradual visibility. Sisonke clarified why the ban on blood donations from men who have sex with men bothered her. Comparing heterosexism to sexism, she argued,

> These people are saying that gay people cannot donate blood. . . . Why do they say that? It's like saying women shouldn't donate blood; only men can donate blood. . . . If you're telling a certain population not to donate blood,

you're actually saying, "Okay, we don't need blood," but there is a demand for that [blood]. And not all gay people are HIV positive.

Sisonke interpreted discrimination against gay men as discrimination against all LGBT persons. Additionally, she found it perplexing that SANBS would turn away blood donors, given the ever-expanding need for blood. For Sisonke, it was important for FEW to participate in negotiations to work against the assumption held by SANBS leaders that "all gay people are HIV positive." FEW's director adhered to a similar logic in explaining why FEW was visible in the negotiations at a staff meeting in February 2006. Even though the issue "doesn't affect us as lesbians," the director stated that FEW needed to support the LGBT movement and fight discrimination wherever the organization found it. FEW must stand with "our gay brothers." The director explained that an obstacle was proving that the ban was unconstitutional because "donating blood is not a right; it's a privilege." The director supported the JWG's position that the gay blood ban was discriminatory, and she promised to represent FEW at upcoming meetings with SANBS on the issue.[6] This decision differed from the director's exclusion of gay men from FEW's antiviolence workshops, indicating that strategic choices about inclusion and exclusion are subtle and vary according to complex sociopolitical forces.

After their negotiations, leaders of SANBS and LGBT movement organizations agreed that before SANBS ruled on whether to allow men who have sex with men to donate blood, it would commission a study on HIV transmission rates among South African gay, bisexual, and heterosexual men and lesbian, bisexual, and heterosexual women (Marrian 2006). By April 2006, LGBT activists realized they had pursued the rescission of the gay blood-donation ban as far as they could and resumed their mobilization around same-sex marriage. SANBS stated that beginning on November 1, 2006, it would allow men who had abstained for six months from having sex with men to donate blood (Zulu 2006). This development did not satisfy leaders of JWG member organizations, who argued that SANBS should ask prospective male donors not whether they had sex with men but whether they practiced safer sex and used condoms. JWG leaders wanted SANBS to stop using sexual identity as a means to disqualify blood donors and begin asking all donors, including heterosexual blood donors, about their sexual behavior. The strategic choice to become visible, to challenge the GLA's divisive claims, and to confront SANBS about its discriminatory practices contributed to LGBT movement organizations' strategic invisibility in the same-sex marriage campaign.

Resurfacing Publicly: The Marriage-Equality Campaign Resumes

LGBT movement organizations emerged from their strategic invisibility in the marriage-equality campaign in August 2006 and mobilized around the drafting of the Civil Unions Bill, which lawmakers had introduced in Parliament. An early version of the bill treated same-sex unions only as "civil partnerships," which created a separate-but-equal status for same-sex couples (de Vos 2006). A later version of the bill corrected this inequality (*Mail & Guardian* 2006a). Beginning in September 2006, JWG member organizations unfurled coordinated visibility strategies. Activists staged public rallies in support of marriage equality (de Swardt 2008; Vilakazi and Chetty 2006). LGBT activists affiliated with OUT organized LGBT persons to provide written testimony about the importance of marriage equality in their lives and to submit editorials to media outlets (Vilakazi 2008). Picking up some of the workload that likely would have belonged to the Equality Project, the Triangle Project recruited black LGBT persons to testify in parliamentary hearings about their support for marriage equality and to participate in protests in favor of same-sex marriage outside the parliament building, which was located in Cape Town (Tucker 2009).

Many groups opposed the bill. The National House of Traditional Leaders, the Congress of Traditional Leaders of South Africa, and the African Christian Democratic Party deplored same-sex marriage as an un-African practice (Maclennan 2006; Stacey 2011; Vilakazi 2008). The argument that same-sex sexualities were un-African was not new to South Africa. In the mid-1990s, antigay opponents made this argument when they fought the inclusion of the EC in the constitution (Stychin 1996). In October 2006, antigay and LGBT activists participated in a public hearing about the bill hosted by the Home Affairs Portfolio Committee (Joubert 2006). Antigay opponents posed provocative questions about same-sex relationships, including, "'What is gay?,' 'How do men have sex with each other?,' and 'How do two women have a baby together?'" (Joubert 2006). LGBT activists challenged these remarks and reminded opponents that in 2002, the Constitutional Court extended adoption rights to same-sex couples. To some LGBT activists, the public hearings "were rushed, disorganized, and predominantly biased against same-sex marriages and LGBTI identities" (Mkhize 2008, 103). In fact, the JWG sent a letter to Parliament objecting to the "last minute rescheduling" of two public hearings and to the "hate speech" directed at LGBT persons (Joint Working Group 2008, 133). Despite hostility to the bill, in November 2006, lawmakers passed the Civil Unions Act, which "provides separately for a civil partnership or marriage" (Reddy and Cakata 2007, 9). After the legalization of same-sex marriage, some antigay opponents continued to voice their discontent, possibly as a means to rally socially conservative South Africans (Mkhize 2008).

The Civil Unions Act has critics within the South African LGBT community.[7] First, the act failed to "repeal the Marriage Act of 1961," which remains the exclusive legal domain of heterosexual couples (Judge, Manion, and de Waal 2008a, 6). Second, the act enables religious and state officials to refuse to perform civil same-sex partnerships or marriages if they have moral or religious objections to same-sex sexuality (Berger 2008). This clause "clearly endorses discrimination on the basis of sexual orientation by state officials" (de Vos 2008, 39). Third, some scholars assert that the act is premised on a Western model of identity politics that is not applicable to all South Africans; individuals who identify as lesbian or gay are most likely to take advantage of this legislation (Bonthuys 2008). In other words, the bill ignores African cultural imperatives, such as "structures of family and clan affiliation," that affect who women and men marry (Matebeni 2008, 255).

The legalization of same-sex marriage in South Africa elevated LGBT visibility throughout Africa, generating new constraints on and possibilities for African LGBT movement visibility strategies. On one hand, marriage equality permitted LGBT activists to cast state recognition of same-sex relationships as continuing the legacy of same-sex marriages, which existed in many indigenous African cultures (Bonthuys 2008; Wieringa 2005).[8] On the other hand, anticolonial political leaders in other African countries interpreted lawmakers' passage of marriage-equality legislation as endangering South Africa's racial authenticity, a development I examine in the next chapter.

Namibian Law-Reform Mobilization

Like South African LGBT activists, TRP seemed poised to pursue a law-reform campaign publicly by lobbying lawmakers and filing lawsuits with local courts in an effort to change laws that excluded gender and sexual minorities. Among TRP's priorities, as articulated in the organization's constitution, was to "lobby for equal rights and opportunities for gays, lesbians, bisexuals and transsexuals and any other group that suffers discrimination in public life and under the law." Labour Act 6 of 1992 prohibited employment discrimination on the basis of sexuality and could have served as a springboard for an LGBT rights campaign (Hubbard 2007). However, TRP did not take this path.

Why was TRP invisible in this moment of political opportunity? Why did TRP eschew legal tactics when activists seemed inclined to favor them? Did TRP staff and members intentionally (or unintentionally) shy away from pursuing a public law-reform campaign because of SWAPO leaders' political homophobia? Two factors prompted TRP to defer legal tactics. First, LGBT activists' fear of SWAPO leaders' hostility—a perpetual, external crisis—kept TRP from publicly pursuing legal tactics. Second, internal crises—disagreements about the campaigns TRP should prioritize, which were rooted in members' differing class and racial identities—derailed the organization's plans for law reform.

Anticipating Hostility: Delayed Legal Mobilization

Before gaining independence from South Africa in 1990, Namibia was a haven for interracial and same-sex couples from South African apartheid laws, policies, and authorities (Frank and |Khaxas 1996). Between 1990 and 1995, law reform seemed possible, especially given the sexuality-based nondiscrimination clause in Labour Act 6 of 1992. In fact, Johannes recalled this time as "heaven" for LGBT Namibians, who thought equality was just on the horizon. Additionally, the state's refusal to prosecute men for sodomy suggested that SWAPO leaders did not choose same-sex sexualities as a viable issue around which to consolidate their political positions in the early years of independence (Hubbard 2007).

In 1995, SWAPO officials began threatening gender and sexual minorities, creating confusion among LGBT Namibians about their legal position. In December 1996, President Sam Nujoma encouraged the "police and public to work hand in hand and arrest anyone caught practising homosexuality, which he likened to a criminal offence like theft" (Günzel 1996, 1). LGBT persons launched TRP to counter SWAPO leaders' antigay remarks. Nujoma's antigay rhetoric led TRP members to believe that lawmakers were going to criminalize all same-sex sexual practices and enforce existing antisodomy legislation. TRP received news from then Ombudsman Bience Gawanas that "sodomy [would] be decriminalized," although it was unclear to TRP members which state officials would initiate this process (TRP meeting minutes, March 18, 1997).

TRP appeared poised to use legal tactics as a means to challenge SWAPO leaders' homophobic statements and to fight for the decriminalization of sodomy. In June 1997, TRP filed a legal complaint with the Office of the Ombudsman objecting to homophobic remarks that President Nujoma had made in December 1996 and to statements that SWAPO leaders had made in January 1997; TRP disclosed this action to the Namibian media (*Namibian* 1997c). NGOs sometimes filed "complaints relating to maladministration by public officials" with the Namibian Office of the Ombudsman, but they had increasingly requested the Office of the Ombudsman "to investigate violations of human rights as well. . . . In the Namibian case, the ombudsman [could] also give legal assistance or advice to those seeking enforcement of fundamental rights through the courts" (Gomez 1995, 157). TRP requested that the Office of the Ombudsman treat Nujoma's statement as a human rights violation because SWAPO leaders' intolerance of sexual diversity could provoke "violence and discrimination against law-abiding citizens" (TRP Submission to the Ombudsman, June 4, 1997).

TRP's strategic visibility in relation to the investigation resulted in a negative outcome. The Office of the Ombudsman declined to investigate the matter for two reasons. First, the ombudsman stated that she could only investigate claims of employment discrimination on the basis of sexual orientation in accordance with Labour Act 6 of 1992, and TRP's complaint did not allege workplace discrimination because of a worker's sexuality. Second, she rejected the complaint because TRP publicized the filing, which violated the principle of confidentiality under which the Office of the Ombudsman operated, such "that it would seem that the Office was used as a stepping stone to raise publicity for [TRP's] cause" (Office of the Ombudsman letter, September 30, 1997). Unless Namibian lawmakers prohibited discrimination on the basis of sexual orientation in the constitution, as South African lawmakers had done one year earlier in 1996, LGBT persons would not be able to pursue legal redress of SWAPO leaders' antigay remarks through the Office of the Ombudsman (Cock 2003).

The following year, in 1998, TRP members further deliberated on how to proceed with a public law-reform campaign. After soliciting and receiving guidance from South African LGBT activists about running a law-reform campaign, TRP members decided to commit some resources to one. At its yearly strategic planning meeting in 1998, which the South African NCGLE moderated, TRP members agreed to prioritize the decriminalization of sodomy, "employment benefits, immigration cases, and gay-bashing" as pressing legal concerns (Rainbow Project 1998, 16). TRP members understood sodomy as sex between men, a law "inherited from the colonial regime" (Tibinyane 1998, 20). NCGLE members explained how their law-reform campaign resulted in the decriminalization of sodomy in South Africa in 1998 and advised TRP to pursue this issue very carefully, given the hostile sociopolitical field in Namibia. Possible tactics for TRP included "going to court" and "lobbying political leaders" and the public (Rainbow Project 1998, 17). TRP members agreed that amending "the Constitution to include sexual orientation"—to prohibit discrimination on the basis of sexuality—as South African LGBT movement organizations had favored was "not ideal" because SWAPO leaders might interpret suggested constitutional amendments as a threat to SWAPO's authority (Rainbow Project 1998, 17). Instead, members seemed satisfied with trying to ensure that LGBT persons' "basic rights [were] covered" (Rainbow Project 1998, 17). At this point, TRP seemed to favor limited public visibility with respect to a sodomy-decriminalization campaign.

Despite NCGLE members' concerns, TRP members decided to pursue the decriminalization of sodomy as a public law-reform campaign. Decriminalizing sodomy could have been an important step in decolonizing and democratizing Namibian laws, policies, and state structures. In 1998, on behalf of TRP, the LAC, a human rights NGO, asked if the prosecutor general "would . . . prosecute charges of sodomy where the sexual act has taken place in private between two consenting adult males" (LAC letter, April 24, 1998). Such an inquiry could have reduced the uncertainty that some LGBT persons experienced; many feared SWAPO officials would actualize their promise to prosecute same-sex sexual behavior, forcing some individuals into unintentional invisibility. The prosecutor general declined to discuss the issue (TRP meeting minutes, May 6, 1998; June 3, 1998). The attorney general, however, asserted that "the sodomy law [was] unconstitutional and [had] to be challenged" (TRP meeting minutes, June 3, 1998). Yet the attorney general apparently did not push this constitutional inquiry further by introducing the issue before lawmakers in a position to consider the constitutionality of the sodomy law.[9]

SWAPO leaders' opposition to LGBT rights and organizing intensified in 1998. Late in 1998, Minister of Home Affairs Jerry Ekandjo threatened to increase penalties for same-sex sexual conduct (Weidlich 1998). Ekandjo's threat countermanded Prime Minister Hage Geingob's assertion in 1997 that "although laws against sodomy were in place in Namibia, these had not been used for the sake of human rights" (*Namibian* 1997d, 2). TRP and other human rights NGOs publicly demanded that Ekandjo withdraw his statement and asserted that such legislation would violate the constitution (Maletsky 1998). In 1999, when discussing the national budget, which had little to do with LGBT rights, Ekandjo's deputy minister, Jeremiah Nambinga, reissued Ekandjo's threat to increase penalties for same-sex sexual conduct (Maletsky 1999). Prime Minister Geingob intervened and stated that SWAPO lawmakers would not increase penalties attached to sodomy, temporarily defusing the tense political atmosphere (Hamata 2000).

Amid SWAPO officials' increasing antigay antagonism in 1998 and 1999, TRP switched strategies, opting for decreased visibility. Activists with TRP decided to pursue the decriminalization of sodomy less publicly with the help of LAC, which provided research support and litigated cases related to Namibian human rights; challenging antisodomy legislation fell within LAC's mandate. TRP met privately with LAC lawyers and researchers, who in turn would mount a public challenge to antisodomy legislation. But by the end of 1999, it was not clear how TRP would proceed with this campaign with LAC, as members and staff spoke vaguely about moving forward with a legal challenge

(TRP meeting minutes, June 20, 1999; December 1, 1999). The law-reform campaign seemed to recede into invisibility as a strategic possibility for TRP.

In 2000, the option to pursue the decriminalization of sodomy seemed to disappear when SWAPO leaders resumed making antigay comments. Nujoma renewed his homophobic sentiments, and at a police graduation, Ekandjo exhorted seven hundred new police officers to "eliminate" gay men and lesbians "from the face of Namibia" (*Namibian* 2000). Ekandjo later clarified that he "did not mean he wanted [gays and lesbians] killed. . . . 'Elimination does not only mean to kill. According to the dictionary meaning, elimination may also mean to ignore, to put aside and [get] rid of'" (Hamata 2000). Such statements forced TRP to adopt a defensive visibility strategy in a "general climate of persecution," especially in light of Ekandjo's incitement of police violence against LGBT persons (LAC annual report 2001, 2). In a press release condemning these remarks, TRP (2000, 11) demanded that SWAPO snub Ekandjo's call for police to arrest gay men and lesbians and "repeal or amend all laws that discriminate against lesbian, gay, bisexual and transgender people in Namibia." Responding to SWAPO leaders' political homophobia kept TRP staff and members busy crafting responses, forced TRP to take a defensive public posture when fending off antigay remarks, and prevented TRP from moving forward with the law-reform campaign. Staff and members occasionally discussed launching a public campaign to decriminalize sodomy in 2000 and 2001, but these discussions led to no visible action (TRP meeting minutes, May 9, 2001).

In light of SWAPO leaders' opposition to LGBT persons and organizing in the late 1990s and early 2000s, TRP staff and members feared provoking a backlash from SWAPO (Human Rights Watch and the International Gay and Lesbian Rights Commission 2003). In particular, several TRP staff and members believed that while Nujoma was president, any attempt to overturn antisodomy legislation would have failed. SWAPO leaders' homophobia, exemplified in Nujoma's frequent claims that sexual minorities did not deserve equal rights, constrained "the space available to the LGBT community to push the boundaries of the interpretation of the constitution in a more liberal direction" (Isaacks 2005, 79). These circumstances limited activists' ability to exercise agency in deciding to pursue a law-reform campaign.

Between 1998 and 2001, immigration rights for same-sex couples emerged as a campaign that TRP could visibly support. In 1997, Liz Frank, a white German woman, a member of Sister Namibia and a founding TRP member, filed for permanent residency; she cited her long-term partnership with Elizabeth |Khaxas, a former director of Sister Namibia and founding TRP member, as the basis for her application for permanent residency (Hubbard

2007; *Windhoek Observer* 2001).[10] However, TRP staff and members opted not to mount a visible campaign in support of immigration rights for same-sex couples or a public campaign to decriminalize sodomy. Instead, TRP only publicly endorsed immigration rights for same-sex couples in press releases that pertained directly to the Frank case and did not mobilize broadly around securing immigration rights for all same-sex couples. Fearing growing SWAPO hostility, activists with TRP did not want to jeopardize the immigration case of one of their own. In 1999, TRP staff and members recommended approaching an international LGBT organization, ILGA, for assistance in pressuring the Namibian political officials about Frank's immigration case. If an international third party pressured the state about the case, TRP staff and members hoped SWAPO leaders would not single out Sister Namibia and TRP for harassment, which suggests that there was some ambivalence about generating international visibility for the case.

In 2000, Ekandjo opposed granting Frank permanent residency, citing that "homosexuality [was] a crime," even though antisodomy legislation did not criminalize sex between women (Hamata 2000). In 2001, the Supreme Court overturned a lower court's ruling granting Frank permanent residency. The court refused to consider Frank's committed lesbian partnership with |Khaxas, a Namibian woman, as a "factor that should count in her favour when her permanent residence application" was reviewed, but the court directed the Immigration Selection Board, which was part of the Ministry of Home Affairs, Ekandjo's ministerial portfolio, to reconsider Frank's application (Menges 2001b). Although the court ordered an internal review of Frank's request for permanent residency, TRP staff and members construed the court's ruling as "extremely homophobic (even questioning [Frank and her partner's] ability as parents) and puts TRP back even farther" in terms of pursuing LGBT rights (TRP meeting minutes, March 7, 2001).

After the Supreme Court ruling was issued in 2001, TRP staff and members questioned whether they should scrap legal tactics altogether. "Regarding the sodomy law, we must now decide whether any attempts to change it, in the present climate, [are] advisable" (TRP meeting minutes, March 7, 2001). Staff and members recognized that they had not followed through with serious, sustained legal lobbying (TRP meeting minutes, March 7, 2001). Despite members' concerns about SWAPO leaders publicly attacking TRP and actualizing their promises to increase penalties for sodomy, staff and members ultimately downplayed the gravity of the public portrayal of this setback because "Namibians on the average [did] not read newspapers and news coverage [about an issue was] usually very brief" (TRP meeting minutes, March 7, 2001). TRP members recognized that media visibility on LGBT issues could be intense for a few days but eventually dissipated. Later, in 2001, Frank succeeded in obtaining permanent residency in Namibia (Eastlick 2002).

TRP staff and members decided that as long as SWAPO leaders persisted in issuing homophobic threats, it would be best to postpone a public law-reform campaign, a decision in which activists' intentionality was seriously constrained. Like Sister Namibia, TRP developed an inclusionary strategic orientation centered on human rights and cast LGBT rights as human rights. Cultivating support from other NGOs to curb SWAPO hostility, staff styled TRP as a broad-based human rights organization. TRP staff and members coached key political and religious readers to denounce antigay rhetoric by voicing their support for all human rights, instead of specifically singling out LGBT rights. TRP's broad embrace of human rights also prevented it from publicly pursuing a legal campaign because it became entangled in antigay hostility within the human rights sector. When TRP first applied to become a member of the Namibian Non-Governmental Organisation Forum (NAN-GOF) in 1999, NANGOF members demanded that TRP representatives deliver an oral presentation about their application's merits. Prior to TRP's application, no representative from another prospective member organization had had to make an oral presentation. Presumably because TRP represented LGBT rights, persons, and interests at a time when SWAPO leaders' antigay statements were frequent, NANGOF members may have attempted to intimidate TRP representatives by requiring them to make a formal presentation about their work. NANGOF's unprecedented treatment of TRP's application provoked outraged responses from Sister Namibia and the National Society for Human Rights, both of whose representatives stated that their organizations would consider withdrawing from NANGOF because they did not want to belong to a coalition that created exclusionary criteria for joining. TRP received full NANGOF membership and played a significant role in rejuvenating the forum's Human Rights and Democracy Sector.[11]

Antigay antagonism within NANGOF toward TRP persisted. In 2002, TRP rescued NANGOF from financial ruin when TRP sponsored a national HIV/AIDS conference to keep NANGOF from repaying an international pharmaceutical company for funds NANGOF had misused. With TRP's support, NANGOF arranged with the pharmaceutical company to use the funds remaining from its donation to host an HIV/AIDS conference, instead of repaying the misused funds. After the conference, TRP received flak from some NANGOF members because TRP conference planners had included a session that addressed how HIV/AIDS affected men who have sex with men. Critics interpreted this issue as a symptom of TRP "hijacking" the forum to give visibility to LGBT matters, as in the case of TRP's role as leader of the

NANGOF's Human Rights and Democracy Sector. Relating this episode during an informal conversation in May 2006, Johannes recalled critics of TRP within NANGOF asking, "Why were LGBT issues suddenly so prominent" and visible? Johannes suspected that TRP's opponents within NANGOF hoped that TRP would "fall flat on our faces" when organizing the HIV/AIDS conference. Continuing hostility from NANGOF members triggered TRP's abandonment of its leadership role in NANGOF's Human Rights and Democracy Sector. In this way, staff and members lessened TRP's visibility in NANGOF. TRP's participation in NANGOF between 1999 and 2003 also prevented the organization from mounting a public law-reform campaign because it directed staff support and energy toward human rights issues more generally, rather than toward specific legal challenges to LGBT rights. TRP's support for human rights work in Namibia extended the organization's invisibility with respect to the proposed law-reform campaign.

Promoting Democracy within TRP

As TRP reinvented itself as a visible promoter of human rights and democracy in Namibia, core members tried to instill democratic practices in TRP and to encourage participation from poor and working-class black and coloured LGBT persons, who were relatively invisible in Namibia. TRP's founding members in 1996 resembled their South African counterparts, who were "privileged mostly white, mostly middle-class, mostly urbanized lesbians and gays, who [were] safe enough to come out and identify as lesbian or gay, [and] fight for their rights" (van Zyl 2005, 31). However, founding members did not want normative visibility within TRP to mean white, middle-class lesbians and men, which would likely alienate black and coloured LGBT persons. TRP founding members recruited black and coloured LGBT persons from diverse class backgrounds in Windhoek. Some white members eventually quit TRP in part because of racism and divergent class interests. Jansen, a black gay man and TRP member, explained that "all the white people" defected from TRP and "decided they are not any part of it [TRP], and they would rather go . . . have fun" (interview with the author, May 29, 2006). Karin, a coloured lesbian woman and TRP member, affirmed that some white lesbians and gay men only wanted to "socialize together. They don't want anything political; they don't want anything more than that. . . . This group doesn't see any need for TRP because they are living in this protected circle that they have. They don't really feel discrimination and being ostracized from their homes" (interview with the author, July 5, 2006).

TRP staff and members believed that they had to diversify TRP's membership in terms of race, ethnicity, and class in postapartheid Namibia. In other words, TRP had to cultivate a multiracial, multiethnic, and class-diverse visibility in terms of its constituency. According to Johannes, if LGBT activists "were going to form a group that only had white members, you were not going to be a voice that people were going to take seriously. You're not going to have any credibility" in a multiracial society. TRP held meetings and recruited black and coloured members in Katutura, a black Windhoek township, and Khomasdal, a coloured Windhoek township. Holding meetings in townships enabled TRP to boost the number of black and coloured members and to enhance the organization's visibility in local townships between 1998 and 2002. As some white members exited TRP, a core group of approximately twelve black, coloured, and white, middle-class volunteers managed TRP from 1997 to 2001.

TRP members decided to empower and encourage black and coloured members from poor and working-class families, who dominated TRP in number, to become more visible in the organization. Enabling constituents' visibility meant creating democratic mechanisms to facilitate their participation. To achieve this goal, founding members drafted a constitution that afforded all members voting power at meetings; ideally, all members had a voice in determining how TRP would develop. New members brought new concerns to TRP. Many black and coloured LGBT persons experienced poverty, joblessness, and lack of access to education, which compounded their struggles with HIV/AIDS and homophobia in their families, communities, and local social institutions (Lorway 2006, 2007, 2008a, 2008b). Members raised these concerns at open monthly meetings. According to Karin, this was evidence that members "felt that TRP, you know, belonged to them. Because that is the message that we gave them, you know. 'This is your place; this is your space'" (interview with the author, July 5, 2006). Founding members hoped democratic mechanisms would involve more black and coloured LGBT persons. For founding members, transparency would take the form of constituents' increased visibility in TRP's decision-making process and staff's increased visibility with constituents.

After TRP opened its office in June 2000, leaders prioritized giving LGBT constituents a space in the organization and office. Filled with educational and entertainment materials, the office's resource center functioned as a safe space for LGBT persons seeking invisibility.[12] As constituents began socializing at the small office, the management committee instituted a rule in 2001 limiting socializing to after 4:00 P.M. two days a week to prevent social gatherings from interrupting staff's work, an indication that total visibility and transparency with constituents might interfere with activist projects (TRP meeting minutes, July 4, 2001). A Women's Caucus formed in 1998 and was renamed the Different Identities Group. Gay men organized the Male Think Tank, and LGBT youth founded the Rainbow Youth (Lorway 2006). In the late 1990s, TRP began offering basic services, such as a weekly soup kitchen and monthly health clinic, to constituents. More affluent constituents subsidized membership fees for disadvantaged constituents and established a fund that assisted those suffering financial hardship (TRP meeting minutes, September 20, 2001).

Much like the offices of FEW and Sister Namibia, TRP's office provided a space for constituents to retreat from public scrutiny. For many members, TRP acted as a social space and haven from their personal troubles. Kauna, a black lesbian woman and TRP member, first became acquainted with TRP after facing "so much rejection . . . in society. . . . I was, like, invited with open arms" (interview with the author, June 15, 2006). TRP offered a "huge support system" to black and coloured LGBT persons, according to Stefan, a coloured gay man and TRP member (interview with the author, June 28, 2006). TRP was particularly a safe haven for LGBT youth, "the place where they could come to, you know, when they had nowhere else to go" (Karin, interview with the author, July 5, 2006). Like members of FEW, some TRP members described TRP as "home." Kauna claimed, "TRP helps with gay and lesbian issues; whatever problems you have, they could perhaps help you. And it's kind of a home where you could talk to somebody. Despite whatever kind of problems, the fact remains: it's like home." Adrian, a black transgender man and TRP member, affirmed TRP's welcoming atmosphere: "It's a lovely feeling to be here. You feel that sense of belonging. Yes, it feels like a home away from home" (interview with the author, July 12, 2006). As members sought social services at TRP, they also asserted ownership of the organization.

From 1997 to 2003, TRP held open monthly meetings at which constituents could voice their concerns or suggest activist campaigns. Beginning in 2001, some meetings devolved into arguments among constituents about TRP's strategies. Some constituents attempted to shift TRP's focus away from pursuing a law-reform campaign to providing social services. Building on members' growing interest in social-service provision, a black gay man who "believed he would eventually become the TRP director" promised to create jobs for members or to give rent money from TRP's budget to those who sided with him; according to Johannes, some educated, middle-class constituents scoffed at this assurance because it revealed how little some poor and working-class members knew about what Northern donors, TRP's main source of funding, would finance—an example of class-based turmoil in TRP.[13]

Some members concocted conspiracy theories. Disgruntled TRP members accused staff of misappropriating funds and increasing their salaries. Staff offered to let members examine the organization's finances, but no one took them up on this offer, probably because most members had little experience navigating complex budgets (TRP meeting minutes, April 3, 2002). Disaffected members expressed concerns about TRP's leadership because operational and strategic choices were invisible to them, despite founding members' efforts to achieve democratic visibility and accountability with constituents. In this sense, staff members' operational choices accrued an invisibility that constituents interpreted as intentionally harmful, even though staff intended these behind-the-scenes efforts to keep TRP running smoothly. The management committee drafted a code of conduct that outlined how constituents were expected to behave in the office and at meetings. Dealing with these internal conflicts contributed to staff members' invisibility with some constituents because staff had to respond to multiple requests for services and information about how they ran TRP.

Constituents' support for, or opposition to, providing social services was largely divided along racial and class lines. Less privileged black and coloured members requested that TRP provide basic services, whereas some black, coloured, and white middle-class members envisioned TRP undertaking projects such as law reform. Some TRP staff and members cast the provision of social services as an either-or dilemma: either they provided social services or they did not. On one hand, some members and staff believed that offering social services to constituents would overwhelm and prevent TRP from pursuing law reform that could lead to the sociopolitical recognition and visibility of LGBT Namibians. Other members "began to withdraw" from TRP because they believed "'poverty issues' were not actual gay and lesbian political problems. The issues they felt were most urgent were related to law reform: rights to same-sex marriage, immigration policy revisions, and rights to adoption" (Lorway 2008b, 85). In addition, these staff and members feared that Northern donors would not fund poverty-alleviation programs designed for LGBT persons because other NGOs already offered such services. On the other hand, some TRP members and staff believed that they should provide social services for less privileged constituents who had nowhere to go. As long as staff obtained funds in the name of Namibian LGBT persons, they believed that members should have equal access to them.

Fulfilling poor black and coloured members' basic needs inundated and paralyzed TRP between 2000 and 2003, telescoping TRP's plans for law reform. According to some constituents, law reform was not a strategic priority for LGBT persons unfamiliar with the Namibian Constitution who had basic needs like education and employment, which these members interpreted as far removed from the legal arena. What would LGBT constituents do with the repeal of antisodomy legislation? How would this repeal benefit them directly, tangibly, and immediately? Christopher, a black gay man and TRP member, argued,

> It really doesn't help you changing legislation if gay people on the ground still suffer a huge amount of stigma, a huge amount of discrimination, violence from the public and the police, verbal abuse from the government, from the public, and from the police, inability to actually access healthcare, the things that really touch people. My feeling is that this is where TRP's resources should be directed: towards the people. (interview with the author, July 18, 2006)

Some TRP staff and members also believed that if marriage equality became a reality, few poor and working-class black and coloured same-sex couples would marry because marriage held few immediate material benefits; according to this point of view, the symbolic victory of winning the right to marry or overturning antisodomy legislation mattered little to poor and working-class black and coloured LGBT persons.

However, many black and coloured members were interested in pursuing legal visibility. Through their involvement with TRP, some members developed "legal consciousness," a sense of their legal rights and entitlements (Merry 1990, 5). When Daniel, a black gay man and TRP member, became aware of marriage inequality, he began to ask questions about sexual minorities' legal status. He was "in a relationship" and anticipated that he and his partner "were going to do certain things together like buy a house" (interview with the author, June 26, 2006). If Daniel died, would his partner be able to "take over or things like that? How would this then affect my family? How would this affect me? When I started realizing those things, I started asking these questions" at TRP. Daniel stated that some TRP staff were receptive to these questions and tried to assist him. "They said that if you as a couple would be willing to stand [for a same-sex marriage case], try for that and say that your rights are not being respected in that sense, then they would be able to appoint a lawyer for you in order to have it run into the court and looked into."

Recognizing and respecting class diversity became a sore point within TRP. Johannes stated that it was easy to run a meeting when twelve middle-class people with similar life experiences, values, and worldviews agreed on a common vision for fighting SWAPO leaders' homophobia, but incorporating "250 to 300 voices from diverse backgrounds [became] very difficult." Johannes concluded that TRP's original constitution could only have worked if all members hailed from the middle class. "An organization like ours can't be completely democratic," Johannes claimed, or else members would run it into the ground with their basic needs. While members could voice multiple concerns through TRP's democratic structure, the polyvocality devolved into cacophony as members diverted meetings with demands for social services.

Some black constituents alleged that TRP's management had been racist in the past. They charged that TRP had hired few black LGBT persons as staff and had neglected to include LGBT persons in important decisions, contrary to founding and core members' claims that the constitution facilitated the incorporation of black and coloured constituents. Alex, a black gay man and TRP member, claimed that because so many black LGBT persons were visible at TRP events, those unfamiliar with or new to TRP might assume that all staff were black, which was not the case (interview with the author, June 30, 2006). Alex also contended that staff only informed black TRP members about events when they wanted to highlight TRP's multiracial visibility for Northern donors, to show how TRP was doing its part to repair race relations. According to this skeptical view, TRP staff leveraged the organization's multiracial visibility to secure more funding for the organization.

While internal conflict siphoned staff and members' attention and contributed to the law-reform campaign's invisibility, founding members and staff asked donors to order and pay for an external review performed by a South African consulting company in 2002 and 2003 because TRP was "being smothered under personal shit," Johannes frankly stated. Karin similarly recalled this turning point in the organization: "TRP had to make the decision. Do we provide these everyday needs of the people, or do we want to make a bigger impact on their lives? Do we want to change the future of the LGBT people in Namibia?" The donor-financed review recommended that TRP become a trust, an organizational form in which TRP staff would be accountable only to an executive board and not to dozens of members and would abandon social-service provision. Donors worried that social-service provision programs like the soup kitchen would bankrupt TRP. As a result of the review, members voted to transform TRP into a trust that would only initiate and execute programs, such as a law-reform project, which would improve the lives and legal situations of LGBT Namibians. Becoming a trust enabled TRP to "move from having to look at one person's needs to looking at a greater scale," according to Daniel. If TRP had not shifted its focus from social-service provision to legal, political, and social advocacy that targeted the state and social institutions, donors would have suspended funding and restarted TRP as a trust after a cooling-off period, forcing TRP into unintentional invisibility. Nevertheless, one result of TRP's organizational transformation was staff members' invisibility with LGBT constituents throughout Namibia, as staff accountability shifted from constituents entirely to Northern donors.

Some members like Peter believed that TRP staff had abandoned them. According to Peter, a black gay man who lived in Swakopmund, he and his friend did not know what "they are doing there in Windhoek. . . . We don't know anything" because of TRP's invisibility with constituents (interview with the author, May 19, 2006).

After this turbulent period, TRP had another opportunity to launch the law-reform campaign in May 2004. Lawmakers were debating whether to keep the sexual-orientation nondiscrimination clause in the new Labour Bill (Dentlinger 2004). TRP could have mounted an effort to persuade the public and lawmakers of the need to retain the clause in the Labour Bill. TRP's mobilization seemed especially important, given Justice Minister Albert Kawana's attempt to use this debate as an opportunity to increase penalties for sodomy and to introduce expanded antihomosexuality legislation (Dentlinger 2004). However, TRP did not publicly oppose lawmakers' removal of the sexual-orientation nondiscrimination clause in the Labour Bill.

TRP's inaction and invisibility during the Labour Bill debate disappointed some constituents. Despite his opposition to TRP's positioning of law reform as a strategic priority, Christopher believed that TRP should have responded visibly and decisively to lawmakers' efforts. Christopher "was really taken aback and heartbroken when the labor law was changed and the clause . . . based on sexual orientation was taken out. There was no lobby[ing] done. . . . Nobody came to ask for my signature. There were no petitions done." Christopher enumerated other tactics TRP could have used to challenge lawmakers' actions:

> Every gay person should have been informed that this was happening. People should have been petitioned, not only gay people, but also their friends, their family, or their allies who actually fill out petition forms. There should have been a demonstration to raise the issue in the public eye and then to stall the process of changing it.

Christopher objected to TRP's complete invisibility during this debate. Despite this lost legal opportunity, TRP staff maintained that it was their intention to move forward with law reform in mid-2006. In funding proposals that staff wrote for Northern donors, TRP staff specified that law reform was a top priority. In addition, an activist with TRP claimed in 2008 that Namibian marriage laws obliged the state to recognize all marriages solemnized by the South African state. "So if two gay or lesbian Namibians come to South Africa and get married they can go and file for recognition in Namibia" (Judge et al. 2008b, 305). However, the TRP activist acknowledged that this action could yield a legal backlash in the form of a ban on same-sex marriage, but marriage equality might be possible under the leadership of President

Pohamba, whose silence on gender and sexual diversity contrasted sharply with Nujoma's homophobia.

Although staff could not persuade white members who left TRP to rejoin, they retained and recruited black and coloured LGBT persons as members. TRP's multiracial visibility reflected Namibia's racial and ethnic diversity. Still, the termination of social-service provision disenchanted and alienated some constituents because they no longer experienced TRP as a refuge from unwanted scrutiny in the way they once had. The opportunity to socialize with other black and coloured LGBT Namibians in a safe space had disappeared. Despite these setbacks, TRP garnered an international reputation among Northern donors and African LGBT movement organizations as an organization that had emerged intact from its internal conflicts. TRP staff members even shared these lessons with small groups of LGBT activists in East Africa, which I explore in the next chapter. In other words, TRP's invisibility at a time of opportunity generated a new type of international visibility for the organization.

Missed Opportunities for Visibility in Namibian and South African LGBT Organizing

The LGBT movements in both South Africa and Namibia were invisible during times of political opportunity, but activists missed these opportunities in different ways. South African LGBT activists intentionally deferred pursuing the marriage-equality campaign after the Constitutional Court's ruling. Movement leaders were unprepared to move forward with the campaign and decided to publicly repudiate the GLA's malicious claim about gay men's blood-donation protest. Organizations were invisible in relation to the marriage-equality campaign only for a few months. Eventually, they surfaced to press lawmakers to pass inclusive marriage-equality legislation. In contrast, TRP's law-reform campaign did not materialize because activists feared SWAPO leaders' political homophobia. Although activists intended to launch a public law-reform campaign, TRP unintentionally lapsed into invisibility; SWAPO leaders' political homophobia constrained activists' ability to control their public visibility in the way they intended. As activists continued deliberating about intensified state repression if they initiated the campaign, these internal discussions contributed to the campaign's postponement such that it receded into invisibility for TRP staff and members. TRP staff also became involved in human rights organizing, which siphoned resources from the proposed campaign. Internal conflict about strategic priorities also contributed to TRP's invisibility. Thus, the invisibilities of the Namibian and South African LGBT movements differed in form and content, suggesting that the circumstances governing movement invisibility deserve closer scrutiny by scholars. Invisibility is not a one-size-fits-all measure of social movement distress.

Similarly, LGBT movements' visibility strategies are not uniform. LGBT activists develop strategies appropriate for their contexts and decide which actions might endanger or advance the movement. In Namibia, TRP staff members decided in part to delay initiating a public law-reform campaign to avoid state repression. South African LGBT activists were in a different position vis-à-vis the state and political parties. By the time the Constitutional Court issued a ruling supporting same-sex marriage, the LGBT movement had already achieved several victories: the inclusion of the EC in the constitution (1996), the decriminalization of sodomy (1998), and the passage of immigration (1999) and adoption (2002) rights for LGBT constituents. South African LGBT activists did not have to worry as much about political hostility as Namibian activists, although some became nervous about the possibility of a backlash against LGBT persons and rights due to the GLA's claimed blood-donation protest. Still, anti-LGBT violence remained a threat, especially for black South African constituents.

Interrogating movement invisibility in times of political opportunity presents scholars with a theoretical opportunity of their own: the chance to examine the social, cultural, and political underpinnings of analytic categories. Categories, such as "invisibility" and "opportunity," may (or may not) have different meanings for activists involved with identity movements in the global South. Activists may not perceive an opportunity in the same way that social movement scholars do, suggesting the need for scholars to exercise additional care when studying movement strategies in newly democratizing contexts. In addition, assessing movement invisibility requires particular care. Namibian LGBT activists did not retreat into unintentional invisibility at the first sign of SWAPO leaders' political homophobia; they persisted in publicly challenging leaders' statements, while carefully weighing whether they should launch a law-reform campaign. Examining analytic categories is necessary when scholars assess social movement development and the types of public visibility movements the global South should have.

These concerns become especially salient when scholars observe LGBT activism in the global South. For instance, questioning why LGBT activists have (or have not) prioritized law reform requires scholars to disclose assumptions they possess regarding LGBT organizing. By presuming that LGBT movements should have plans to launch a law-reform campaign, scholars may knowingly or unwittingly impose a Northern LGBT organizing paradigm on movements in the global South. This imposition involves transferring developmentalist assumptions about gender and sexual diversity organizing in the global North to countries in the global South. *Developmentalist assumptions* are presuppositions that social, political, and economic processes in the global South will eventually resemble those in the global North, thanks to Northern development projects and interventions. M. Jacqui Alexander (2005) advises scholars to avoid projecting Northern expectations about how LGBT movements can and should develop onto the global South. In her estimation, scholars should avoid concluding that LGBT movements that lack robust law-reform campaigns are stunted and "defect[ive] in political consciousness and maturity" (28). Although LGBT activists in the global South may be interested in similar goals, the strategies they choose will be rooted in local cultural and political structures (Chabot and Duyvendak 2002).

Legal tactics may not be practicable for some LGBT movements in the global South. In some African nations, law-reform campaigns are not currently viable for LGBT movements such as the Ugandan movement. In 2005, lawmakers in Uganda passed a constitutional amendment prohibiting same-sex marriage (Human Rights Watch 2005). Ugandan LGBT activists face arrest, detention, police harassment, and political homophobia, according to Luisa, a Ugandan lesbian woman and Behind the Mask intern (interview with the author, February 2, 2006). However, some LGBT activists in Uganda legally challenged their harassment and detention by police. Hence, African LGBT activists refuse to be forced into quiescence and invisibility, although they may be unable to deploy the same strategies as LGBT activists elsewhere (Hollander 2009).

4

Homosexuality *Is* African:
Struggles "to Be Seen"

At the beginning of TRP's weekly radio show, "Talking Pink," producers played a recording of former Namibian Minister of Home Affairs Jerry Ekandjo, which fetured him stating,

> We don't have homosexuals in Namibia. There are only a few people. In Windhoek, there are maybe not more than ten. . . . If there are more than ten, let them come in the [Home Affairs] office. But most of them are from the European Union. You will find Afrikaners, the English, the British, but you will never find Oshivambo, Nama, Herero, Damara.

Producers then played a recording of TRP members declaring their ethnic and sexual identities: "I am a black Ovambo lesbian in Namibia. I am a Herero man, gay and proud. I am a . . . proud Damara lesbian." The fusion of ethnic and sexual identities audibly refuted Ekandjo's claim. "Talking Pink" broadcasts reminded listeners in Windhoek that there were lesbians and gay men of different ethnicities in Namibia.

Ekandjo's statements constituted the erasure of LGBT Namibians, indicative of homosexuality-is-un-African discourse that some SWAPO leaders favored (Aarmo 1999). According to the logic undergirding political homophobia, because same-sex sexuality was un-African, it did not exist, and there were no African lesbians or gay men (Epprecht 2004). In this way, homosexuality-is-un-African discourse generated controlling visibilities for gender and sexual minorities of African descent. For some Namibians and South Africans of African descent, the notion that gender and sexual diversity was African was contradictory. How could activists of African descent who claimed to be "lesbian" and "gay," which were Western terms, also be "African"?[1] Lindiwe explained how FEW and other South African movement organizations worked against the perception that all LGBT activists were white. Mimicking antigay opponents, Lindiwe stated, "They'll always tell you that being a lesbian, it's a white thing. 'It's a trend that the European people brought to Africa.' They'll tell you that they've never seen a black old woman being an activist as a lesbian."

Much like the lingering threat of anti-LGBT violence in South Africa, homosexuality-is-un-African discourse functioned as a specter in national and continental sociopolitical imaginaries. The concept of "specter" captures the hazy political horizon that informed and guided activists' decisions and actions (Gordon 2008). Through the specter, different social and political actors could revise the past and reimagine the nation's and continent's future by invoking claims to racial, national, and cultural authenticity that depended on heteronormativity. Defending an African imaginary from Western cultural and political incursions, some political and traditional leaders in Namibia, South Africa, and other African nations articulated the past in strictly heterosexist terms, erasing the possibility of local, indigenous gender and sexual diversity. In their eyes, the new nation must be heterosexual. Homosexuality-is-un-African discourse enabled some leaders to ward off what they viewed as Western "gay imperialism," which took the form of Northern donors, diplomats, and LGBT activists imposing their will on independent African democracies (Barnard 2004, 7). The specter linking Africanness to heterosexuality did not completely subside, even though Namibian political leaders might refrain from issuing homophobic statements publicly, or the South African government guaranteed LGBT rights. Registering as a barely visible threat sometimes, the specter threatened to erupt in the public sphere, a possibility against which Namibian and South African LGBT activists guarded.

Constantly working within and against this specter, LGBT activists in Namibia and South Africa struggled to be seen in three ways simultaneously: as representing LGBT persons, as "Namibian" or "South African," and as "African." This visibility strategy entailed creating frames that resonated with target audiences, frames that audiences would recognize and, hopefully, respond to favorably (Benford and Snow 2000). Activists made decisions or took actions leading them in the direction of cultural, racial, and/or national authenticity, yet the possibility that other audiences would regard them as un-African remained. In this sense, as LGBT activists sculpted their visibility strategies to adhere to external notions of Africanness, these strategies acquired a disciplinary quality.

Like other cultural and political forms, authenticity is a social construction that gains traction through repeated deployment and refinement (Nagel

1994). Authenticity is a difficult public presentation to cultivate, in part because authenticity is an abstract concept that groups can define as narrowly or widely as they wish.[2] My use of "authenticity" refers to activists' public presentations and performances that situate the movement, movement organization, or constituents as belonging in a particular arena or field. Namibian and South African LGBT activists tailored their constituent- and organizational-level visibility strategies to prove that "LGBT" persons and activism were authentically "African," a label that referred to race, culture, and/or nationalism, depending on the context. As with many identity strategies, a visibility strategy of authenticity relies on exclusion and inclusion. Making certain movement items visible renders other items and expressions invisible. In particular, activists' deployment of professionalized LGBT nomenclature subsumed other local expressions for gender and sexual dissidence. In this sense, activists' identity terminology regulated which "models of sexuality get to be seen as authentic" and which models become invisible (Binnie 2004, 39).

This chapter examines the visibility troubles that arise when LGBT activists' public claims to authenticity seem to contradict their material reality.[3] Namibian and South African LGBT activists asserted the Africanness of gender and sexual diversity and LGBT activism but used Western gender and sexual identity terminology in their work. In addition, activists solicited and received funding from Northern donors and maintained ties with international LGBT movement organizations based in the global North. Activists' use of Western imagery and ties with Northern donors stood to jeopardize their cultural and political standing nationally, if antigay opponents interpreted activists' transnational ties and use of Western identity categories as evidence of Northern manipulation. Activists struggled to balance public presentations of LGBT organizing as authentically African to destabilize homosexuality-is-un-African discourse, while convincing Northern donors that their projects were worthy of funding. Movement public presentations were essential to movement continuity. Political homophobia threatened to weaken LGBT activists' ability to organize adherents, if negative publicity forced constituents and supporters to abandon the movement. LGBT movement organizations relied on Northern funding. Without donor funding, organizations like Sister Namibia would lapse into unintentional invisibility, unable to sustain their political projects.

Using ethnographic and interview data, I show how Namibian and South African LGBT movement organizations navigated this strategic dilemma of public visibility: that of being seen as authentically African LGBT movement organizations, despite their relationships with Northern donors and LGBT movement organizations. First, I review the diverse meanings of "homosexuality-is-un-African" discourse and how Namibian and South

African LGBT activists refuted this discourse. Next I examine how Behind the Mask and TRP approached the strategic dilemma of being seen as *gay for pay,* which refers to being perceived as un-African because they solicited and accepted funds from Northern donors.[4] Accepting funds from Northern donors put Behind the Mask and TRP in a position of accountability to donors. Finally, using ethnographic data, I show how Namibian and South African LGBT movement organization leaders resolved to portray the movement as "African" to the ACHPR.

Being Perceived as "Un-African"

African antigay opponents, including ruling party leaders, deployed political homophobia to exclude same-sex sexualities from national imaginaries (Aarmo 1999; Currier 2010b; Epprecht 2004; Massaquoi 2008). Common techniques included denying the existence of indigenous same-sex sexualities and labeling same-sex sexualities as foreign, un-African, Western, un-Christian, and evidence of continuing colonialism (Reddy 2002). Davis, a black gay man and TRP member, explained how TRP responded to the multiple meanings of political homophobia:

> We tried to . . . educate [SWAPO leaders] by telling them that . . . there are also other people in society that are different from some [Namibians]. That was just the idea that we wanted to get across. . . . We're all Namibians and taxpayers and live in Namibia. [Nujoma] also said something about [homosexuality] that it's un-African and it's a European disease and all sorts of things. We just wanted to show him that we're Africans, and we're also gay as well. And we've never been to Europe to be, you know, manipulated to become gay, but it's something in us. (interview with the author, May 17, 2006)

According to Davis, TRP claimed racial and national authenticity for lesbian, gay, and bisexual (LGB) Namibians by emphasizing their lack of cultural contact with white Europeans and North Americans and by portraying LGB Namibians as having an authentic, prediscursive sexual essence that had not been "manipulated" by cultural and racial outsiders or by Western terminology.

To some antigay opponents, activists' use of the LGBT acronym substantiated their suspicion that activists were converting heterosexuals into homosexuals. According to antigay opponents, Namibians were always, already heterosexual, until they came into contact with Western influences or with an LGBT movement organization (Epprecht 2008). Davis also explained that SWAPO leaders "were saying that [TRP is] actually convincing people to become gay. There is that confusion. So we are trying to make them understand that these people are already gay. I mean, we can't make them gay; it's impossible." According to Davis, same-sex sexual desire inhered in individuals. He claimed that TRP did not teach or recruit people to become lesbian, gay, or bisexual. In his defense of black LGB persons' racial authenticity, Davis depended on a notion of same-sex sexual desire as prediscursive. The visibility dilemma for LGBT activists emerged when opponents viewed the articulation of this desire in Western identity terms as un-African.

How did black and coloured Namibians and South Africans come to describe themselves as "gay," an English-language term and a Western concept (Donham 1998; Stychin 2001)?[5] What about the possibility of a less visible, but no less vibrant, lexicon of local gender and sexual diversity terms? Organizations like TRP did not employ indigenous identity terms in their public work: staff used Western identifiers.[6] Some constituents began to use the LGBT acronym through a process of direct intervention. LGBT activists imported Western identity vocabulary and encouraged constituents to use Western identity terms in movement discourse and activities. Organizations like FEW, Sister Namibia, and TRP sponsored identity workshops and social events that acquainted gender and sexual minority constituents with Western identity terms (Lorway 2008b).

As activists import and promote foreign identity categories locally, another way of discussing collective identity formation is warranted. Whereas what I call the *organic model* of collective identity formation treats collective identities as arising organically from the experiences, desires, emotions, and beliefs of nascent activists (Polletta and Jasper 2001; Taylor and Whittier 1992; Taylor and Van Dyke 2004), the *import model* of collective identity formation refers to activists' seizure and introduction of foreign identities into a local movement repertoire. The import model reverses the process of collective identity formation associated with the organic model. When movement leaders introduce foreign collective identities, they often impose them from above through top-down dissemination, educating rank-and-file activists and constituents about identities' meanings, whereas in the organic model, these identities often emerge from below. Implementing imported identities may rely on a mixture of egalitarian and hierarchical methods (Katyal 2002; Lorway 2008b). Favoring egalitarian principles, leaders may benignly educate constituents about imported identity, without pressuring them to adopt these identities. Tending toward a hierarchical model, leaders may mold constituents' personal identities through persuasion and immersion campaigns, deemphasizing alternative identity models. The import model involves intervening in and revising constituents' identities, as activists expose constituents to new identity terminology, possibly for the first time.

Race matters in the import model of collective identity. Many white Namibians and South Africans had greater cultural access to European racial, gender, and sexual discourses than persons of African descent, which predisposed whites to adopt gender and sexual minority identities. Black and coloured gender and sexual minorities in Namibia and South Africa encountered Western gay cultural artifacts in the form of films, books, magazines, and television shows accessible in the resource centers at FEW, Sister Namibia, and TRP. In fact, TRP brought these artifacts directly to rural constituents through the video project. Staff screened films like *The Adventures of Priscilla, Queen of the Desert* in different Namibian towns for black and coloured constituents. Film screenings provided rural LGBT constituents an opportunity to socialize in a safe space, screen a film, and discuss the film's pertinence to their own lives. Although many LGBT constituents in Namibia might never meet white gay Westerners, they could access Western gay culture in this venue. Some black and coloured constituents did not see insuperable cultural difference in *Priscilla*; they interpreted the characters' experiences with gender and sexual diversity as similar to their own. Several coloured gay men who belonged to TRP appreciated the film selection. Jannie, a coloured gay man, found the film uplifting and "interesting." "As far as I'm concerned, the video . . . show[s] the world that . . . we are normal in Namibia. . . . And that's how God created us" (interview with the author, April 23, 2006). Jannie combined Christian rhetoric with an essentialist claim that same-sex-desiring people's sexualities could not be changed, an example of the coexistence of multiple, competing cultural logics in contemporary Namibia.

However, consuming Western cultural artifacts did not guarantee that movement constituents would personally assume these labels (Boellstorff 2005). Other interventions, such as identity workshops, increased the likelihood that constituents would adopt LGBT terminology, in a process that resembles coming out of the closet (Binnie 2004). Until they began attending TRP's events, some Namibian gender and sexual minorities were unfamiliar with the LGBT acronym. According to Lorway (2008b, 86), who began studying TRP's work with LGBT youth in 2001, some TRP members averred that they "had neither heard of the terms 'gay' or 'lesbian' nor knew what they meant prior to their introduction to TRP." Although many TRP members recognized that their sexual desires and gender expression did not necessarily resemble heteronormative arrangements favored by most Namibian ethnic groups, they did not have access to English terms that neatly summarized their desires (Isaacks 2005; |Khaxas 2005). Donor-funded gender and sexual identity workshops acquainted members with Western terminology (Lorway 2008a).

Claudia described a hypothetical situation in which TRP would invite someone "confused about where you sort of place yourself when it comes to your sexual orientation" to gender and sexual identity workshops, similar to those developed by FEW (interview with the author, May 11, 2006). "If a workshop comes up on sexual orientation, like knowing where, like sort of identifying yourself, then we would say, 'That person really needs that type of info, so it would be good to invite that person.'" FEW engaged in similar practices intended to facilitate constituents' public identification as black lesbian women activists. To outsiders, identity workshops might prove that LGBT movement organizations were in the business of Westernizing sexually and gender-variant Africans. The foreignness of "coming out" as an individual-level identity strategy became salient to anti-LGBT opponents (Boellstorff 2005, 125; Chabot and Duyvendak 2002). Opponents could impugn LGBT movement organizations for acquainting people with same-sex sexualities, people who, according to antigay logic, would not have otherwise learned about lesbian and gay identities. In other words, opponents could interpret activists' use of Western identity terms as confirmation that they were in the business of converting heterosexual Africans into homosexual persons.

Although Namibian and South African LGBT activists were cognizant of and repudiated homosexuality-is-un-African rhetoric, they did not seem to question how using Western identity categories affected how opponents viewed them. This was evident in how Sibusiso, a black lesbian and Behind the Mask member, described her organization's mandate as putting other LGBT movement organizations in touch with each other, providing "a voice for the voiceless, the homosexual community in Africa as a whole," publicizing the LGBT movement in Africa, and "giving hope to the hopeless" (interview with the author, November 28, 2005). Sibusiso narrated a hypothetical story that appeared on Behind the Mask's website

> about a Nigerian who is in threat of being stoned because of the fact that he is homosexual. And later on we report that that person was let out [of jail]. . . . Eventually they weren't stoned. And there's someone who is sitting somewhere who knows that they are gay. Not that the same experience would happen to them or anything, but then they have hope that, "Okay, if I become true to myself and maybe come out, let one person know that I'm gay."

Behind the Mask used individual-level strategic visibility to communicate information about gender and sexual diversity to African LGBT movement constituents. Sibusiso's unnamed, ungendered, and nationless African who read this story on Behind the Mask's website intuited that she or he is "gay" but understood the negative consequences that could accompany disclosing that she or he desired women or men sexually. It is unclear from Sibusiso's narrative whether this person had access to Western identity categories. However, it was Behind the Mask's job to translate the Nigerian man's story into one of instruction and inspiration for other LGBT Africans who may not yet use Western identity categories. "[If we] hadn't run that story about the Nigerian, they [other gay Africans] wouldn't think that there's a better life for them out there" as openly gay. This hypothetical example demonstrates how Western identity categories represented a way of rescuing LGBT individuals from what activists perceived as invisibility, isolation, and hopelessness and ushering them into Western "cultural intelligibility" (Butler 2006, 23).

For some queer scholars, translating indigenous same-sex sexual desire constitutes a normalizing and homogenizing process when LGBT movements and communities expect sexually and gender-variant individuals to engage in "compulsory disclosure" of a "gay identity, regardless of one's location within the country's racial and class hierarchies" (Decena 2008, 405). Evelyn Blackwood (2004, 106) observes, "Due to the visibility of 'lesbian and gay' rights movements in Europe and the U.S., many activists in Africa, rather than using local words, have claimed the English words 'lesbian' and 'gay' as visible signifiers for their movements." This stems in part from the fact that some indigenous terms for same-sex sexual desire are "derogatory and cannot be recouped in a positive manner at this point in time" (106). Thus, for some gender and sexual minorities, Western terms are preferable to indigenous insults. Blackwood counsels activists and scholars to regard the term *lesbian,* in particular, as provisional, instead of treating it as "a static identity that can prevent us from recognizing the multiplicity of local identities and relationships" (106).

In the global South, "coming out" in Western terms rendered LGBT persons racially and nationally traitorous in the eyes of antigay opponents. Yet increasing the number of people who identified as LGBT could enable activists to counter the claim that LGBT persons were Westernized and un-African, bolstering the visibility of a growing African LGBT movement. Namibian and South African LGBT movement organizations could then count these individuals as constituents. From the perspective of LGBT movement organization staff and leaders, individual-level visibility strategies strengthened organizations' and movement visibilities in Namibia, South Africa, and beyond. According to this perspective, movement visibility relied on increasing the number of constituents who identified as LGBT. In these ways, Western identity terminology had simultaneously enabling and disempowering consequences for constituents and for political action.

Looking Visibly Western

Some antigay opponents alleged that LGBT activists and constituents were gay for pay because they used Western identity categories, according to Johannes. Gay-for-pay logic stipulated that if white foreigners did not pay Namibians and South Africans for same-sex sex, they would otherwise be heterosexual. In other words, Africans were heterosexual by default and were only "doing it for money" (Aarmo 1999, 263). While some Africans engaged in same-sex sex work out of economic exigency, obviously, not all Africans with same-sex sexual desires sought out foreigners for sexual relationships (Lorway 2008b).

Beyond gay sex tourism, being "gay for pay" suggested that Namibians or South Africans claimed they were gay or represented LGBT persons only to obtain funding. This label tarred LGBT political ventures that Northern donors funded as racially and nationally inauthentic from their beginning. The label also implied that Africans were opportunistic, selfish, and willing to betray their nations and ethnic groups for Northern funding. In addition, this negative label promoted the idea that LGBT movement organizations were flush with cash, a sentiment that Sylvia Tamale (2007), a Ugandan feminist scholar, experienced firsthand when she publicly defended LGBT Ugandans vilified by the media, public, and politicians. She recalls receiving a text message on her cell phone that read, "'On your way to becoming a millionaire!' . . . There was an assumption that my support for the rights of homosexuals meant that money was going to pour in from . . . Western Europe and North America" (Tamale 2007, 17). LGBT movement organizations were seen as cash cows that needed to be milked until Northern funding dried up.

Antigay opponents may have perceived Namibian and South African LGBT movement organizations as Western and un-African because many "have been white-dominated until the very recent past. . . . The donors whose funds sustain most of their activities are western, and . . . the language and imagery that they use in their publications appear distinctly foreign" (Epprecht 2001b, 1100). TRP staff members, in particular, experienced both positive and negative consequences that stemmed from looking too visibly Western when they drove a small, yellow car with "Astraea Lesbian Foundation" stenciled on the back, evidence of the U.S. donor's funding.[7]

To some TRP constituents, the car's distinctiveness contributed positively to TRP's public visibility. According to Claudia, after seeing the car, people would "look up TRP in the [telephone] directory and would call . . . asking, 'Just tell me more about the organization. It's not like I'm gay or anything. I just want to know'" about TRP. The car signified the existence of LGBT persons and organizing to other Namibians and confirmed that TRP received foreign funding. According to Karin, in 2000, the idea for purchasing a car for TRP emerged from discussions held by a group of lesbian, bisexual, and transgender (LBT) women who formed the Women's Caucus within TRP. One project they brainstormed, Karin recounted, was a women-operated taxi service that would transport "women, not just lesbian women, women in general that works late and that. I mean, taxis is a problem; taxis is dangerous." This project addressed the safety of women in public, especially in public places at night, a visibility strategy intended to keep vulnerable women constituents safe, similar to FEW's spatial-monitoring strategy. Karin explained that "funders didn't find it a very feasible project, and they were asking how we are going to sustain this thing. . . . They didn't see that . . . this thing could become self-sustainable in the end." Caucus members encountered a similar problem with generating self-sustaining activism, a problem that proved similarly vexing for Sister Namibia's director as she tried to locate additional funding for her organization's activities. Caucus members revised the proposal, "dropped the whole idea of an income-generating" activity attached to a taxi service, and focused on "target[ing] all LBT women in Namibia with awareness raising [and] education. Part of that proposal also included a car to go to the various regions [of Namibia]. And . . . we got money [from Astraea] to buy the car."

To other staff and members, the car brought unnecessary, negative attention to TRP. Davis stated, "As soon as anybody sees that [Astraea Lesbian Foundation logo], they go, like, really uncomfortable; they don't want to be in that car anymore because there's 'lesbian' written on the car." The word *lesbian* outed and Westernized occupants. After riding in the car one day, Tanya, a coloured lesbian and TRP member, complained to staff that young men in town were heckling car passengers because the car had "lesbian" emblazoned on the back. TRP's purchase of a car also seemed unnecessary to some members. Jansen interpreted the purchase of the yellow car as a sign that TRP and staff were misusing funds and keeping TRP members from participating in the decision-making process. He explained, "When the money comes in . . . we are not just informed that we received" donor funding. "It's just that you see that there is money; people are getting salaries and their cars." Jansen cited the car's purchase as an example of how black constituents were excluded from and invisible in decision-making processes. In other words, the invisibility of staff members' choices led some black constituents to believe that staff members were trying to disempower them.

Karin interpreted the criticism offered by gay men like Jansen as "narrow-minded" and "sexist," but she acknowledged that workshops that addressed sexism encouraged gay and bisexual men to accept "the situation that the women are here . . . to stay." Men's objections to the car stemmed from the fact that the car was "first and foremost for women-only projects." Karin and other women realized that "it was just inevitable that the car would become or would be used for all the activities of TRP, as long as the women were not being sidelined." TRP staff and members were not united in their reception of the "lesbian" car and how the organization used Northern funding, reflecting gendered divisions among some staff and members (Lorway 2008a, 2008b).

The "lesbian" car publicized TRP's work on lesbian rights and confirmed its receipt of Northern funding and support. While some TRP staff viewed such public visibility positively in that the car motivated ordinary Namibians' inquiries about the organization's work, others viewed this visibility with suspicion because it eluded their control. The prominent visibility of the "lesbian" car communicated to the public that Northern donors influenced TRP, possibly tarnishing the organization's reputation with some audiences.

"Gay for Pay": "Un-African" Movement Organizations

For antigay critics, the involvement of Northern donors and LGBT movement organizations in Namibian and South African LGBT organizing called activists' racial, cultural, and national authenticity into question. Some African political leaders regarded LGBT organizing as a "straightforward product of Western cultural imperialism" because movement organizations used "Western-sounding language and Western-looking imagery" and received funding from Northern donors (Epprecht 2004, 226). In 1997, Nujoma registered his wariness of "foreigners who claim to know development and democracy better than us," foreigners who included Northern donors (Günzel 1997). According to critics like Nujoma, since LGBT movement organizations relied on foreign funding, they were little more than puppets of Northern donors (Epprecht 2001b; Richardson 2005). For critics, Northern donors were sources of identities that disrupted indigenous African cultural traditions, and LGBT movement organizations that received international funding operated neither independently nor in an authentically African way (Epprecht 2004; Hoad 2007). In other words, Northern donors "paid" Namibians and South Africans to be professionally "gay."

There were few philanthropic foundations in Namibia that would bankroll LGBT movement organizations' projects, and SWAPO leaders, in particular, opposed LGBT organizing. Soon after TRP's launch in late 1996, founding members realized that they could not "finance the activities of the organization out of our own pockets, but by this time, TRP had built a . . . very strong reputation with [Northern] funders. . . . Between 1997 and 1999, we always made sure that funders knew what we were doing, even though we never asked for money," Johannes related. TRP members did not question the ethics of obtaining funding from Northern donors; instead, they interpreted constituents' needs and hostility to gender and sexual diversity as necessitating foreign funding. As Sister Namibia staff experienced, the lack of funding contributed directly to an organization's unintentional invisibility when activists had to suspend certain projects.

Like TRP, Behind the Mask was unable to obtain funding in an under-resourced South African sociopolitical field. Sibongile suspected that homophobia had prevented Behind the Mask from getting funding from the South African government and other private sources. According to Sibongile, South African funders did not want to support LGBT organizing "even though it's in our constitution that we've got the same right as the other citizens to love whoever that we want to love." Social and religious homophobia was still an obstacle to South Africa LGBT organizing, despite the existence of LGBT rights. Sibongile also observed that some philanthropic groups also "used religion to . . . turn a blind eye [to] our cause." Behind the Mask's transnational scope also made it difficult to secure South African funding because some funders only supported organizations that operated nationally.[8] Like TRP, Behind the Mask had multiple donors that funded certain projects or paid the salary for certain staff positions.

Accepting foreign funding created a visibility dilemma for Namibian and South African LGBT movement organizations.[9] On one hand, leaders of Behind the Mask and TRP knew that funding from Northern donors would allow them to retain staff and advocate on behalf of Namibian and South African LGBT persons. On the other hand, if Behind the Mask and TRP were perceived as un-African, neocolonial, and "gay for pay" because they received funding from Northern donors, it might jeopardize their work locally and transnationally in a pan-African context.[10]

The strategic choice to solicit funding from Northern donors put Behind the Mask and TRP in a position of being indebted to donors. This dynamic mirrored the economic dependency of postcolonial nations in the global South on nations in the global North, a relationship with historical roots in colonialism. Without funding, LGBT movement organizations faced the possibility of terminating their projects and being forced into unintentional invisibility. At least with funding, activists could continue their work. However, they confronted the prospect of being unable to control organizations' visibility and reputation.

Emerging Pan-African Visibility: The East African Initiative

In 2005 and 2006, Hivos and the Ford Foundation asked Behind the Mask and TRP to work with struggling LGBT movement organizations in Kenya,

Uganda, and Tanzania.[11] Both Behind the Mask and TRP had received funding from Hivos, but not from the Ford Foundation. Behind the Mask had submitted a funding proposal to the Ford Foundation, but it was denied because a Ford representative claimed that Ford's "focus . . . was something else," not on LGBT rights and organizing, according to Sibongile. However, Sibongile learned that "there was another [African] LGBT organization that they funded at that time. . . . We were kind of disappointed that we couldn't get" funding. Sibongile hoped that working with the Ford Foundation would show the donor what Behind the Mask could do and position the organization to receive funding in the future.[12]

Northern donors were responding to dysfunctions they had encountered in 2003 when they began funding new LGBT movement organizations in Kenya, Uganda, and Tanzania. Donor representatives grew concerned when they learned that some organizations had obtained funding under possibly false pretenses, and representatives hired an independent researcher to investigate where their funds went and which LGBT movement organizations were or were not legitimate. Donors defined legitimate movement organizations as those whose leaders could account for how they spent funds and carried out projects they included in their annual reports. In other words, leaders of legitimate movement organizations documented their activities and spending in ways that assured them public visibility of some kind. Their public presence conferred the political legibility and legitimacy donors desired. Donors preferred giving funds to established movement organizations "because they have the staff and mechanisms to receive and utilise grants" (Britton 2006, 163). According to Johannes, owing to the possible fraud, donor representatives reasoned that they could not indefinitely send money to organizations in Kenya, Uganda, and Tanzania that kept "disappearing into bottomless pits." Organizations' invisibility signaled possible fraud to Northern donors. Behind the Mask and TRP staff worked to project an aura of technocratic competency to donors as a way to ensure that donors continued funding their projects.

Thanks to the independent researcher, donors discovered that some movement organizations had been submitting annual reports that "could not be true," Johannes explained. Repressive laws prevented public LGBT organizing and other forms of oppositional political organizing in Kenya, Uganda, and Tanzania, as donors knew, making it unlikely that LGBT movement organizations would be able to sustain public visibility over a long period of time. LGBT movement organizations could not have held large public events without drawing attention and ire from the Kenyan, Ugandan, or Tanzanian police or government (Nagadya 2005; Tamale 2007). When the donor-hired researcher interviewed individuals in Kenya, Uganda, and

Tanzania who claimed to represent LGBT movement organizations that had received funding from Northern donors and that supposedly had hundreds of members, owned property, and/or held large events, she discovered that many claims were only partially true. For instance, LGBT movement organizations that had existed for less than a year likely did not have hundreds of members because people might not want to join an organization officially in the event that police cracked down on LGBT organizing and seized movement organization records. In these cases, individuals opted for invisibility to keep themselves safe. The donor-hired researcher learned that in a few cases, individuals did not work with LGBT persons at all. In interviews with the donor-hired researcher, some admitted that they knew few LGBT persons.

Luisa, a black Ugandan lesbian activist, suspected that she had unknowingly witnessed this fraud firsthand when a Ugandan man approached her and some lesbian friends at a bar about joining an LGBT organization:

> This gentleman . . . wanted us to join an organization; he had already formed it. So we asked him which members he has. He told us so far he has only got the men; that is why he has come to us: to get the women. . . . So we talked to him; we told him we shall get back to him. . . . After he left, we sat down and discussed what he had talked to us about. One, we are not students. Two, we are not students of Makerere. Some are students, but not of Makerere. Secondly, it was led by men, and we . . . had always heard about these gay organizations in Uganda. But every time, we would hear about people talking that they just embezzle money; they use women to embezzle money because most funders want to see women empowerment. . . . So these men would use women. They would just write women's names, and then they send documents to funders. They get money; they don't do anything for their community. (interview with the author, February 2, 2006)

Luisa intuited that this man was trying to swindle Northern funders. Stories of fraudulent gay organizations were familiar to Luisa, as was the development strategy to empower women through social-service provision and income-generating activities (Bulbeck 2007), but this man's approach struck her as suspicious. Declining to join the stranger's "gay" organization, Luisa and her friends decided to launch their own organization for LBT women.

Northern donors turned to Namibian and South African LGBT activists to help solve this funding problem in Kenya, Uganda, and Tanzania. Donors asked the directors of Behind the Mask and TRP to act as consultants with emerging LGBT movement organizations and disseminate the donor-hired researcher's findings among activists in Kenya, Uganda, and Tanzania. Why would leaders who were worried about their movement organizations' public profiles as African organizations do the bidding of Northern donors? Accepting this assignment would reinforce the unequal relationship between LGBT movement organizations and Northern donors. Movement organizations' leaders would have to follow the orders of Northern donors, further endangering their organizations' public reputations if African antigay opponents, including political leaders, learned of these interactions. This could also engender an unequal relationship between established LGBT movement organizations in southern Africa and emerging LGBT movement organizations in East Africa. With their funding, experience, and knowledge, Behind the Mask and TRP were in a position to influence how donors dealt with LGBT movement organizations. Leaders of these movement organizations could give donors negative feedback about certain Kenyan, Uganda, and Tanzanian LGBT movement organizations or recommend some for funding. Despite this power differential between Namibian and South African LGBT movement organizations and Kenyan, Uganda, and Tanzanian LGBT movement organizations, the space in which leaders of Behind the Mask and TRP could exercise their agency with Northern donors was much smaller compared to the possible choices donors could make. Leaders of Behind the Mask and TRP felt compelled to do as donors asked. They did not want to risk their reputations and visibility with donors. These LGBT movement organizations benefited from Northern donors' funding, guidance, and international contacts; their public, international reputations depended in part on how they interacted with donors.

The directors of Behind the Mask and TRP were tasked with conducting in-country meetings with activists in each country. However, they canceled the meeting with Tanzanian LGBT activists, who opted for invisibility. Going into the meetings, donors expected Kenyan and Ugandan LGBT activists to develop country-specific strategies and an overall regional strategy. At the meetings with Ugandan and Kenyan activists, leaders of Behind the Mask and TRP talked about the research findings and explained that activists would not immediately and automatically receive funds from donors simply because they attended the meetings. Although leaders of Behind the Mask and TRP were not direct agents of Northern donors, the directors played an important role in demystifying and providing information about the donor–movement organization relationship. In this way, they played an initial regulatory role in instructing activists how their movement organizations should behave and interact with donors. They also helped meeting attendees enumerate factors that donors had defined as obstacles that kept movement organizations from applying for and receiving donor funding. Being realistic about their needs would help activists write proposals donors could fund, according to leaders of Behind the Mask and TRP; for example, recruiting ten thousand people as members would be an unrealistic goal in countries in which ruling party leaders were hostile to sexual diversity. After the meetings, both leaders recommended that donors meet individually with movement organizations to assess whether donors should invest in them.

Donors seemed to assume that LGBT activists from Kenya and Uganda would listen to and work well with southern African LGBT activists, presumably because of their common collective identity as Africans. Donors also seemed to suppose that activists' common experience of organizing amid political homophobia and repression would enable Namibian and South African activists to obtain access to more information about Kenyan and Ugandan LGBT movement organizations' needs than Europeans or North Americans would have. However, Kenyan and Ugandan LGBT activists were wary of Namibian and South African activists because they feared being outed publicly, owing to the hostile sociopolitical fields in which they operated (Baraka 2005; Nagadya 2005). In other words, they preferred adopting a strategic position of intentional invisibility to guarantee the safety of activists and constituents.

Since movement organizations were in an unequal relationship with donors, self-preservation initially motivated Behind the Mask's and TRP's directors' decision to participate as facilitators. In 2003, southern African LGBT activists had learned that the fate of their organizations might be intertwined with that of Kenyan, Ugandan, and Tanzanian movement organizations, prompting them to cultivate an interest in identifying the problems in that region. Hivos staff began to doubt the existence of some East African LGBT movement organizations, owing to their sporadic visibility. These organizations' invisibility had consequences for other African LGBT movement organizations. As a result of these experiences, Hivos staff communicated in a 2003 e-mail their decision to "discontinue" direct funding to African LGBT movement organizations and explore indirect means of support such as "short courses or exchange meetings." Sister Namibia, for instance, had been adversely affected by similar donor funding decisions, forcing the leader to phase out paid staff positions and hire short-term consultants; these actions resulted in the invisibility and suspension of some projects. Owing to the financial scams, Hivos, in particular, suspended funding to some LGBT organizations, with the exception of southern African movement organizations, such as TRP, Gays and Lesbians of Zimbabwe (GALZ), and Behind the Mask. After Hivos staff disclosed their concerns, Behind the Mask and TRP staff worried that scam artists had referred to Behind the Mask and TRP in their fraudulent funding applications, sullying the organizations' reputations. Behind the Mask and TRP staff members also grew concerned that widespread fraud could result in cessation of funding of all LGBT projects in Africa, which would jeopardize their operations and possibly result in their organizations' unintentional invisibility, as Johannes explained. Thus, they developed a vested interest in ascertaining the existence of East African LGBT movement organizations and decided to honor Northern donors' request that they work with Kenyan, Ugandan, and Tanzanian LGBT activists.

Interest in generating international visibility for a pan-African LGBT movement also motivated Behind the Mask's and TRP's directors' choice to participate in investigating and mentoring Kenyan and Ugandan LGBT activists. TRP, in particular, benefited from advice and mentoring from activists affiliated with GALZ and the NCGLE.[13] Behind the Mask and TRP staff believed that their organizations should continue their tradition of supporting struggling LGBT movement organizations elsewhere, which, in turn, would enhance the movement's pan-African visibility. Activists believed that as more African LGBT movement organizations continued to form, the public visibility of a pan-African LGBT movement would be easier to sustain.

Sharing their organizing experiences with emerging East African LGBT movement organizations appealed to TRP staff because, according to Johannes, they "wanted to play a role in providing assistance and support to some of the young LGBT initiatives out there," which donors supported in principle and with funding. Similarly, Behind the Mask was founded to ensure that African LGBT activists could access information about homophobia and LGBT movement success in other African countries and to train activists to report on political developments related to LGBT organizing in their countries. Behind the Mask maintained an extensive network of contacts with LGBT persons and groups in many African countries.[14] Both Behind the Mask and TRP consulted with new LGBT movement organizations in neighboring countries early in their history, as Johannes recalled. In other words, they played a role in fostering and exporting LGBT organizing to other African countries, increasing the public visibility of LGBT activism on the continent. According to Johannes,

> From the beginning, Hivos, for instance, would push us to engage with young groups in . . . Botswana . . . and . . . a precedent was set. So when the East Africa Initiative . . . came up and [donors] had to identify organizations, by then, Behind the Mask, for instance, was already involved in training in different southern African countries. They [donors] found that TRP and [Behind the Mask] were the most suitable organizations to help these organizations through some of the difficulties that they experienced because, in East Africa, there wasn't an established LGBT organization.

Owing to TRP's experience helping initiate LGBT organizing in Botswana and Behind the Mask's training of activists in many African countries to chronicle their organizing experiences, donors sought them out as mentors.

Northern donors believed they could rely on Behind the Mask and TRP to advise struggling organizations in East Africa. Emphasizing their technocratic competency in their visibility strategy with donors, Behind the Mask and TRP staff showed donors that they were using funds in ways that supported and sustained the LGBT movement's growth in other African countries.

Leaders of Behind the Mask and TRP regarded their work with emerging movement organizations as a way to create a stronger African LGBT movement. According to Johannes, "every established LGBT organization on the continent, in the end, benefits your position. Because if there's a strong voice in Kenya and there's a strong voice in Uganda and Tanzania, you know we can break away of this whole issue of it [same-sex sexuality] being un-African." From Johannes's perspective, individual LGBT movement organizations in African countries would generate a cumulative public visibility for a pan-African LGBT movement. In addition, if grassroots activists formed movement organizations on their own soil, these efforts would be African. If African LGBT activists facilitated the growth of emerging movement organizations, this transmission of expertise and experience would also be African. Hence, Northern donor funding could not invalidate Namibian and South African LGBT organizing; only Namibian and South African activists were equipped to undertake culturally specific and sensitive political advocacy, owing to their familiarity with their sociopolitical fields.

Despite what seemed to be a mutually beneficial working arrangement, the leaders of Behind the Mask and TRP felt uncomfortable evaluating East African LGBT organizations for funding. They believed it was problematic for leaders of established African LGBT movement organizations to vet newer organizations for donor funding. Donors occasionally asked Behind the Mask to verify the existence, reputation, and visibility of new movement organizations that applied for funding, owing to the organization's extensive contacts with LGBT activists in different countries.

This situation placed established movement organizations in an unequal power relationship with new or struggling LGBT movement organizations. LGBT movement organizations with international funding, such as Behind the Mask, could put "more grassroots organisations" at a disadvantage because donors flocked to the former, boosting their public visibility, while "contribut[ing] to the invisibility and/or the de-resourcing of less mainstream organisations," such as struggling LGBT movement organizations in East Africa (Chasin 2000, 202). Behind the Mask and TRP staff had thought about how to address the paradox that receiving donor funding enhanced their organizations' visibility, while forcing underresourced activist organizations into invisibility because they lacked funding. Johannes believed that TRP's continued funding benefited the African LGBT movement, even though movement organizations might

> be competing for the same resources.... I don't necessarily think that is unhealthy. I do believe, however, that there's a bigger picture.... It's great that at the moment, TRP has access to donors; we have close relationships with them. The donor money seems to come to us much easier than to most other organizations ... and that is good. But I think there's a bigger picture that as TRP we're trying to see.... We really feel that a movement in other African countries benefits the continent. We see how things spill over.

Behind the Mask and TRP staff did not believe that applying for funds from Northern donors conflicted with their commitment to helping struggling LGBT activists and movement organizations elsewhere in Africa because if they became invisible, then there would be no continental watchdogs for LGBT rights, which constituted the "bigger picture" for LGBT organizing in Africa, according to Johannes.[15]

Behind the Mask and TRP had to negotiate the visibility dilemmas that accompanied accepting funding from Northern donors. The spectral quality of homosexuality-is-un-African discourse underscored these dilemmas and haunted Namibian and South African LGBT movement organizations; activists never completely escaped its reach. Nevertheless, they kept applying for and receiving funding from donors so that they could continue with their existing projects, even though it may have jeopardized their visibility, credibility, and claim of being "African" if antigay opponents learned of activists' extensive connections with donors. Suspending or scaling back their efforts did not appeal to LGBT movement organizations' staff; hence, they decided to keep applying for and receiving funding from Northern donors. Sibongile hoped her staff could parlay their advocacy with East African movement organizations into funding from the Ford Foundation. She stated, "We now have a good relationship with them ... [because] we have worked with them on the East Africa problem.... We have really again made ourselves known to them" and enhanced their "credibility" and visibility with the donor. In fact, "we were actually asked to send a proposal out to them again," an invitation that was infrequent. Behind the Mask and TRP staff couched their organizations' work in a pan-African LGBT movement context, one that resisted assertions that their activism was not authentically African.

Public Presentations: Building a Pan-African LGBT Movement

The strategic dilemma of being perceived as un-African for soliciting and accepting money from Northern donors is related to a dilemma involving how the pan-African LGBT movement presented itself publicly to an African institutional political body. In February 2006, a group of southern African LGBT activists, along with other southern African, European, and North American LGBT activists, met in Johannesburg, South Africa, to discuss the possibility of introducing an LGBT activist contingent to the ACHPR. Activists anticipated that they would face difficulties being seen as African and as LGBT activists.

Activists faced two strategic choices related to presenting themselves as a pan-African LGBT movement to an African human rights body. First, staff members of Behind the Mask, Sister Namibia, and TRP, along with other southern African, European, and North American LGBT activists, had to decide if they would press LGBT rights violations at the ACHPR in 2006. The ACHPR would be one of the first opportunities for activists to present the African LGBT movement to an African political body; hence, the movement's first impression on commissioners was important to Namibian and South African LGBT activists. If African LGBT activists remained silent about LGBT rights abuses, then officials in their respective countries could continue to ignore such violations. However, if African LGBT activists publicized abuse claims, they could frame LGBT rights violations as human rights abuses and insist that the ACHPR lean on African nations in which such abuses were rampant, generating international and continental visibility for LGBT Africans, activism, and human rights violations. In other words, African LGBT activists thought that they could help instigate top-down change if the ACHPR ordered member nations of the African Union to stop persecuting LGBT persons.[16]

Second, they had to determine how to present a unified African LGBT movement for the first time to the ACHPR. Attending the meeting as self-identified African LGBT activists could help elevate the pan-African LGBT movement's continental visibility. Conversely, emerging publicly as a united African LGBT movement could detract attention away from the contingent's LGBT rights abuse claims if commissioners and those in attendance viewed an African LGBT movement as a spectacle. Presenting themselves publicly would likely be tricky, as activists would have to decide who could join the contingent, which violations to publicize, and to which audiences they would introduce the pan-African LGBT movement.

In February 2006, IGLHRC representatives convened a meeting of southern African LGBT activists, including staff members from Behind the Mask, Sister Namibia, TRP, and GALZ, to discuss broadening and forging a pan-African LGBT movement.[17] Behind the Mask hosted the meeting, befitting the movement organization's reputation for updating African LGBT activists about what was happening throughout the continent. IGLHRC representatives broached the possibility of approaching the ACHPR with LGBT human rights abuse claims at the ACHPR's next meeting in Banjul, Gambia, in May 2006. Illustrating IGLHRC's reputation as an international authority on LGBT rights, Jeanette, a white woman and IGLHRC representative, first described her organization's objectives, record with approaching regional human rights commissions elsewhere, and interest in collaborating with African LGBT activists. She cast IGLHRC as an advocacy organization, focused on documenting LGBT rights abuses cooperatively with local activist groups. After elucidating how IGLHRC had worked with special rapporteurs at the UN at the 1995 Beijing, 2000 Beijing +5, and 2005 Beijing +10 meetings to disseminate information about LGBT human rights violations, which gave IGLHRC some international credibility (Bob 2005), Jeannette stressed, "The UN isn't going to save us," although she admitted that it was an important vehicle for addressing human rights violations.[18]

According to Jeanette, IGLHRC had shifted its focus from the supranational level to support regional LGBT advocacy. She explained how IGLHRC had partnered with Latin American LGBT movement organizations to pressure the Inter-American Court of Human Rights to rule in favor of LGBT rights. Despite IGLHRC's success with human rights legal tactics in regional and international arenas, Jeanette posed two important questions to the southern African LGBT activists at the meeting: "Will changing laws necessarily change culture? Is it possible to work with the African Commission?" Her queries were noteworthy for two reasons. First, Jeanette acknowledged that law reform would not necessarily result in speedy cultural change; such changes would likely be glacial. Second, casting the ACHPR as a potential political opportunity constituted a reversal of position for IGLHRC (Murray and Viljoen 2007). In 2000, IGLHRC advised African LGBT movement organizations against filing complaints with the ACHPR because if activists did not give commissioners adequate warning and time to prepare for the probably contentious discussion of LGBT rights, commissioners might sanction "the idea that homosexuality is opposed to 'African values.' Such a precedent would be extremely difficult to reverse" (39; see also Murray and Viljoen 2007, 106). IGLHRC representatives were sensitive to the sociopolitical context in which southern African LGBT activists operated and understood that they might confront soft repression.

Before making a decision about whether to regard the ACHPR as a political opportunity for pursuing LGBT human rights violations in Africa, activists named obstacles to LGBT organizing in African countries. They linked these obstacles to LGBT human rights abuses appropriate for the ACHPR to address. These obstacles included lack of access to information;

freedom of expression; police impunity, harassment, torture, extortion, and illegal detention; difficulties organizing and registering with the government as LGBT movement organizations; violence and anti-LGBT prejudice; political and religious homophobia; lack of research on LGBT issues; and the eroding rule of law and weak judiciaries. This inventory put parameters on subsequent discussions about what would constitute the pan-African LGBT movement's agenda at the ACHPR and enabled activists to strive for clarity and consistency in articulating their goals. Then activists named countries, such as Cameroon, Nigeria, and Uganda, in which LGBT human rights abuses were egregious. This list convinced activists of the need to bring these abuses to the ACHPR's attention. They decided to regard the ACHPR as a political opportunity for addressing LGBT rights violations in Africa and to attend the upcoming meeting in Banjul in May 2006. Activists' support for this plan grew when Robert, an African American man and IGLHRC representative, mentioned that a commissioner had informed him during a human rights training workshop they had both attended that he, the commissioner, would welcome an LGBT rights case. With at least one commissioner willing to hear an LGBT rights case, activists forged ahead with their plans to form a contingent.

In light of such possible receptiveness at the ACHPR, activists believed that addressing the antigay backlash in Nigeria was urgent. In December 2005, IGLHRC had invited six African LGBT activists to the Fourteenth International Conference on HIV/AIDS and Sexually Transmitted Infections in Africa conference in Abuja, Nigeria. The recent pro-same-sex-marriage ruling in South Africa and LGBT activists' presence at the conference had provoked an antigay response from Nigerian lawmakers, who drafted preemptive legislation that would outlaw same-sex marriage and prevent LGBT activists from forming or registering activist organizations with the government (International Gay and Lesbian Human Rights Commission 2007).[19] Robert, who had attended the Nigerian conference, seemed astounded that activists' "queer noise" and visibility in Abuja had resulted in this legislation, although he noted, "When there's activism, there's a response." Participants shared Robert's understanding that violence and homophobia were negative responses to LGBT activist visibility. Activists at the IGLHRC meeting discussed how this response constituted a negative response to South Africa's dominance as a progressive nation beloved by Northern democracies. They acknowledged the regional divides between African nations with respect to LGBT rights and how the public visibility of gender and sexual diversity activism garnered different responses in different African contexts.

Analyzing the antigay outcry in Nigeria led activists and IGLHRC representatives to question whether the ACHPR constituted an international political opportunity after all (Bob 2005). Robert warned activists that a "direct push to file" a claim with the ACHPR might not be the best approach because it could spawn an intense backlash in countries like Cameroon, where police had arrested, detained, and convicted several alleged gay men and lesbians of sodomy, a punishable legal offense, a few months earlier (Awondo 2010). He reminded participants of the perception in Africa that once LGBT issues showed up in the press, they would be on everyone's radar, increasing the likelihood of hostile responses to LGBT persons and activism. Localized visibility could spiral into uncontrollable hypervisibility for LGBT persons and activists in other African contexts. Even if LGBT activists' media visibility faded quickly, there was still a possibility for antagonism toward African gender and sexual minorities. In this way, the visibility of activists' actions at the ACHPR could trigger unintentional visibility for LGBT persons and activists elsewhere.

While understanding that a potential negative response might accompany the increased public visibility of an LGBT activist contingent at the ACHPR, some participants advocated filing LGBT human rights abuse complaints there, albeit with some parameters. Proposed parameters involved presenting LGBT rights violations within a framework intelligible to commissioners. Lucas, a white man and GALZ representative, suggested that activists should frame antisodomy laws and the death penalty as colonial laws.[20] Southern African LGBT activists agreed that they wanted to encourage the ACHPR to recommend that African nations no longer punish sodomy with the death sentence. They savvily linked antisodomy laws and the death penalty; they could introduce a hot-button issue, the decriminalization of sodomy, through a more benign issue, the abolition of the death penalty. In addition, by casting antisodomy laws and the death penalty as left over from colonialism, LGBT activists hoped to capitalize on commissioners' preference for decolonizing legal statutes. By linking the contentious issue of decriminalizing sodomy to an internationally recognized human rights violation, the death penalty, activists intended to present the African LGBT movement as being moderate and working within a preexisting African political framework. They sought to exploit African nationalist rhetoric that touted decolonization as a goal to enable them to repeal antigay legislation.

Concerns related to the framing of LGBT rights abuse claims included preparing audiences for the complaint and identifying which audiences at the ACHPR might be the most sympathetic. Staff members from Behind the Mask, Sister Namibia, and TRP knew about the UN's Economic and Social Council's (ECOSOC) rejection of ILGA's application in January 2006 for consultative status on LGBT issues without a hearing "for the first time in [ECOSOC's] history" (International Lesbian and Gay Association 2006a).[21] They did not want to face a similar fate and be dismissed from the ACHPR without having a chance to present their cases. Gert, a European LGBT activist living in Zimbabwe, suggested the NGO Forum as a safe place to announce the African LGBT movement's presence and to facilitate networking with supportive human rights NGOs. At the NGO Forum, African and international organizations "discuss particular themes which are then usually presented in a number of resolutions to the Commission, some of which it goes on to adopt in its own forum" (Murray and Viljoen 2007, 110).

The NGO Forum could be an important sounding board for LGBT activists; the ACHPR tended to respond more positively to complaints and resolutions that appeared first before the NGO Forum (Murray and Viljoen 2007). Jeanette warned against springing LGBT human rights resolutions on unsuspecting NGOs or the ACHPR because the global LGBT movement had "got[ten] killed in Geneva" when representatives of the Brazilian government introduced a resolution in front of the UN without warning other organizations (see also de la Dehesa 2010). Jeanette was referring to an attempt by Brazilian diplomats to push the UN to discuss LGBT rights violations worldwide (Saiz 2004). Representatives from other governments resisted this attempt because they asserted that "sexual orientation was not a proper subject for consideration by a human rights body" (Saiz 2004, 50). Jeanette mentioned this unfortunate incident as an example of the need for LGBT activists to prepare potential audiences for the public visibility of discussions about gender and sexual diversity. To avoid the same fiasco at the ACHPR, Jeanette suggested strategically inserting references to LGBT persons as part of mainstream issues that affected many people. IGLHRC had succeeded in getting language about LGBT persons and orientation included in torture legislation because, as Jeanette claimed, "no one wants to say, 'It's okay to torture gays.'"

The group of southern African LGBT activists deliberated how to enter and participate in the NGO Forum. Rina, Sister Namibia's representative, advocated approaching feminist movement organizations that had prior experience working with the ACHPR. Southern African LGBT activists also agreed that those who went to Banjul should resist the temptation to dominate discussions by portraying LGBT issues as more dire than other situations. Lucas, the GALZ representative, warned against exaggerating LGBT human rights abuses not only because the African LGBT movement could be discredited as too self-important but also because hyperbolized LGBT rights abuses could enable the ACHPR to set aside serious, widespread human rights violations in places like Darfur, Sudan, where mass rape and genocide were taking place unchecked at the time. Lucas acknowledged that some human rights abuses were just as pressing, if not more so, than LGBT rights violations.

This cautious approach to working with the ACHPR constituted a moderate strategy consistent with activists' support for addressing the decriminalization of sodomy within a broader context of decolonizing African laws. Making LGBT rights palatable and understandable as human rights concerns would enable the contingent, activists believed, to achieve more than they would if they had presented LGBT rights independently of other human rights violations. In this way, activists hoped that their framing of LGBT rights would become culturally intelligible to commissioners and to participants at the NGO Forum and "culturally resonant" with the human rights frames in circulation (Benford and Snow 2000, 622).

The dilemma of how to present the African LGBT movement dovetailed with another strategic concern: how to deal with the growing perception that South Africa's political progressiveness in terms of protecting LGBT rights and affording same-sex couples the right to marry was a threat to socially conservative political officials. Nigerian lawmakers interpreted the presence of African LGBT activists at the AIDS conference in Abuja in December 2005 and South Africa's marriage-equality ruling negatively. Nigerian lawmakers viewed African LGBT activists as interlopers whose public visibility at the AIDS conference constituted a threat in need of a response that would force activists into unintentional invisibility. Johannes, TRP's representative, asserted that it was not just South African LGBT activism that had alienated antigay opponents in Nigeria and elsewhere in Africa but also the continental and international visibility of LGBT activists from Namibia, South Africa, and Zimbabwe since the mid-1990s. According to Johannes, antigay opponents had "the idea that we're importing [same-sex sexuality and LGBT organizing] from southern Africa all of a sudden because that's the new argument that we're hearing more and more." In this sense, antigay opponents regarded southern African LGBT activists as a front for Northern dominance, owing in part to their reliance on Northern donor funding. The visibility of Namibian, South African, and Zimbabwean LGBT movement organizations' staff as leaders of an emerging African LGBT movement could pose problems for organizations' development, if suspicion about southern African activists' supremacy persisted among African LGBT activists and antigay opponents.

In response to the political hostility that the possible legal preemption of LGBT organizing and same-sex marriage in Nigeria represented at the time, activists recognized that they had to present an LGBT movement that the ACHPR recognized as authentically "African." If African LGBT activists did not present the movement as African, commissioners and NGOs could dismiss the movement as the puppet of Northern donors and LGBT activists. Everyone agreed to an equal representation of men and women in the contingent to address sexism within the African LGBT movement. Meeting attendees also agreed that black African LGBT activists should lead and make up most of the contingent. The visibility of black Africans at the ACHPR meeting would help the contingent debunk the myth that only white persons were LGBT and ensure that contingent members were seen as African. The racial composition of the African LGBT contingent thus constituted an important factor in visibly demonstrating that same-sex sexualities and LGBT organizing were African.

The strategic choices that southern African LGBT activists made at the March meeting resulted in some advances for the pan-African LGBT movement. When the contingent of African LGBT activists attended the ACHPR's meeting in Banjul in May 2006, they liaised with a Nigerian human rights NGO. According to Rina, who was part of the contingent, the NGO allowed a member of the contingent, a Cameroonian lesbian who obtained asylum in the United States, to take its first "speaking slot and address the case of illegally detained and imprisoned gay men and lesbians in Cameroon" (informal conversation with the author, May 15, 2006). Commissioners "perked up" when the Cameroonian lesbian activist addressed the plight of LGBT Africans. Rina recognized the newness of LGBT rights for African commissioners but allowed for the possibility that they paid such attention to the Cameroonian speaker because she was addressing sexuality openly, which remained unusual in some African contexts (Kendall 1999).

Activists with Sister Namibia and TRP regarded their trip to the ACHPR as successful because no one refused to grant them access to the NGO Forum or to the ACHPR. They also forged ties with Nigerian and other African feminist and human rights organizations, networking that could yield positive results for the LGBT movement's visibility strategies. They packaged and framed the pan-African LGBT movement's concerns about LGBT rights violations in a way that fit within preexisting discussions about human rights. Careful deliberation about which strategic choices to make regarding how to present a pan-African LGBT movement to the ACHPR resulted in moderate success for activists' first foray into this venue. Late in 2006, IGLHRC representatives and a Ugandan LGBT movement organization, Sexual Minorities Uganda, composed a "shadow report" that highlighted how Ugandan authorities had violated the human rights of LGBT persons, which Ugandan politicians had declined to note in their official country report to the ACHPR (International Gay and Lesbian Human Rights Commission 2007, 19). Commissioners used the shadow report to interrogate Ugandan representatives about Uganda's record on LGBT rights. Having such an effect on commissioners' actions could be interpreted as a gain for a pan-African LGBT movement seeking continental political visibility.

The Continuing Struggle to Be Seen as African

Namibian and South African LGBT activists struggled "to be seen" as African individuals, as citizens in their own nations, and as representing African movement organizations (Guidry 2003, 501). The complexity of homosexuality-is-un-African discourse elicited a variety of constituency-level strategic responses to designating LGBT identities as African. Namibian and South African LGBT activists sought to dispel antigay opponents' misconceptions about African LGBT persons' racial, cultural, and national authenticity. Although the public prominence of Western identity categories in southern African LGBT activism constituted Westernization to opponents, Namibian and South African LGBT activists maintained that constituents' LGBT identities did not invalidate their racial, cultural, and national identities.

The public visibility of LGBT constituents gained importance among some activists in relation to Northern funding opportunities and to managing the national and international reputation of African LGBT activism. In an effort to educate and socialize constituents, activists offered identity workshops that introduced new black and coloured recruits unfamiliar with Western gender and sexual identity nomenclature to these terms' meanings. Many activists hoped that recruits would adopt these identity terms; the more individuals who publicly claimed and used LGBT terms, the greater the public visibility of LGBT movement organizations would become. Activists believed that individual-level visibility strategies bolstered the public visibility of LGBT movement organizations and the movement in Namibia, South Africa, and beyond, much in the way that identity strategies operated in LGBT organizing in the United States (Armstrong 2002; Bernstein 1997). In fact, as Jansen explained in the context of TRP, albeit with some skepticism, organizations could publicize the racial diversity of their LGBT constituents with Northern donors as a way to secure funding from them.

While some constituents might experience empowerment after adopting LGBT identities, a potentially disempowering dynamic accompanied the visibility strategy of identity workshops. The primacy of certain identity categories could render other terms invisible to constituents, a process that some queer scholars of transnational sexualities warn can erase vibrant, local gender and sexual dissidence (Blackwood 2005). In addition to possibly displacing local terms for gender and sexual variance, identity regulation occurred in LGBT movement organizations' constituency-level visibility strategies. For instance, staff in organizations like FEW homogenized the identities individuals assumed within the confines of the organization. It is important to remember that identity regulation occurs in a number of social movements around the world, as activists sort out movement boundaries; this process is not new

(Gamson 1997). While recognizing the disempowering and empowering aspects of constituency-level visibility strategies is necessary, I stop short of labeling identity workshops as manipulative. Such a label is too cynical. Activists earnestly believed these workshops benefited constituents. However, the possible disadvantages associated with gender and sexual identity workshops merit further attention.

Namibian and South African LGBT activists contended with the implication that their organizations were racially, culturally, and nationally inauthentic. Appearing too Western endangered organizations' public standing, as some TRP staff and members knew all too well, based on their experiences with the "lesbian" car, visible confirmation of TRP's receipt of Northern donor funding. Choosing to apply for and accept funding from non-African sources put Behind the Mask and TRP at risk for being perceived as un-African. Without funding, LGBT activists faced the prospect of shutting down their organizations and lapsing into unintentional invisibility, but accepting funding meant that LGBT activists had to become visible to donors when donors demanded it. Donors held LGBT movement organizations to certain expectations and influenced their agendas. In this way, LGBT activists found their choices constrained by their funding ties to foreign donors. As a result, these ties made LGBT movement organizations increasingly vulnerable to attack from antigay opponents. However, activists with Behind the Mask and TRP interpreted their work with East African LGBT movement organizations as benefiting a young African LGBT movement. The more LGBT movement organizations there were in Africa, the stronger the African LGBT movement would become. It would also be increasingly difficult, activists with Behind the Mask and TRP reasoned, for antigay opponents to continue arguing that same-sex sexuality was un-African if enough LGBT movement organizations were publicly visible.

Another dilemma that Namibian and South African LGBT movement organizations encountered was how to make a pan-African LGBT movement visible to the ACHPR. Leaders from Behind the Mask, Sister Namibia, and TRP joined other South African and Zimbabwean LGBT activists and representatives from IGLHRC in deliberating whether to view the ACHPR as a political opportunity and then how to portray the pan-African LGBT movement to the ACHPR in terms of which LGBT human rights violations to pursue, to which audiences to present the movement, and how to compose the LGBT activist contingent.

How to portray a unified pan-African LGBT movement prompts lingering questions. First, there is the prickly question of what exactly is "African" about the LGBT movement. Contemporary Namibian and South African

LGBT activists challenged the allegation that LGBT-identified persons were un-African, even though they did not question their use of the Western acronym. Using this terminology enabled Namibian and South African LGBT movement organizations to access international discourses about gender and sexual diversity, lessons that they deployed at home. Leaders of LGBT movement organizations affirmed that those who hailed from African nations and identified as LGBT were indeed African. Organizations' work within Namibia and South Africa qualified LGBT movement organizations as African.

Another criterion of "African" that emerged was the recruitment of black Africans as leaders, staff, and members of LGBT movement organizations, a trend with historical significance. In the 1980s, black South African lesbian and gay activists, along with activists of other races who opposed apartheid, employed antiracist ideology to challenge white movement organizations' apolitical visibility. In the late 1980s and early 1990s, South African organizations like LAGO and GLOW crafted public profiles as black-led, multiracial LGBT movement organizations in the democratic transition away from apartheid. Multiracial visibility enabled TRP to establish "credibility" in racially diverse Namibia, as Johannes explained. Staff and founding members also promoted the inclusion of black LGBT constituents in TRP's decision making. In both Namibia and South Africa, multiracial visibility did not negate the Africanness of the LGBT movement; such racial inclusion was the hallmark of democratic Namibia and South Africa. In addition, organization staff counted on the fact that black constituents outnumbered white and coloured constituents. The sheer number of black LGBT constituents helped activists support the argument that gender and sexual diversity was African. Thus, the visibility of black LGBT constituents really mattered.

Yet do these definitions correspond to how LGBT movement organizations and activists in other African countries define "African"? Might there be a discrepancy in how LGBT activists in western, eastern, central, and southern Africa conceptualize "Africanness" that has yet to emerge as a palpable concern within the movement? Research on LGBT organizing in North America and Western Europe documents the cleavages that have resulted from disputes about white normativity within local and national LGBT movement organizations that claim to be multiracial and the creation of monoracial LGBT movement organizations (Adam, Duyvendak, and Krouwel 1999; Armstrong 2002; Ward 2008). A common racial identity—being black African—did not automatically translate into cultural similitude, given the multiracial composition of Behind the Mask, Sister Namibia, and TRP. Many African countries were similar in that they had histories of colonialism, but racial and ethnic politics varied by country. The legacy of apartheid in Namibia and South Africa transformed racial and ethnic relations, rendering antiblack racism salient. East African nations did not have the same recent history. Racial–ethnic divisions elsewhere in Africa did not break down into "black" and "white," as they had in Namibia and South Africa.

A backlash against South Africa's "Western-style democracy" and southern African nations' economic growth may impact the pan-African LGBT movement (van Zyl 2009, 364). Opposition to southern African nations' hegemony is apparent in complaints that they are exporting homosexuality and LGBT organizing to different African nations. Behind this antagonism is a negative reaction to foreign political and social influence, even if it comes from another African source. Antigay opponents in countries like Nigeria have grown wary of South Africa's economic and political dominance and cite its embrace of LGBT rights as a negative social and political development. African politicians' disavowals of sexual-rights gains in South Africa may serve as another way to distinguish their African nationalist credentials (Epprecht 2008). South Africa may be "in Africa but it is not (always) like Africa" (Farred 2004, 596).

The pan-African LGBT movement will not be immune to sociopolitical shifts and negative reactions from antigay opponents to South Africa's reputation as a newly democratizing nation and economic power. To ensure that the pan-African LGBT movement does not alienate future allies, southern African LGBT movement organizations may have to opt for decreased visibility in the movement to prevent the emergence of an African antigay countermovement and to preserve gains that the pan-African LGBT movement may make with political institutions such as the ACHPR.[22] This may constitute a long-term strategic dilemma of deciding how to portray a pan-African LGBT movement publicly amid shifting continental politics.

Conclusion:
Why Visibility Matters

The political opportunity constituted by democratization and decolonization conjured the promise of equality for all Namibians and South Africans, regardless of race, class, gender, or sexuality. Just after Namibian independence, gender and sexual minorities regarded the democratic transition jubilantly, expecting that SWAPO leaders' promises of equality would translate into LGBT rights. As SWAPO leaders unleashed homophobic rhetoric in the mid-1990s, LGBT persons' hopes were not realized. Ruling party leaders' positions on LGBT rights affected activists' visibility strategies, forcing activists with Sister Namibia and TRP to adopt defensive positions in public as they demanded that SWAPO leaders recant their antigay threats.

In contrast, in South Africa, lawmakers passed LGBT rights legislation soon after the ANC assumed leadership in the democratic transition away from apartheid. No longer an international political pariah, South Africa celebrated a new distinction in 1996: that of having one of the most inclusive, progressive constitutions in the world. The NCGLE pressed lawmakers from different political parties to include a sexual-orientation nondiscrimination clause, the EC, in the constitution. Indicative of its moderate visibility strategy, the NCGLE continued urging lawmakers to pass expanded LGBT rights legislation. Other LGBT movement organizations engaged in specialized advocacy. Within this context, Behind the Mask and FEW were able to focus on monitoring LGBT rights throughout Africa and fighting violence against black lesbians, respectively. However, the threat of antilesbian violence provoked FEW to adopt a protectionist strategic orientation favoring decreased visibility to keep black lesbian constituents safe.

The apartheid past imposed material and symbolic constraints on Namibian and South African LGBT activists' visibility strategies. Apartheid controlling visibilities haunted contemporary LGBT organizing in Namibia and South Africa, evidenced in activists' mobilization against the specter of un-African same-sex sexualities. Antigay opponents portrayed activists of African descent advocating for LGBT rights as mimicking white Western culture at the expense of their own racial, cultural, and national authenticity. This specter influenced Namibian and South African LGBT activists' strategic choices about their local, national, and international visibilities.

Visibility Mattered to Namibian and South African LGBT Activists

The phrase "visibility matters" held a couple meanings for Namibian and South African LGBT activists. It referred to the strategic priority that visibility and invisibility had at different times for activists. Movement visibility and invisibility constituted more than flattened outcomes resulting from activists' interactions with social and political institutions. They reflected the strategic efforts of activists to control how target audiences viewed the LGBT movement, organizations, campaigns, and constituents. In Namibia, activists crafted visibility for the LGBT movement built on notions of democratic inclusion. However, disputing SWAPO leaders' antigay statements garnered a "controversial" reputation for Sister Namibia and deterred TRP from launching a public law-reform campaign, contributing to its invisibility. In South Africa, FEW developed a strategic orientation that tended toward decreased visibility, even invisibility, when circumstances warranted. FEW staff emphasized protecting black lesbian constituents who faced the threat of violence.

"Visibility matters" had a second meaning. Activists' visibility strategies generated material consequences for the LGBT movement and movement organizations. Behind the Mask and TRP confronted a visibility dilemma associated with accepting funding from Northern donors. Without funding, they would have to suspend their projects and enter involuntary invisibility, but taking Northern funding rendered their activism inauthentic and un-African in the eyes of some spectators. The public visibility and invisibility of LGBT activism, rights, and persons in Namibia and South Africa had both material and symbolic dimensions.

Visibility Strategies Manifested Physically

Namibian and South African LGBT movement organizations rooted their visibility strategies in physical spaces. Their visibility took physical forms observable when activists occupied public spaces, organizations rented or owned offices open to constituents and some visitors, and activists engaged in public protest. Activists' relationships with public spaces revealed organizations' strategic orientations to public visibility. FEW staff's decision to bar men, including black gay men, from the office and event spaces reinforced FEW's strategic insularity and tendency toward decreased visibility. Similarly, TRP staff monitored who attended film screenings associated with the group's video project, excluding individuals whom staff perceived might be hostile to gender and sexual diversity.

LGBT movement organizations provided safe spaces for gender and sexual dissidents seeking respite from the scrutiny of family, social institutions, and state actors (Gamson 1996; Palmberg 1999). These spaces extended beyond organizations' offices to include meetings staff held with constituents, as in the case of FEW's antiviolence training workshop and of the video project TRP took to rural Namibian towns. In turn, these spaces of invisibility nurtured the creation of LGBT collective identities as staff acquainted constituents with Western "LGBT" terminology. Activists' visibility strategies revealed not only their struggles to control resources, how others viewed LGBT constituents, and who could access movement spaces, but also their symbolic struggles to find belonging and social acceptance in national and continental imaginaries (Tucker 2009).

Visibility Strategies Were Products of Activists' Perceptions of Constraints and Opportunities in the Sociopolitical Field

As the ANC led the new, nonracial democracy, leaders of the NCGLE favored a moderate visibility strategy when working with lawmakers to enshrine the EC permanently in the constitution. Leaders strove to avoid antigay hostility from the South African public; after the EC's passage, the NCGLE engaged in a strategy of "incrementalism" in pursuit of additional LGBT rights, including the right for same-sex couples to marry (Stychin 1996, 465). Strategic wariness of sociopolitical hostility extended to FEW, whose staff monitored organizational spaces and advised black lesbian constituents to exercise caution in unfamiliar settings. These organizational- and constituency-level strategies reflected the tendency of FEW staff to anticipate antilesbian hostility and plan accordingly.

Namibian LGBT activists maneuvered organizations to evade state repression but still challenged antigay animosity publicly. Although political homophobia put activists on the defensive, their media visibility reminded Namibians that activists would not disappear from public view. Activists with TRP initially wanted to pursue a public law-reform campaign that would press for the decriminalization of sodomy. However, SWAPO leaders' threats to increase penalties for sodomy and to harass gender and sexual minorities caused activists to reconsider proceeding with the campaign. Challenging discursive threats was one thing; fielding state repression was another. Eventually, the law-reform campaign slipped into invisibility, an example of how the visibility of a particular movement item can fluctuate. TRP staff members' use of resources also contributed to the campaign's invisibility. To elicit more broad-based support for LGBT rights in Namibia, activists refashioned TRP publicly as a human rights organization, a strategy that diverted resources and activists' attention away from the law-reform campaign. Internal disagreements about whether TRP should pursue law reform or social-service provision also siphoned resources and energy from the campaign.

At Times, Activists Desired Invisibility or Decreased Visibility

Activists' desires for lessened visibility or invisibility reflected the intentionality undergirding visibility strategies. FEW's strategic orientation favoring lessened visibility guided members' decision about participating in public protest. Opting for intentional invisibility, activists with FEW declined to reveal themselves as lesbian activists when they moved through the throng of pro-Zuma protestors on the second day of Zuma's rape trial in February 2006. As they struggled to locate feminist and HIV/AIDS protestors, they grew nervous about protestors' antifeminist hostility and decided that leaving the protest would keep them safe. Fear motivated activists' decision to withdraw from public visibility, but activists believed that this was the right decision at the time.

At Times, Visibility and Invisibility Escaped Activists' Control

Unintentional visibility and invisibility exposed the limits of LGBT activists' strategies and agency. Activists were unable to plan for every contingency. When crises emerged, at times, activists could only react to them, unable to deploy a proactive strategic solution. While activists responded to a crisis, this sometimes resulted in a temporary visibility disruption in another arena of movement activity. When Sister Namibia lost donor funding and the director engaged in fund-raising for other organizations, *Sister Namibia* and the sexual-rights campaign lapsed into invisibility, an unintended consequence.

LGBT movement organizations' unintentional visibility also took the form of negative visibility. The GLA's false claim about gay men giving blood in defiance of a SANBS ban on donations from men who have sex with men generated unwanted visibility for the South African LGBT movement. LGBT activists did not want the public and lawmakers to associate the movement with the GLA and a protest tactic that could endanger the nation's blood supply. Thus, activists engaged in strategic action to correct potentially negative visibility for the movement. To ensure that the media did not collapse the GLA with mainstream LGBT activism, leaders of JWG member organizations publicly distanced themselves from the GLA and criticized the GLA's alleged action. Working on rescinding the blood-donation ban allowed the movement to gain control over the campaign but also routed movement resources and activists' attention away from the marriage-equality campaign. In this situation, activists became visible in relation to the blood-donation campaign at the expense of their visibility in the marriage-equality campaign.

Visibility Strategies Corresponded to Different Levels of Social Movement Structure: Constituents, Movement Organization, and Movement

LGBT activists wanted constituents, organizations, and movements to be seen in a particular way: as authentically African. This goal transcended different levels of movement structure but unfolded differently as a strategic process at each level. At the level of constituents, activists battled the controlling image that homosexuality and sexual minorities were un-African. Behind the Mask, FEW, Sister Namibia, and TRP engaged in interventions in black and coloured gender and sexual minority constituents' identifications as "lesbian," "gay," "bisexual," or "transgender." FEW and TRP invited new recruits to identity workshops that introduced them to Western identity terminology, while Behind the Mask's website and Sister Namibia's magazine and campaigns familiarized individuals with LGBT movement priorities. To counteract the idea that homosexuality was a colonialist trend that "European people brought to Africa," groups like FEW worked to "make sure that all the black lesbians are visible so that [members of the public] know how many we are," according to Lindiwe, a black lesbian affiliated with FEW. Many activists believed that if more individuals of African descent identified publicly as LGBT, movements could deflate homosexuality-is-un-African discourse more effectively by pointing to their sizable constituency of black African LGBT persons. Although this constituency-level identity strategy doubled as a visibility strategy, this did not mean that organizational- and movement-level visibility strategies behaved in the same way that constituency-level identity strategies did.

LGBT activists also disputed the assertion that they were "gay for pay." Repudiating this negative reputation involved reminding target audiences that profit did not motivate LGBT activism. According to Nomsa, a member of FEW, activists were "not there for money. FEW's not there to make money because it's an NGO. They're there to promote awareness about homosexuality and lesbianism, you know, [to] see lesbians as human beings." Organizations dealt with not only the insinuation that their political advocacy was inherently un-African but also Northern donors' reluctance to fund some African

LGBT movement organizations. The leaders of Behind the Mask and TRP realized that their organizations' fortunes might be caught up with those of East African LGBT movement organizations, which donors suspected of misusing funds. Fearing the loss of donor funding, the directors of Behind the Mask and TRP agreed to donors' requests that they counsel East African activists about their strategic prospects, even though antigay opponents could charge that LGBT activists were the pawns of Northern donors. To sustain their visibility and other strategies, organizations needed Northern financial support. Behind the Mask and TRP could continue representing the interests of LGBT constituents, an example of how advocating for particular representations of constituents depended materially on the existence of movement organizations. Organizations' material necessity trumped qualms that activists may have had about endangering their authenticity and credibility with antigay African nationalist leaders who might perceive them as being under the thumb of Northern donors and the "Gay International" (Massad 2002). Activists prioritized donors, as representatives of a global development industry, as target audiences, even to the detriment of their sustained visibility with constituents, some of whom complained about staff not updating them regularly about TRP's plans.

Activists made strategic choices they believed would benefit the visibility of not only individual constituents but also the movement and movement organizations. Southern African LGBT activists recognized that the reputation of a pan-African LGBT movement affected gender and sexual minorities and LGBT movement organizations in different African nations. When discussing publicly presenting a pan-African LGBT movement to the ACHPR, activists understood the visibility of constituents as bound up with that of movement organizations, although the processes governing individual-level visibility differed from those related to organizational- and movement-level visibility.

Visibility continues to matter to LGBT activists in Namibia and South Africa. Sister Namibia recovered from the visibility disruption the organization experienced in 2006 and resumed publishing its magazine. TRP closed its doors in 2010, slipping into invisibility. According to a former TRP staff member, staff had to suspend their planned campaigns because of financial mismanagement (informal communication with the author, July 15, 2011). Unhappy with the prospect that there would be no organization whose primary mandate was organizing for LGBT rights, in 2010, several former TRP staff and constituents launched Out-Right Namibia, an LGBT movement organization, after TRP's closure.

Continuing to monitor LGBT rights throughout Africa, Behind the Mask offers a stable, visible presence in the African LGBT movement. The organization's website provides coverage of LGBT rights gains and abuses in different African contexts, thanks to Behind the Mask's extensive network of journalist activists on the continent. FEW remains an important voice for black lesbians in South Africa. FEW helped generate public concern for antilesbian violence; in particular, corrective rape is increasingly recognized nationally and internationally as a pressing social problem facing black South African lesbians (Anguita 2011).

Visibility Matters to Social Movements and Scholars

Visibility matters not just to individual lesbian, gay, bisexual, and transgender Namibians and South Africans but also to LGBT activists, movement organizations, movements, and campaigns. Visibility was more than a movement goal for Namibian and South African LGBT activists, more than an achievement that coincided with the movement's success in cultural, political, and legal arenas. Activists used visibility, and at times invisibility, as a flexible strategy to show target audiences how LGBT persons, rights, and activism were "African" and to advance other movement and organizational priorities. Employing decreased visibility, and at times, invisibility, FEW modeled ways for black lesbian constituents to protect themselves from violence, a short-term expedient to a structural problem on which the organization continued to work. Activists with Sister Namibia and TRP used SWAPO leaders' political homophobia as an opportunity to voice their discontent with the ruling party's leadership and to correct misrepresentations of Namibian gender and sexual dissidents. In addition to managing their reputations with target audiences in national fields, activists also cultivated ties with donors and international LGBT movement organizations based in the global North.

Public visibility permeates many aspects of social movement activity, including the framing of movement claims, interactions with the media and social institutions, collective identity formation, and marshalling of resources. Visibility is a quality and strategy that scholars can locate in different elements of social movement organization and culture: in organizations' mention in a newspaper article; in one-off protests that halt traffic; in observers' familiarity with a movement's claims, goals, and tactics; and in the life cycle of a movement that attains cultural and political influence at its peak and disintegrates in its decline. The concept of visibility strategy is useful for understanding the material and symbolic dimensions of activists' relationships with constituents, supporters, and target audiences and the steps they take to control how they are seen.

Visibility Strategies Leave Traces

By what means do movements become publicly visible? How does one know that a movement has slipped into invisibility? How might scholars discern differences in the visibilities activists present to distinct audiences? Answering these questions requires scholars not to take visibility and invisibility for granted in social movement analysis. Finding evidence of the strategic aspects of movement visibility may involve searching for what is not there. When Namibian and South African LGBT movement organizations were invisible in moments of political opportunity, I came to understand their invisibility in relation to strategic constraints by tracing the pattern of organizational visibility in relation to movement campaigns. Organizations' sudden withdrawal from public interactions may attract scholarly attention, but at other times, gradual public retreat may be harder to grasp. Although social scientists may not witness movement visibility strategies unfold in real time, these strategies can become perceptible through lingering effects. Such traces appear as "cultural and social imprints" that remain long after an isolated action occurred (Gray and Gómez-Barris 2010, 6). As a trace, visibility is implicated in the invisibility or absence of a movement item (Gordon 2008; Sedgwick 1990).

Parsing social movement processes related to visibility, especially processes that are not explicitly strategic, can be tricky. Not everything activists do or say necessarily reflects an overarching strategy. Some choices activists make are "operational" and devoted to "short-term" bureaucratic decisions that have little influence on the architecture of movement strategy (Minkoff and McCarthy 2005, 298). Quotidian routines may generate certain visibilities or invisibilities for the movement or organizations that activists do not question because they have receded into expected actions. As an example of a taken-for-granted routine, Namibian and South African LGBT activists did not interrogate the wisdom behind applying for Northern funding, although this may be a more contested choice in the future, as activists contemplate the power differentials associated with external funding (Incite! Women of Color against Violence 2009). Distinguishing between what is and what is not strategy can keep the concept of visibility strategy from being overused.

Visibility Strategies Are Windows into Social Movement Processes

As a concept, a visibility strategy emphasizes activists' efforts to engineer a particular visibility or reputation for their movement organization or movement. Such strategizing requires an investment of activists' time, energy, attention, and emotions in controlling how others view their movement organization, movement, claims, or campaigns. In some cases, Namibian and South African LGBT activists juggled competing, even contradictory visibility strategies, depending on the target audiences to which activists directed their representations and messages.

Scholars can use movement visibility and invisibility in other ways. Political process approaches to social movements regard visibility as a sign of movement vibrancy and invisibility as movement distress (Tilly 2004). Within movement organizations, visibility and invisibility can serve as proxies for other social movement dynamics. An organization's invisibility may result from adverse conditions within the movement, siphoning activists' energy and resources to resolve crisis. Unintentional movement visibility may result from a strategic blunder (Jasper and Poulsen 1993). Visibility blunders might stem from activists exaggerating the conditions of constituents' victimization, a concern expressed by southern African LGBT activists debating how to present a pan-African LGBT movement to the ACHPR, or inappropriately likening one group's suffering to that of another (Halley 2000).

Visibility and intentionality do not always align in movement processes. Public visibility or invisibility can shed light on how activists' intentionality works within a movement or organization. Intentionality does not always motivate movement organizations' visibility and invisibility. Evidenced in the unintentional invisibility of South African LGBT movement organizations in relation to the marriage-equality campaign, Sister Namibia's visibility disruption, and the invisibility of TRP's public law-reform campaign, activists were not able to exercise complete control over their visibility and invisibility. Decoupling intentionality from movement visibility and invisibility can facilitate the diagnosis of cultural, social, and political conditions over which activists have little control.

Visibility can have less benign implications within social movements. The visibility of one group may come at the expense of another group's marginalization (Phelan 2001). Practices of inclusion and exclusion may accompany and even motivate movement visibility strategies, as activists elevate certain strategic priorities above others or foreground the interests of some constituents, while ignoring those of others (Gamson 1997; Ghaziani 2008; Ward 2008). Decision-making processes and leaders who are invisible to activists suggest less democratic practices in organizations. Some TRP constituents interpreted the opacity and invisibility of the decision-making apparatus as leaders' efforts to sideline black and coloured constituents' grievances. In such dynamics, scholars can discern the outlines of organizations' strategic orientations (Downey and Rohlinger 2008; Ganz 2000).

Visibility Strategies That Work in One Sociopolitical Field May Not Translate to Another

This point is important to keep in mind when studying transnational organizing, particularly transnational LGBT activism (Adam, Duyvendak, and Krouwel 1999). Many activists in the global South are conversant with movement strategies favored by LGBT movements in the global North but may choose not to duplicate them in their national contexts, as in the case of using Western LGBT terminology (Boellstorff 2005). Activists who deploy Western LGBT terminology may eschew other features of Northern LGBT organizing. In such instances, activists pick and choose which elements of a foreign tactical repertoire they want to use. Among sociopolitical fields that share a common history, as in the case of Namibia and South Africa, strategies that make sense in one place may not achieve intelligibility or may seem impossible to activists (Chabot and Duyvendak 2002). Launching a public campaign to decriminalize sodomy ultimately lost it strategic appeal to activists with TRP, in the face of political homophobia from Namibian leaders; however, the same campaign yielded success for the LGBT movement in South Africa. An emphasis on activists' agency can resist developmentalist assumptions about what social movements in the global South should look like (Alexander 2005). Gender and sexual diversity organizing is not uniform in the global South. As long as the political horizon continues to shift and expand, activists' visibility strategies will continue to metamorphose in unexpected ways.

Methodological Appendix

I first became acquainted with southern African LGBT organizing in 2000, while I was researching the Zimbabwean literary publishing industry in Harare. In 1995, President Robert Mugabe denigrated GALZ's attempt to obtain a booth at the Zimbabwe International Book Fair (ZIBF) (Epprecht 1998, 2004; Goddard 2004; Hoad 2007; Murray 1998; Phillips 1997). In a speech that opened the ZIBF, Mugabe (1995) denounced lesbian and gay activism. He stated,

> I find it extremely outrageous and repugnant to my human conscience that such immoral and revulsive organisations like those of homosexuals who offend both against the law of nature and the morals of religious beliefs espoused by our society, should have any advocates in our midst and even elsewhere in the world.

Mugabe's comments incited Namibian state leaders to denounce homosexuality (Reddy 2002). When I was ready to begin this project in 2004, the political situation in Zimbabwe had worsened, making fieldwork untenable. I shifted my attention to LGBT organizing in Namibia and South Africa.

To understand the strategic choices that activists made about movement organizations' public visibility, I studied comparable LGBT movement organizations in Windhoek, Namibia, and Johannesburg, South Africa. I confined my case study selection to Windhoek and Johannesburg. When I began my fieldwork, Johannesburg was home to an estimated 8 million people, whereas approximately 250,000 people inhabited Windhoek. Although Johannesburg was significantly larger than Windhoek, I decided that this size difference would not bias my data collection as the unit of analysis for this study was the LGBT movement organization. I excluded from my analysis other South African cities in which LGBT movement organizations were located so as not to upset the balance I established by limiting my case study sites to Johannesburg and Windhoek.

Understanding Namibian and South African LGBT movement organizations' strategic choices motivated my use of multiple qualitative methods, which can "illuminate previously unexamined or misunderstood experiences" and "increase the likelihood of obtaining scientific credibility and research utility" (Reinharz 1992, 197). Researchers describe multiple methods as increasing the coherence and validity of findings (Blee and Taylor 2002). I gathered and analyzed newspaper articles and organizational documents, conducted and analyzed in-depth qualitative interviews, and engaged in ethnographic observation. In this appendix, I first explain how I collected my data before discussing how I accessed Namibian and South African LGBT movement organizations and how my personal identity affected my rapport with LGBT activists.

Data-Collection Sequencing Strategy

I employed a sequencing strategy for collecting my data (Mason 2002). By sequencing strategy, I mean that I staggered my data collection so that I only gathered information relevant to Namibian and South African LGBT movement organizations' strategies of (in)visibility. The information I gathered informed and limited the subsequent data I collected.

The first step consisted of amassing and analyzing articles from Namibian and South African news media. I began collecting online newspaper articles in September 2004 from Namibian and South African mainstream and LGBT media, and in December 2004, I collected newspaper articles from Namibian and South African mainstream sources from Northwestern University's Melville J. Herskovits Library of African Studies. In the second step, I gathered archival data at the Gay and Lesbian Archives (GALA) in Johannesburg on several occasions between September and November 2005 about the history of Namibian and South African LGBT organizing and from online South African gay websites. For the third step, I engaged in intensive ethnographic observation of two LGBT movement organizations in Johannesburg between September 2005 and April 2006 and of two organizations in Windhoek between April and July 2006. While I observed each movement organization, I collected records related to the organizations' strategic choices about their (in)visibility. After I had engaged in ethnographic observation of movement organizations for a few weeks, I engaged in the fourth and final step: interviewing organizational staff and members.

Newspaper and Archival Research

I limited my online search of English-language newspaper articles to those published between 1995 and 2006.[1] I selected 1995 as a starting point for my newspaper data collection because SWAPO leaders in Namibia made their first antigay remarks in this year. My primary online South African mainstream news sources were the *Mail & Guardian* (http://www.mg.co.za/) and the South African Press Association (http://www.sapa.org.za/), and my online Namibian mainstream news sources were the *Namibian* (http://www.namibian.com.na/) and *New Era* (http://www.newera.com.na/). South African LGBT-specific online news sources included *Exit* (http://www.exit.co.za/), Mambaonline (http://www.mambaonline.com/), and Behind the Mask (http://www.mask.org.za/). I spent several days at GALA between September and November 2005 collecting and analyzing historical documents from each country's LGBT movement. I gathered historical documents related to the South African LGBT movement dating back to the late 1980s but did not include these data in my document analysis. Additionally, I gathered articles from *Exit,* a South African newspaper targeting white, middle-class gay men, and from GALA's collection of news clippings related to LGBT issues, rights, and movement activities (AM 2704). I also consulted the records of key movement organizations that were or had been based and active in Johannesburg, including NCGLE, the Lesbian and Gay Equality Project, GLOW, and ACTIVATE, an LGBT movement organization at the University of the Witwatersrand. I collected approximately five hundred documents from GALA, Behind the Mask, FEW, Sister Namibia, and TRP.

I gathered 1,617 newspaper articles from Namibian and South African news sources about LGBT movement activity in both countries. I coded and analyzed national mainstream and LGBT-specific sources, but I confined my coding and analysis of local newspapers to those covering Johannesburg and Windhoek. For the duration of my fieldwork in Johannesburg and Windhoek (September 2005–July 2006), I also clipped articles related to LGBT organizing, rights, and issues from daily, weekly, and weekend newspapers, with the exception of the *Windhoek Advertiser,* which stopped publishing in the early 2000s.

I included articles that mentioned LGBT movement organizations by name, homosexuality, LGBT activism, LGBT cultural visibility, or antigay comments. For example, when searching Namibian and South African news sources online, I entered keywords such as "homosexual," "homosexuality," "lesbian," "gay," "bisexual," "transgender," and "same-sex" into sources' search engines. I entered these articles into QSR NUD*IST 6 and 7, qualitative data analysis programs, and generated inductive codes from a glossary of themes that emerged from my intensive observation of movement organizations. I also created deductive codes from secondary sources about LGBT organizing in the global South, such as being recipients of Northern funding. I then entered the articles into SPSS software and coded them according to the following: day, month, year, LGBT movement organizations mentioned, LGBT-related issue, and type of source. After coding these articles, I used them to establish a historical timeline for LGBT organizing in Namibia and South Africa (1995–2006).

Aware of social movement scholars' criticisms of media bias, I did not use news articles to select LGBT movement organizations to study (Earl et al. 2004). Instead, I used them to generate a list of organizations operating between 1995 and 2005. I decided not to select LGBT movement organizations solely based on their media visibility because synonymizing movement organizations' visibility with media coverage flattened visibility into an outcome or default accomplishment. Instead, I treated the media as one of many audiences LGBT movement organizations targeted and as one source of information about organizations' strategies (Gamson 1975).

Ethnographic Observation

When I arrived in Johannesburg in September 2005, I was not sure which Namibian and South African LGBT movement organizations I would select for ethnographic observation. I wanted to study movement organizations that had been in existence for at least two years and had some form of verifiable, routinized visibility, such as regular meeting space or an office. Organizations were eligible for ethnographic observation only if they engaged in advocacy and social change on behalf of LGBT Namibians and/or South Africans. Thus, purposive sampling drove my selection of LGBT movement organizations for ethnographic observation (Hammersley and Atkinson 1995). Random sampling would have been impossible and unsuitable for my purposes, given my interest in choosing organizations that had been visible for some time.

My first stop in Johannesburg was GALA, an organization that documents South African LGBT history and uses historical documents to combat misrepresentations of LGBT South Africans (Reid 2002).[2] I reviewed South African LGBT movement documents for two weeks, familiarizing myself with movement developments. From my coding of South African newspapers and reading of LGBT movement documents at GALA, I knew several LGBT movement organizations were active in Johannesburg and surrounding townships: Behind the Mask, FEW, GALA, ACTIVATE, and the Lesbian and Gay Equality Project.[3]

Conversations with GALA staff steered me toward Behind the Mask and FEW. The Equality Project suspended operations a few months before I arrived in Johannesburg in 2005. I excluded GALA and ACTIVATE because, at the time of observation, both groups seemed to have limited strategic scopes; GALA's advocacy work remained limited to social justice research, and ACTIVATE was focused mostly on organizing at the University of the Witwatersrand (Manion and Morgan 2006). After meeting with the director of Behind the Mask, who granted me permission to study the organization, I selected Behind the Mask and FEW for ethnographic observation. As I relate later, I experienced difficulty securing permission to observe FEW's organizational dynamics.

Selecting LGBT movement organizations to observe in Namibia was straightforward. In February 2006, I met the leaders of Sister Namibia and TRP when they were in Johannesburg for a meeting of southern African LGBT activists and learned that their groups were the only LGBT movement organizations operating in Namibia at the time. Both leaders granted me permission to study their organizations' internal dynamics and historical records.

Understanding movement organizations' strategic choices about their public visibility drove my ethnographic observation. I observed movement organizations' activities and interacted with LGBT activists "for an extended period of time, watching what happen[ed], listening to what [was] said, [and] asking questions" (Hammersley and Atkinson 1995, 1). I estimate that I spent eight hundred hours total observing LGBT movement organizations' dynamics, averaging about twenty hours per week. I openly took notes on paper, on a mobile telephone with a portable keyboard, or on a laptop computer. LGBT activists did not seem to find my note taking distracting. At the end of each day of observation, I transferred my field notes to an observational template. I limited my observation to what happened at organizations' offices or when they participated in off-site events.

Studying two organizations meant that I was not able to study each movement organization so intensively because "the more settings studied the less time that can be spent in each" (Hammersley and Atkinson 1995, 40). What I may have sacrificed in terms of micro-level detail I made up for in rich observation about movement organizations' strategic choices about public visibility as I concentrated on staff members and visitors' talk about audiences, constituencies, and campaigns.

Qualitative Interviewing

To ensure that I understood how, when, and why LGBT movement organizations made certain strategic choices about their visibility or invisibility, I interviewed movement organizations' staff and members. Using a digital voice recorder, I conducted fifty-six in-depth, semistructured qualitative interviews with staff and members of Behind the Mask, FEW, Sister Namibia, and TRP.

Semistructured interviews allowed me to understand strategic choices "from the perspective of movement actors" (Blee and Taylor 2002, 92). Before going to South Africa, I created a semistructured interview schedule containing a list of possible questions to ask respondents. Their answers guided the order in which I posed questions on the interview schedule. Interviewees' responses also provoked new questions not on the schedule. I amended the interview schedule if I discerned that questions did not elicit detailed responses from interviewees.

To capture a range of LGBT movement organizations' staff and member attitudes, I engaged in purposive sampling when I selected activists to interview (Auerbach and Silverstein 2003). I strategically selected activists with different roles in the organization who had been involved for at least six months to describe its decision-making process, audiences, constituency, and campaigns for interviews. Selecting activists to interview based on their role in the organization, instead of using other criteria, such as gender, race, age, or length of time in the organization, made sense because I was interested in their narration of how staff and members made strategic choices. Their role in the organization likely influenced their proximity to decision-making processes, which provided them with a more intimate understanding of different strategic choices. I compared interviewees' responses to questions about the organization's routines as checks against my field notes and analysis of the movement organizations' strategic choices about their public visibility strategies. I began interviewing staff and members only after I had spent enough time observing an organization to have established trust and rapport with staff and members. I digitally recorded and conducted interviews in English. Most interviews lasted between forty-five and ninety minutes.

I asked Namibian and South African LGBT activists a number of questions about their organizations' public visibility strategies. I inquired about how organizations chose their office locations, about groups with which organizations worked or which ones they avoided, how activists recruited members, about the audiences to which organizations directed their messages, how organizations worked with mainstream and LGBT-specific media, and about the differences in movement organizations' public presentations to diverse audiences. I also asked about periods in which movement organizations retreated from public visibility and the relationship between the visibility of LGBT persons and organizations. During the interview, I treated LGBT activists as experts on movement organizations. Some staff and members seemed to appreciate validation of their expertise during the interview. A few times, respondents remarked, "I didn't realize I knew so much" or "I can't believe I'm saying this much about" an organization. I asked activists about shifts in their organization's visibility and invisibility strategies, how the organization tailored its strategies for different audiences, how the organization decided to publicize its work and goals, and the organization's routines for making itself accessible to the public and targeted constituency. Interview data confirmed many of my ethnographic observations and provided crucial background information that contextualized organizations' strategic choices.

I protected the anonymity and confidentiality of subjects by using pseudonyms for staff, members, and leaders in my field notes and transcriptions of interviews, by not recording personal identifiers on tape, and by keeping my field notes, transcribed interviews, and digital interview files on a laptop computer encrypted with a password, ensuring that I was the only person with access to this information. After I finished interviewing staff and members, I sent the digital recordings via e-mail or international courier to a transcriptionist in the United States who had no ties to Namibia or South Africa. She transcribed the interviews and e-mailed the transcripts back to me, and I analyzed the interviews in QSR NUD*IST 6 and 7.

Interview participants varied in terms of their nationality, race, gender, and sexuality. Of the fifty-six individuals I interviewed, twenty-six were Namibian, twenty-three were South African, and seven were non-Namibians or non–South Africans. Foreign staff members hailed from Uganda, Burundi, Germany, Jamaica, the Netherlands, and the United States. Table A1 displays demographic information about respondents' race, gender, and sexuality.

I interviewed an equal number of men ($n = 27$) and women ($n = 27$) and two transgender men. Of the staff and members I interviewed, 45 percent ($n = 25$) identified as gay, 43 percent ($n = 24$) identified as lesbian, 7 percent ($n = 4$) identified as heterosexual, and 5 percent ($n = 3$) identified as bisexual. Gay men and lesbians dominated the staff and membership of LGBT movement organizations in both countries. Almost 73 percent ($n = 41$) of respondents identified as black, 20 percent ($n = 11$) identified as coloured, and 7 percent ($n = 4$) identified as white. Unlike lesbian and gay movement organizations in the 1980s in South Africa or the first attempt at organizing in Namibia, LGBT movement organizations in Namibia and South Africa were multiracial, with the exception of FEW, and power and leadership had largely shifted to black and coloured Namibian and South Africans. Of the leaders of movement organizations I studied, two identified as black lesbians (FEW and Behind the Mask), one as a coloured gay man (TRP), and one as a white lesbian (Sister Namibia). Leadership positions in LGBT movement organizations were no longer solely the domain of white gay men (Gevisser 1995).

	Black			Coloured		White		Total
	Men	Women	Trans.	Men	Women	Men	Women	
South Africa								
Gay	6					2		8
Lesbian		15			1			16
Heterosexual		1						1
Bisexual	2						1	3
Namibia								
Gay	10			7				17
Lesbian		5			2		1	8
Heterosexual			2		1			3
Bisexual								0
Total	**18**	**21**	**2**	**7**	**4**	**2**	**2**	**56**

Table A1. *Total number of interview respondents affiliated with South African and Namibian LGBT movement organizations by race, gender, and sexuality.*

Data Analysis

I analyzed the news media articles and organizational documents separately from the interview and ethnographic observational data. This separation made sense given my interest in understanding LGBT movement organizations' strategic choices contemporaneously and over time. In QSR NUD*IST 6 and 7, I utilized the same thematic coding categories for all data as a way to ensure consistency in coding. I integrated news media articles and organizational records and then coded them together thematically, and I repeated this process for interview and ethnographic data. Deductive codes that I gleaned from secondary sources, such as social movement literature, included audience construction, constituency construction, talk about opponents, and antigay sentiments. Inductive codes that emerged from my initial perusal of my data include mention of Northern donors and international NGOs, democratic procedures at movement organizations, and how organizations perceived and reacted to political opportunities.

Accessing LGBT Movement Organizations as an Outsider

Gaining access to Behind the Mask, Sister Namibia, and TRP was easier than I initially anticipated. Before meeting with the leaders of LGBT movement organizations, I prepared a short, jargon-free research proposal explaining my research. I made it clear that I was interested in observing the movement organization's meetings and activities and not maligning the organization. I stated that I wanted to learn about how the movement organization presented itself publicly, interacted with different audiences, and decided to work on or withdraw from certain movement campaigns. After one meeting, the leaders of Behind the Mask, Sister Namibia, and TRP gave me permission to study their organizations.

Obtaining permission to study FEW proved difficult.[4] In an effort to protect FEW after negative encounters with researchers, FEW's director worked to ensure that researchers did not portray the organization unfavorably. The director's past interactions with foreign researchers inclined her to deny my request to study the organization, and our conversation illustrated how important the organization's public visibility and reputation were to her. Several things allowed me to gain access to FEW. First, I met with FEW's director and public relations officer several times in November and December 2005. My earnest engagement with FEW staff members convinced FEW's director that I was not the "fly-in, fly-out" type of researcher she distrusted. Second, my regular presence at Behind the Mask, which has offices very close to FEW in Constitution Hill, enabled staff to get to know me; some Behind the Mask staff also belonged to FEW and vouched for me in private interactions with FEW staff members. Third, I was frank about my sexual identity. FEW's director asked me about my sexual identity and stated, "You can tell me that it's none of my business." I shared that I was bisexual. She asserted, "At least you're one of us. There's nothing I can't stand more than straight people studying us."

Fourth, I stressed that I was interested in studying organizational dynamics, not in individual constituents' experiences with coming out, violence, or discrimination. Many LGBT Namibians and South Africans experienced negative sanctions associated with disclosing their nonnormative sexual and gender identities, such as violence and expulsion from their homes, making them interesting objects of study to outsiders who wanted to understand the persistence and permutation of violence in postcolonial African contexts. However, I did not want to objectify or exploit LGBT persons and their narratives of suffering or tragedy (Currier 2011). Using research participants' stories only because of their experiences of violence or differences violates feminist ethical principles because it reduces research participants to objects, denying them agency in the research process (Naples 2003; Reinharz 1992). Although I do not deny that such narratives are worthy of study, I was more interested in focusing on organized expressions of agency. I wanted movement organizations' staff and members to understand that I did not want to exploit constituents' stories. I believe that limiting the scope of my research helped persuade the directors of Behind the Mask, FEW, Sister Namibia, and TRP to allow me to study their organizations.

Researcher Identity: The "Strange White Woman"

My nationality, race, gender, class, and sexuality affected my research in different ways. My whiteness distinguished me as an outsider because most staff and members at the LGBT movement organizations were of African descent (Naples 2003). Whiteness has a long, troubled history in both countries, and potential research participants interpreted my race and nationality through apartheid racial categories (Steyn 2001). Early in my observation of FEW in January 2006, the director explained the presence of the "strange white woman" to staff at a staff meeting, differentiating me in terms of my race, not my position as a researcher. Some black and coloured LGBT activists in both countries initially regarded me with suspicion until I spoke; my accent indicated that I was from the United States. Some Namibian LGBT activists greeted me in Afrikaans when we first met, as was customary among individuals speaking with those they perceived to be white Namibians. After admitting that I spoke no Afrikaans, staff and members first regarded me as an oddity but eventually seemed to adjust to my presence.

Being a female-bodied person facilitated my entry into FEW and Sister Namibia, organizations whose constituents were women. My gender presentation and behaviors offered a lens through which I learned much about the cultural instability of black lesbian identities. While I was in the field, I dressed like staff and members at both organizations, wearing mostly casual attire because it was comfortable, and I frequently walked long distances to and from office spaces. Some women believed I identified as butch because I dressed sportily and was tall and large in comparison to other women. However, some black women viewed my customary silence and helpfulness as contradicting my gender presentation, as they compared my style to that of black lesbians. For instance, they regarded my offers to get others coffee or tea as "femme" behavior and emotion work. These conversations both confirmed that I was developing rapport with black lesbian activists and served as opportunities for me to learn about slippages between individual sexual subjectivities and collective black lesbian identities.

Questions of Safety

Given that SWAPO leaders racialized Namibian same-sex sexualities as white in their antigay commentary (Currier 2010a; Lorway 2006), I initially worried that my presence as a white American researcher at Sister Namibia and TRP would make these organizations vulnerable to state scrutiny. If both organizations were under state surveillance, would police notice and equate the presence of a white foreigner with political mischief, prompting them to question the activities of LGBT movement organizations? Activists assured me that my fears were unfounded. One staff member stated that members and visitors would not continue to frequent the offices of Sister Namibia and TRP if people knew the police disrupted organizations' activities. In addition, activists pointed out that SWAPO leaders' political homophobia had not initiated a crackdown on LGBT organizing akin to the Zimbabwean state repression of LGBT activists (Goddard 2004). While in Namibia, I still took steps not to draw undue attention to my presence at Sister Namibia or TRP.

Similarly, I feared my presence as a white woman with an ambiguous gender presentation in Johannesburg townships would draw attention to black lesbian activists. When I shadowed activists from FEW who traveled into townships to visit prospective members, I monitored the conversations I initiated on public transport. Because I did not want to imperil activists' work in townships, I was careful not to initiate LGBT-themed discussions. After I went on an outing to Tembisa, a Johannesburg township, in December 2005, a black gay man and Behind the Mask staff member candidly queried,

"What the fuck were you doing out there?" He and a colleague advised me that they never visited Tembisa "due to its reputation for being crime-ridden."

South African LGBT activists shared some of my safety concerns. For instance, FEW sponsored a self-defense training class at the request of a staff member who had been hassled by youths on her way to and from the organization's office. FEW invited me to participate in the training because not only did they consider me to be a fixture in the organization by that time but they also recognized that I traveled as they did. I commuted mostly by minibus taxis, although occasionally, I took more expensive private taxis to and from Constitutional Hill in Hillbrow, a Johannesburg neighborhood. Research participants offered advice about which places in Johannesburg to avoid and how I should safeguard my valuables. In this and other ways, LGBT activists were sources of important knowledge.

Although LGBT activists and I experienced traveling in Johannesburg somewhat similarly, our safety concerns differed because of where we lived. Many activists returned home to sometimes difficult township lives, whereas I was able to rent a room in an apartment in the white, gay neighborhood of Melville and, later, a room in a house in the adjacent, white neighborhood of Westdene, with numerous security features. My class position insulated me from the more volatile aspects of living in Johannesburg and its townships.

Note about LGBT Terminology

I use the language that activists prefer because using nomenclature that activists did not deploy seemed disingenuous (Epprecht 2008). Replacing activists' terms with others that I deemed suitable would suggest that I knew which terms were appropriate for southern African sociopolitical contexts. This choice might elicit criticism from scholars of transnational sexualities that this study abets the supremacy of Western gender and sexuality terminology in the global South. Influenced by queer theorizing, scholars of transnational sexualities interrogate the sociopolitical contexts in which genders and sexualities emerge and emphasize variability in local-global constructions of gender and sexuality (Grewal and Kaplan 2001; Kim-Puri 2005). Many scholars are uneasy about the appearance of Western identity categories like "gay" and "lesbian" in the global South that are associated with a "global gay" project and professionalized LGBT activism (Hemmings 2007; Hoad 2007; Puar 2001).

According to Dennis Altman's (1997) imagination of a global gay model, sexually and gender-variant cultures in the global South have roots in Western gay cultures. In this model, global capitalism hastened individuals' acquisition of Westernized gay subjectivities in the global South, producing a globalized gay "sameness" (Boellstorff 2007, 202). However, this model is flawed for a couple of reasons. First, the global gay model is androcentric and excludes women's same-sex sexualities (Sinnott 2004). Second, the model exaggerates the growing sameness of gayness worldwide and underestimates the importance of localized expressions of gender and sexual diversity. For Tom Boellstorff (2005, 29), who examines national sexual subjectivities in Indonesia, "the issue is not [whether] the world's becoming more the same or more different under globalization . . . but the transformation of the very yardsticks by which one decides where something is the same or different." In other words, fixing sameness or difference hinders studies of transnational sexualities because measures of them cannot keep pace with global economic, political, and cultural developments.

The deployment of Western identity nomenclature may be culturally inappropriate in some places in the postcolonial global South (Swarr and Nagar 2003). "Using 'lesbian' as a global signifier is problematic . . . because it imposes a Eurocentric term, which connotes a fixed sexual identity, on practices and relationships that may have very different meanings and expectations in other cultures" (Blackwood 2002, 70). These terms are inadequate in Western contexts because they exclude many local forms of gender and sexual nonconformity. So why should they be used in the global South? Rigid Western identity categories do not accurately reflect fluid, indigenous, and hybrid sexualities in the global South. Oliver Phillips (2000) makes this point when referring to Zimbabwean president Mugabe's allegations that homosexuality is a foreign product of European colonialism. He states, "It is this categorical fixity of definition [of sexuality], rooted in the individual, that has been imported into Zimbabwe, rather than any new [sexual] activities" (19).

The supremacy of Western identity categories in the global South may also efface local and indigenous configurations of gender and sexuality (Bacchetta 2002; Blackwood 2008; Hoad 2007; Katyal 2002; Massad 2002). Local genders and sexualities often favor procreative heterosexualities and can be manipulated to persecute sexually and gender-nonconforming individuals (Blackwood 2005). Sexually and gender-variant persons in different nations in the global South have embraced English-language identity terms to escape derogatory terms in local languages (Blackwood 2004). Privileging local genders and sexualities can promote the false impression that local concepts are better than foreign concepts (Boellstorff 2005) or that the local is wholly "pristine" and unaffected by transnational processes (Tan 2001, 124). Although it may be difficult to respect local gender and sexual arrangements when analyzing how foreign ideas interact with local understandings, it is not impossible (Blackwood 2008).

These criticisms should give scholars studying LGBT movements in the global South pause. On one hand, identity categories describing sexual and gender diversity have gained some currency among Namibian and South African LGBT activists. It would be unfair to discount activists' use of LGBT categories as naive, instead of attributing agency to their actions. On the other hand, questioning what "LGBT" signifies in Namibia and South Africa may be a wise course; taking the coherence of "LGBT" for granted might lead scholars to ascribe even representation and equality to the "l/g/b/t" signifiers in the acronym prematurely, equality that has not materialized in the global North (Ward 2008). Global processes can constrain activists' selection of nomenclature. Transnational sexualities scholars have demonstrated how new identity terms become available to LGBT activists through transnational circuits of power, such as Northern interventions in culture and politics in the global South (Bacchetta 2002; Manalansan 1995). Identity terms also circulate through HIV/AIDS education, prevention, and treatment projects (Seckinelgin 2009; Wright 2000).

My decision to use LGBT terminology departs from the terminological choices of other scholars of gender and sexual diversity in southern Africa. The South African LGBT persons and activists Natalie Oswin (2007) and Andrew Tucker (2009) interviewed used the term *queer* to refer to their political projects or personal identities; this seemed to be especially true for white, well-educated, and affluent activists. I point out this variation not to impugn these scholars' decisions but to illustrate the varied terrain of LGBT organizing in southern Africa.

Notes

Introduction

1. I use the LGBT acronym in reference to Namibian and South African gender and sexual diversity activism. Some activists used the acronym LGBTI, which includes intersex identities and persons (Dirsuweit 2006). Because not all organizations I studied used the LGBTI acronym, and no organization I observed engaged in intersex advocacy, I use the LGBT acronym. Owing to the relative invisibility of bisexual and transgender activism within the organizations I studied, I address neither bisexual nor transgender mobilization in much detail in this book. In the methodological appendix, I explore the merits of and drawbacks to LGBT terminology.

2. I assigned all activists I interviewed pseudonyms to protect their anonymity. I refer to activists only as "members" of an organization. I also do not identify certain named interviewees as directors or staff members of an organization to protect their anonymity.

3. Black South African gay men were also at risk for corrective rape (Muholi 2004). Robert Lorway (2010) documents the emergence of corrective rape in Namibia.

4. I use the concept of *same-sex sexualities* to encompass sexual desires and identities oriented to people of the same sex or gender and the politics that attach to these desires and identities (Rupp 2001).

5. *Political homophobia* refers to the public denigration of same-sex sexualities, LGBT activism, nonheterosexual persons, and gender and sexual variance (Boellstorff 2007; Currier 2010b). Some scholars attribute the emergence of contemporary political homophobia to the presence of Christian missions in southern Africa alongside settler colonialism (Epprecht 2008; Hoad 2007; Wieringa 2005). Colonialist and Christian ideologies intertwined and reinforced antihomosexuality

sentiments. Deploying political homophobia has been a way for African nationalist leaders to overcome colonial emasculation and to mark a new pathway to national, cultural, and racial authenticity (Currier 2012). I use this term to specify particular instances in which political leaders intended to police gender and sexual diversity and political dissidents. By no means am I asserting that an entire African country or racial group is homophobic. Instead, certain leaders have deployed this discourse. It is also not my intention to "[pathologize] individual leaders," which as Neville Hoad (2007, xii) explains, "does little to further understanding" of African gender and sexual politics (see also Thomas 2007). I understand political homophobia as a deliberate strategy some leaders use to silence political opponents, to defend cultural sovereignty, and to deflect public attention away from internal conflicts.

Political homophobia upholds *heteronormativity*, the "institutions, structures of understanding, and practical orientations that make heterosexuality seem not only coherent—that is, organized as a sexuality—but also privileged" (Berlant and Warner 1998, 548). Heteronormativity also relies on and enforces gender conformity and punishes gender and sexual dissidence. *Gender and sexual dissidents* are individuals whose bodies, gender presentations and identities, and sexual desires and identities do not conform to heteronormative sociopolitical arrangements. Gender and sexual dissidents include both individuals who intentionally challenge heteronormativity and individuals who are perceived by institutional authorities as gender and sexual troublemakers, even if they do not purposely contest heteronormativity. In other words, gender- and sexually nonconforming persons may qualify as gender and sexual dissidents even if they have no intention of challenging heteronormative arrangements publicly.

6. I use *Western* to refer to Euro-American systems of power and knowledge, whereas I use *Northern* to refer to the geopolitical placement of many social movement scholars and donor agencies; this latter term reflects that "wealth and poverty, advanced industrialism and underdevelopment do not lie in neatly divided geographical hemispheres" (Bulbeck 2007, 61). The terms *global North* and *global South* replace geopolitical classifications of First World and Third World. Excluding Australia and New Zealand, "the developed countries of the world lie to the North of the developing, undeveloped or least developed ones" (Dirlik 2007, 13).

7. Mario Diani and Donatella della Porta's (1999, 19) definition of social movements informs this study: "(1) informal networks, based (2) on shared beliefs and solidarity, which mobilize about (3) conflictual issues, through (4) the frequent use of various forms of protest." This definition highlights the major components of social movements: how collective identities hold members together, how groups develop and pursue their goals through protest, and how politics and culture serve as sources of conflict that mobilize groups to act. A movement organization is "a complex, or formal, organization which identifies its goals with the preferences of a social movement . . . and attempts to implement those goals" (McCarthy and Zald 1977, 1218).

8. Launched in 2000, Behind the Mask linked LGBT movement organizations in Africa through its website, investigated LGBT rights violations on the continent, monitored media representation of LGBT persons, and reported stories of interest to African LGBT persons. Issues of interest to Behind the Mask staff included homophobic and transphobic violence, poverty, HIV/AIDS, and LGBT persons' unemployment. Most Behind the Mask staff members were, by definition, amateur journalists or journalist activists intent on drawing public attention to the lives of African LGBT persons.

Apart from the founder and the managing editor, both of whom were trained journalists, no staff member had formal journalism training, although the junior reporter was pursuing a degree in communication at a local university. To address the lack of formally trained journalists, Behind the Mask overhauled its hiring policies to recruit staff with experience as professional journalists. Behind the Mask also mandated writing workshops for staff and foreign correspondents who wrote for the website. These practices distinguished the organization's website from other gay websites. Behind the Mask's website was "not a gay site with pictures of naked men or pictures of women with their breasts out. . . . Our strength is we're able to give people information without it [sexual content] . . . blaring on the screen" (Andrew, a black gay activist, interview with the author, October 31, 2005). Behind the Mask staff differentiated the organization's website from commercial gay websites, a public presentation consistent with other professional South African LGBT movement organizations. Such distancing from for-profit, gay pornography websites contributed to the aura of legitimacy LGBT movement organizations sought to create for themselves.

Thirteen people worked at the organization as paid staff when I observed Behind the Mask from October 2005 to March 2006: the white Dutch founder, who served as a part-time paid consultant; a director; a managing editor; an office administrator; a domestic worker; a webmaster; a part-time French translator; a junior reporter; a human rights researcher; and four temporary, unpaid interns. Ten staff identified as black, and three staff identified as white. Most staff members wrote stories for the website, although the reporter and managing editor wrote regular feature stories as their primary duties. Most staff members were South African; the rest hailed from Burundi, Germany, the Netherlands, Uganda, and the United States. Reporters wrote in English, and some stories were translated into French. Behind the Mask recruited correspondents elsewhere in Africa to report on LGBT issues.

9. FEW developed as a project of Behind the Mask in 2002 when two staff members decided to focus exclusively on issues affecting black South African lesbians. In 2003, they established FEW as an independent organization and obtained funding from Northern donors in 2004 for the Rose Has Thorns campaign, a project committed to eradicating antilesbian violence. For such a young movement organization, FEW had a large staff, all of whom identified as black women. When I observed the

organization, FEW employed five full-time staff consisting of a director, a public relations and outreach officer, a junior training officer who worked as the director's personal assistant, a computer specialist responsible for maintaining the office's computers and teaching computer skills classes, and a receptionist who doubled as an officer manager. The organization employed six part-time staff: a domestic worker, an activities coordinator, and four community representatives who served as liaisons between FEW and Johannesburg townships. Most strategic choices fell to the director, who reported to an executive board. During weekly staff meetings, staff deliberated about their strategic plans, and the director explained to staff why she was making a particular decision, to acquaint staff with a formal work environment. FEW built in staff turnover by implementing six-month contracts for the junior training officer and community representatives so that more constituents would gain employment experience and on-the-job training as FEW staff. Several part-time volunteers involved with managing FEW's soccer team and dramatic troupe also attended staff meetings to report on their activities; FEW's director was grooming these volunteers to become community representatives in the future.

10. A small group of women formed Sister Namibia as a feminist movement organization in 1989 just before independence. Core members focused on publishing a magazine of the same name for the organization's first decade of existence (Frank and |Khaxas 2006). Staff included a director, a bookkeeper, a receptionist, a delivery person, a part-time domestic worker, and a contract media officer when I observed the organization between April and July 2006. The director solicited staff for their input about decisions, but she often had to make decisions on her own. Black and white lesbian women held prominent roles in Sister Namibia, with at least three working formally as director over the organization's existence. Three staff identified as black, two as coloured, and one as white. Sister Namibia was the only organization I observed that owned the building in which its office was located.

11. While I observed TRP, the organization employed a director; an office manager; an information and publicity officer; a project director; an outreach officer; a part-time housekeeper; and a full-time, unpaid volunteer. Staff often deliberated over major decisions during regular staff meetings, and the director often consulted with staff about minor decisions that fell to him. Four staff members identified as black, two as coloured, and one as white.

With donor funding, TRP focused on several different projects. TRP's LGBT human rights and advocacy program addressed how LGBT Christians could integrate their spirituality and sexuality and devised school curricula focused on democracy, human rights, and gender and sexual diversity. Late in 2006, staff planned on launching a new program that addressed LGBT health concerns, including HIV/AIDS prevention and treatment. Staff anticipated initiating a public law-reform campaign in 2007. TRP's leadership program exported skills training to other African LGBT movement organizations, as TRP staff nurtured emerging organizations in Botswana and East Africa. Fourth, under the outreach program, TRP sponsored a yearly LGBT human rights week; an award-winning radio show on Katutura Community Radio, "Talking Pink," one of the few shows in Africa that dealt with LGBT issues; and a video project that brought LGBT-themed films to different Namibian communities.

12. For more detail about the qualitative methods I employed, please see the methodological appendix.

13. African theorists have critiqued how European colonialism delimited and organized African societies according to Western cultural logics (Mudimbe 1988). In some African contexts, this process extended to the imposition of dichotomous Western gender and sexual norms on African societies, which relied on visual logics (Oyěwùmí 1997). Highlighting Namibian and South African LGBT activists' visibility strategies risks a similar kind of cultural imperialism. However, LGBT activists operate within a complex circuit of African cultural traditions; colonial and apartheid discourses of race, gender, class, and sexuality; and transnational human rights rhetoric. Visibility is an important dimension of political organizing in Namibia and South Africa because of these intersecting cultural and political trajectories.

14. In critiques about LGBT organizing in the United States, queer theorists also challenge the primacy LGBT movement organizations afford to certain identities and subjects within the movement (Clarke 2000; Phelan 2001). In particular, they contest the flattened visibility of certain constituents promulgated by LGBT organizing: one that values white, middle-class, gender-conforming lesbians and gay men over working-poor LGBT and queer persons, LGBT and queer persons of color, gender-diverse persons, and differently abled LGBT and queer persons (Duggan 2003; Ward 2008). When privileged, white, gender-normative individuals become the assumed referent category for the movement's constituency, they become visible as movement subjects at the same time that their ubiquity recedes into the background. In turn, privileged individuals' visibility displaces less privileged LGBT and queer persons from the movement's constituency, rendering less privileged queers invisible as constituents (Ghaziani 2008; Manalansan 2005). While informative, this viewpoint does not map directly onto the racial politics of postapartheid Namibia and South Africa; however, concerns about the normalized visibility of constituents that queer theorists highlight in the United States resemble those raised by South African activists who resist the efforts by LGBT persons to sideline gender-variant persons in the annual LGBT Pride March in Johannesburg.

15. John D. McCarthy and Mayer N. Zald (1977, 1221) differentiate between beneficiaries and constituents; they define *beneficiaries* as those who stand to gain from movement success and *constituents* as those who bestow resources on movement organizations. I use *constituents* to refer to beneficiaries and individuals to whom LGBT movement organizations are accountable, notably LGBT persons. Movements act on

behalf of constituents; this requires movements to manufacture the constituents they represent, a process that involves constant refinement. Constituents authorize movements to act on their behalf in the hope that movement success will improve their lives. Constituents differ from movement adherents (or movement organization members) who are involved in regular operations that maintain the movement, but adherents and members are certainly constituents in the sense that the movement answers to them. Not all constituents believe a movement represents them. Some gender and sexual dissidents claim that some LGBT movements cannot claim them as constituents because movement priorities only benefit privileged LGBT persons (Ward 2008).

16. Theorizing the agentic and strategic aspects of movement invisibility in repressive contexts is tricky. On one hand, groups have some agency in repressive situations, albeit seriously constrained, as feminist theorists have argued (Alexander and Mohanty 1997). On the other hand, overestimating activists' agency can minimize the repressive sociopolitical forces that obstruct movement actions. Sometimes activists have no choice but to retreat into invisibility. Is this a strategic choice or a matter of survival? At what point does the strategic choice of invisibility become a forced position activists must take?

17. Visibility disruptions enable activists to channel their energy and resources into working with select audiences on goals, reevaluating strategic priorities, and restructuring the organization or movement. These disruptions may be involuntary or voluntary. Exigent circumstances may necessitate a hasty retreat from engaging with audiences, indicating activists' inability to plan for disruptions in advance. A slow disengagement from interactions or campaigns may reveal activists' control over their invisibility. A benefit to voluntarily withdrawing from public view and engagements is that activists can control and determine the circumstances under which they reemerge, if they do reemerge (Taylor 1989).

18. The state is "composed of numerous institutions, agencies, and organizations that have different functions acquired through processes that are social, political, and historical" (Matthews 1994, 5). Hence, the state is not a unitary, "monolithic" actor; in fact, different state actors "may be at odds" or collaborate with each other, depending on the situation (Matthews 1994, 5).

19. My understanding of "public presentation" differs from that proffered by Kimberly Dugan (2008). She defines "collective identity presentations" as "articulations or frames . . . designed to convey messages about the lived identities of movement participants" (22). I envisage public presentations not as being confined to the identities of movement adherents but as both including and exceeding the collective identities of adherents and constituents in the sense that activists want to be seen in particular ways. In addition, a dramaturgical model of social interactions informs how I conceptualize activists' management of multiple public presentations (Goffman 1959).

20. It is important to maintain a conceptual distinction between decoloniza-

tion and democratization. In Namibia, decolonization, "not democratization," was SWAPO's strategic priority, according to Henning Melber (2004, 238).

21. SWAPO has continued to receive an increasingly larger percentage of the vote in national elections since assuming office in 1989. In contrast, the ANC suffered substantial losses in municipal and regional contests in 2009, although the party won the national election that ushered Jacob Zuma into the presidency (Daniel and Southall 2010).

22. Northern governments pressured the ANC to "become more liberal, to engage with capital, and to adapt to the seeming imperatives of the global capitalist economy" (Johnson 2003, 214). Defending their democratic vision for South Africa, some ANC leaders attacked social movements and civil society NGOs critical of ANC policies (Johnson 2003).

23. I use historically accurate nomenclature when referring to lesbian and gay activism in apartheid South Africa at this time.

24. Owing to South Africa's history of "minority white rule," framing LGBT rights solely within a minority rights framework would likely have generated obstacles for the movement (Tucker 2009, 176). As "long as sexuality concerns were framed around equality in opposition to discrimination, they stood a good chance of being accepted" (Tucker 2009, 176; see also Hoad 2007).

25. Because the majority of Namibian and South African LGBT movement organizations' staff and constituents were black and coloured, I emphasize the material conditions that affected them. In chapter 2, I explore how LGBT persons' visibilities differed under apartheid, depending on their race and class.

26. *Coloured* is an apartheid-era racial "category for mixed race people" that still retains currency for some Namibians and South Africans (Hubbard and Solomon 1995, 165).

27. Approximately 79.5 percent of South Africans are of black African descent. Coloured persons make up 9 percent of the South African population, and white persons another 9 percent. The remaining 2.5 percent are of Asian (South and East Asian) descent (Statistics South Africa 2011). Approximately 78 percent of Namibians are of African descent, although about one-half of Namibia's population of two million people belongs to the Ovambo ethnic group. Sixteen percent are white, and 6 percent are of coloured or mixed-race descent (World Bank 2008).

28. Homophobia has also been a hallmark of white masculinity in Namibia and South Africa (Mooney 1998; Wise 2007). Homophobia enabled the apartheid state to enforce strict racial, gender, and sexual regulations (Conway 2008).

29. Examples of identity movements include racial–ethnic identity, women's, nationalist, and LGBT movements. Identity movements prioritize cultivating public collective identities as a goal by contesting "stigmatized identities," demanding "recognition for new identities," or "deconstruct[ing] restrictive social categories" (Bernstein 1997, 536–37).

30. Hank Johnston, Enrique Laraña, and Joseph Gusfield (1994, 18) describe this feature of collective identity formation as "public identity"—how the "external public" affects how "social movement adherents think about themselves." Responses from bystanders and target audiences play important roles in the "feedback loops" of identity strategies, influencing how identity strategies unfold in different venues in the future (Bernstein 2008, 290–95). The concept of "public" identity reveals the limits of movements' ownership of their own public presentations, a notion Judith Butler (2004) takes up with respect to bodies. Butler states, "Although we struggle for rights over our own bodies, the very bodies for which we struggle are not quite ever only our own. The body has its invariably public dimension; constituted as a social phenomenon in the public sphere, my body is and is not mine" (21). The same principle extends to movements' public presentations; although public presentations belong to movements in the sense that they created them, the interpretive work in which target audiences engage means that audiences also own these presentations.

31. I refer to the private funding agencies that supported Behind the Mask, FEW, Sister Namibia, and TRP collectively as "Northern donors." Although this abstraction does not distinguish between the types of donors that promote economic, social, and political development, which include agencies of foreign governments and international NGOs whose headquarters are in the global North, it does reflect the tendency of activists and political leaders in Namibia and South Africa to refer to donors in this way.

32. All the LGBT movement organizations I studied obtained funding from Northern donors, an indication that the philanthropic sectors in Namibia and South Africa were weak and that governments did not view LGBT service provision and rights as funding priorities. Staff at Behind the Mask, FEW, Sister Namibia, and TRP did not question the decision to solicit external funding.

33. Apart from addressing the religious overtones of political homophobia and the influence of Christian ideology on colonialist governance in southern Africa, I do not discuss religious groups as target audiences of LGBT movement organizations. Only one organization in my ethnographic sample explicitly targeted religious groups: TRP targeted Christian churches. I did not follow TRP's religious outreach because no other group in my sample pursued a similar strategy. In addition, while I observed TRP, staff only held one observable event related to the organization's religious project. There was too little for me to analyze in the way of visibility strategies related to religious outreach.

1. The Rise of LGBT Organizing

1. I do not intend for this chapter to be read as an exhaustive account of LGBT organizing in South Africa and Namibia; instead, I focus selectively on episodes and LGBT movement organizations that highlight activists' historic concerns about public visibility.

2. In this chapter, I do not explore why South African LGBT activists risked

the threat of state repression while the NP was still in power because I confined my newspaper data collection from 1995 to 2006 and my ethnographic observation and interviews from 2005 to 2006. I explore the effect of soft repression on Namibian LGBT movement organizations in more detail in chapters 3 and 4.

3. Although I discuss nineteenth-century theories of race, gender, and sexuality, I do not discuss their trajectories in the German colony of South West Africa or colonial South Africa.

4. Sexologists located abnormality in the bodies of women of African descent, exempting white women's bodies from consideration as abnormal, unless they were lesbian bodies (Somerville 1994). Siobhan B. Somerville (1994, 253) explains that sexologists perpetuated the myth that lesbians and women of African descent had "unusually large" clitorises.

5. Deborah Gaitskell and Elaine Unterhalter (1989) suggest that three distinct types of Afrikaner nationalism correspond to three dates in Afrikaner history: 1902, the British defeat and colonial annexation of independent Afrikaner republics in the Anglo-Boer War; 1914, the launch of the NP; and 1948, the NP's rise to power in South Africa. "In each case, the nation is perceived differently. First, the Afrikaner nation mourns as a suffering victim [after its military loss]; then on the basis of racial and cultural distinctiveness, the nation mobilises to redress political and economic disadvantage [of Afrikaners]; finally, the Afrikaner nation attains state power completely independently but is eventually compelled because of challenges to its authority to expand its appeal to all members of the white race and then attempt to enlarge the boundaries of the nation to encompass black groups" (60).

6. Incorporating Christian doctrine, Afrikaner nationalism framed Afrikaners as God's chosen people. Nationalist tenets framed the Great Trek into the South African interior away from the British-controlled Cape Colony in the 1830s–1840s as comparable to the Israelites' trek out of Egypt, which Afrikaner nationalists interpreted as evidence that they were God's "chosen people" (Dubow 1992, 219).

7. The social construction of blackness as heterosexual influenced African nationalism and contributed to nationalist homophobia (Epprecht 2005).

8. Before apartheid, interracial sex was "socially discouraged but not outlawed"; apartheid policy "banned all sexual relations between whites and other racial groups between 1950 and 1988" (Goldberg 2002, 85).

9. *Health club* was a white gay euphemism in Johannesburg for a place where white gay men could meet other men for sex (Galli and Rafael 1995, 135).

10. I intentionally use the terms *lesbian and gay* and *LGBT* to indicate historical shifts in LGBT organizing in including individuals and issues that did not map neatly onto *gay* and *lesbian*.

11. In 1912, black men and women formed the South African Native National Congress in Bloemfontein; this group later became the ANC (Meli 1988).

12. A group of mental health professionals publicly objected to lawmakers' efforts

to increase penalties for same-sex sexual behavior (Jones 2008). However, psychiatrists who supported the decriminalization of same-sex sexuality insisted that same-sex sexuality was an illness in need of treatment; they argued that with treatment, lesbians and gay men could be cured of homosexuality and become heterosexual (Epprecht 2008; Jones 2008). Some psychiatrists also assisted the military by treating lesbian and gay military personnel. In some cases, psychiatrists and other physicians affiliated with the South African Defence Force (SADF) used aversion shock and hormonal therapies to treat lesbians and gay men (Jones 2008), even resorting to genital reassignment surgeries to change gay men's and lesbians' sexualities by changing their genders (Swarr 2003). These abuses came to light during the Truth and Reconciliation Commission hearings that occurred between 1996 and 1998 (van Zyl et al. 1999).

13. Parliamentary debate also included a "brief discussion of lesbianism" (Jones 2008, 404). Subjecting white lesbians to controlling visibility, lawmakers discussed lesbians "in terms of their sexual activity, looks, and butch role-playing" (Retief 1995, 103). Legislators worried that white lesbians did not conform to Afrikaner nationalist expectations about white femininity, heterosexual marriage, and motherhood (McClintock 1995).

14. In "gayle," what Ken Cage (2003, 81) labels South African gay slang, *mandy* means "to masturbate."

15. Lesbians remained a numerical minority and were not as visible in GASA and other gay movement organizations because some lesbian feminists opted to participate in "women-centred and women-only organisations" (Armour and Lapinsky 1995, 299). Some lesbian movement organizations disintegrated because lesbians hesitated to "work on issues that [had] to do with lesbians alone," as this form of identity-based organizing forced "black and white women . . . to ignore other forms of oppression" (Armour and Lapinsky 1995, 299). Black lesbians were reluctant to join white lesbian organizations "not only because they felt excluded, but also because exposing themselves as lesbians may have alienated them from their more conservative black comrades" in the antiapartheid movement (Jara and Lapinsky 1998, 51). Lesbians who remained active in gay movement organizations had to deal with gay men's sexism, which persisted through the 1990s. Speaking about her experience in the black-led Gays and Lesbians of the Witwatersrand in the 1980s and early 1990s, Beverley Palesa Ditsie, a black lesbian activist, asserted that gay men in the organization did not see "lesbians as women. . . . If they had seen us as women then they would have had to deal with their own sexism" (Mbali 2008, 188).

16. Gevisser (1995, 57) explains that after ILGA granted RGO membership, RGO "was never heard of again, and Machela now lives in Stockholm."

17. In 1983, the UDF emerged as an umbrella organization of "local civic and professional groups" that mobilized against apartheid and for nonracial democracy (Marx 1992, 14).

18. The ANC's vision of nonracialism involved eliminating institutionalized and individual forms of racism, dismantling official racial-categorization schema, implementing racial integration through policy initiatives, and creating a "universal nation, based on equality and belonging" (MacDonald 2006, 108).

19. The "largely-black" Association of Bisexuals, Gays, and Lesbians (ABIGALE) was one of the first lesbian and gay movement organizations to include bisexual persons when it emerged in 1992 in Cape Town (Achmat and Raizenberg 2003; Bullington and Swarr 2010; Gevisser and Reid 1995, 279). The group foundered when disputes between black and coloured members materialized (Gevisser 2000). Although ABIGALE and other organizations included bisexual persons, there has been little organizing specifically around bisexual issues (Stobie 2007). Instead, bisexual issues were subsumed within lesbian and gay activism, particularly with respect to same-sex sexual practices and relationships.

20. The march has taken place each year in Johannesburg since 1990 (de Waal and Manion 2006). Cape Town began to stage its own march in 1993, but interest in the event waned in the 1990s; the event resumed in 2001 (Tucker 2009, 172). From 2002 until 2004, organizers relocated the Johannesburg Pride March from downtown Johannesburg to Zoo Lake, which is situated near the white northern suburbs of Rosebank, Saxonwold, and Parkview, a decision that alienated many black lesbians and gay men; in 2004, organizers charged attendees a fee to access commercial venues associated with Pride, a move that some activists viewed as exclusionary (de Waal and Manion 2006).

21. The court initially convicted Madikizela-Mandela of four charges of kidnapping and being an accessory to the crime of assault in May 1991, but an appeals court only upheld the kidnapping convictions and ordered her to serve a two-year suspended service and to pay fines to the courts and the three young men who survived the ordeal (Holmes 1997).

22. The EC (Section 9:3–4) states, "3. The state may not unfairly discriminate directly or indirectly against anyone on one or more grounds, including race, gender, sex, pregnancy, marital status, ethnic or social origin, colour, sexual orientation, age, disability, religion, conscience, belief, culture, language and birth. 4. No person may unfairly discriminate directly or indirectly against anyone on one or more grounds in terms of subsection (3). National legislation must be enacted to prevent or prohibit unfair discrimination" (Republic of South Africa 1996).

23. This was the earliest reference to "lesbian, gay, bisexual, and transgender" that I found in the South African LGBT movement.

24. A 1995 national survey of South Africans revealed that only 38 percent favored lesbian and gay rights, and 41 percent believed homosexuality was un-African (Reid and Dirsuweit 2002). Those who supported lesbian and gay rights "were more likely to be white, literate, from urban areas, Catholic, Hindu, or Protestant, and younger

than those who were against gay rights," suggesting that older South Africans and black persons who lived in rural areas and had little education were likely to oppose LGBT rights (Massoud 2003, 304). In a national survey of social attitudes in post-apartheid South Africa, multiracial respondents ranked "homosexuals" as the third most hated group in the country (Gibson and Gouws 2003, 49–50). Participants from different racial and ethnic groups ranked the "Afrikaner Weerstandsbeweging (Afrikaner Resistance Movement, AWB), a far-right movement," as the most hated group and the Inkatha Freedom Party, an opposition party that clashed violently with the ANC during the democratic transition, as the second most hated group (Gibson and Gouws 2003, 18–9, 49).

25. ANC support for LGBT rights had limits, which contributed to the NCGLE's treatment of other political parties also as target audiences (Croucher 2002). In 1997, Minister of Justice Dullah Omar withheld support for the NCGLE's legal campaign demanding the decriminalization of sodomy (Daniels 1997). Omar expressed reticence about honoring the NCGLE's demand owing to "technical rather than ideological concerns"; he also wanted to ensure that the decriminalization of sodomy would not erode children's rights, a claim the NCGLE stated was unfounded (Blignaut and Prabhakaran 1997). An NCGLE spokesperson, Mazibuko Jara, stated that this campaign was "the first time that the South African courts are being challenged by a proud and assertive lesbian and gay movement to get rid of antiquated laws" (Powers 1997). Jara's comment indicated that ANC leaders' opposition would not deter LGBT activists' campaigns. The NCGLE's campaign culminated in a 1998 Constitutional Court decision that struck down the antisodomy law (Goodman 2001). The Department of Home Affairs also opposed the NCGLE's 1999 campaign to get the state to grant the same-sex partners of South African citizens permanent residency (Berger 2008). Later in 1999, the Constitutional Court ruled in favor of the NCGLE's demand (Berger 2008). That the NCGLE had to sue to obtain these rights for LGBT persons supports Gevisser's (2000, 121) argument that "if there is going to be full equality for gays and lesbians in South Africa, it will come from the judicial system, in its application of the constitution, and not from the ANC lawmakers in parliament." In principle, ANC leaders supported LGBT rights, but in practice, ANC lawmakers objected to fully implementing the EC.

26. Scholars have criticized other elements of the South African LGBT movement. Jacklyn Cock (2003, 35) contends that the movement is not a "representative or mass-based movement." For Teresa Dirsuweit (2006, 331), that the LGBT movement is not a mass-based movement is evident in "how few people are involved" in movement activities, which is due both to proliferating niche-activist organizations and "a sense of lulled apathy" among constituents because the constitution guarantees their equality (see also Oswin 2007, 660). Political demobilization is not confined to LGBT constituents. Scholars have documented this trend in different South African movements

(Hassim 2005; Mattes 2002). I am wary of comparing forms of contemporary LGBT activism to the heyday of mass antiapartheid organizing, given the massive changes in the South African sociopolitical field. The time of antiapartheid organizing has passed. However, effervescent organizing has emerged in rural communities and urban townships as groups contest the effects of neoliberal privatization on their lives (Ballard, Habib, and Valodia 2006; Robins 2008; Zuern 2011). It is also important to note that these criticisms resemble some social movement theorists' concerns about the effect of professionalization on social movements. A consequence of professionalized movements is that they can become disconnected from, less visible to, and less accountable to their constituents, a criticism that is unlikely to disappear soon.

27. Organizations that belonged to the JWG in 2005 included FEW, Behind the Mask, the Gay and Lesbian Archives, OUT LGBT Well-Being, the Triangle Project, the Durban Gay and Lesbian Community and Health Centre, and the University of South Africa's Applied Psychology unit. Membership was expanded in 2006 to include other organizations.

28. Zackie Achmat, a prominent gay rights activist, formed the Treatment Action Campaign (TAC) in 1998 in South Africa to demand access to treatment for persons living with HIV/AIDS (Robins 2008). TAC publicly contested the government's refusal to dispense antiretroviral (ARV) treatments to persons living with HIV/AIDS (Robins 2008). TAC publicly challenged President Thabo Mbeki's AIDS denialism, a position that held that "HIV is harmless and . . . AIDS symptoms are caused by malnutrition, drug abuse and even ARVs themselves" (Nattrass 2008, 159).

29. "Ovambo" is also spelled "Owambo."

30. I selectively address events and groups that affected the outcome of Namibian independence. This is not an exhaustive account of the Namibian national liberation movement.

31. SWAPO received 57 percent of the vote for NA seats in 1989; it won 74 percent of the NA seats in 1994 and 76 percent in 1999, although this latter figure diminished slightly in 2004 (Melber 2007, 65).

32. Conversations with Namibian activists led me to believe that individual lesbian and gay Namibians negotiated with lawmakers to get the sexual orientation nondiscrimination clause included in the Labour Act.

33. Lorway (2008a, 31) refers to SCOG as the "Social Committee of Gays," but in an interview, Rina referred to this group as the "Social Club of Gays."

34. Henriette Gunkel (2010, 46) points out that in some African political circles, Zimbabwe represents "the symbol of decolonization on the African continent."

35. SWAPO officials disagreed about sex and the distribution of condoms in men's prisons. In 1995, Prisons and Correctional Services Minister Marco Hausiku (SWAPO) warned male prisoners not to "engage in sodomy" (Nguaiko 1995, 7). In 1996, despite climbing HIV infection rates among male prisoners, Hausiku forbade

supplying prisoners with condoms because it would have been "like encouraging homosexuality" (Mutikani 1996, 1). He attributed sex between male prisoners to staff shortages; if the prisons had more guards, they would "be in a position to control" prisoners and ensure that they did not have sex (Mutikani 1996, 1). Prisons and Correctional Services Deputy Minister Michaela Hübschle (SWAPO) disagreed with Hausiku's policy. Recognizing that there was a "sub-culture of homosexuality in prisons" and that prisoners forged "homosexual relationships in prison," Hübschle supported distributing condoms to male prisoners (Mutikani 1996, 1). In 1997, Minister of Health and Social Services Libertine Amathila endorsed distributing condoms in prisons and stated, "We must face reality—sexual activity is occurring in prisons and this will continue. By distributing condoms we are not encouraging sodomy, but are rather attempting to contain the spread of HIV/AIDS" (Nel 1997, 3). Hübschle also favored decriminalizing sodomy so that prisons could legally distribute condoms to prisoners (Tibinyane 1999).

36. Namibia "inherited" the antisodomy law as part of Roman-Dutch common law that was operative in the country before independence (Hubbard 2007, 120). Two statutes governed sex between men: the "sodomy" statute made anal sex between men illegal, and the "unnatural sexual offices" statute criminalized "mutual masturbation," thigh sex, and other sexual activities between men (Hubbard 2007, 120). Dianne Hubbard (2007, 120) explains that antisodomy legislation was gendered and affected only men who have sex with men. She speculates that women who have sex with women were legally invisible, perhaps because of Namibian women's social marginalization and the low number of "court cases dealing with lesbians."

37. This matter resurfaced in May 2004, when Justice Minister Albert Kawana repeated that same-sex sexualities were "illegal and criminal" during an NA debate about including a clause in the new Labour Bill prohibiting discrimination on the basis of sexual orientation (Dentlinger 2004). Labor law no longer includes this provision (Fenwick 2006).

38. *Moffie* became popularized among Western Cape Coloured gay communities in South Africa in the 1950s. The word originated as "sailor slang" in 1929, as a derivation from "morphy . . . a term of contempt among seamen for effeminate, well-groomed young men" (Cage 2003, 83). The term was used by gay men to valorize and recognize other gay men but could also be deployed pejoratively, as it was in Ekandjo's statement.

2. "This Lesbian Issue"

1. *Heteropatriarchy* refers to the "social power structure that creates and maintains the heterosexist binary of masculinity and femininity and the associated social expectations (gender performances) determined according to biological sex" (Elder 2003, 4). In contexts in which the state is invested in policing gender and sexuality,

heteropatriarchy allows "a homosocial, homophobic, and, in a real sense, bankrupt state to position itself as patriarchal savior to women, to citizens, to the economy, and to the nation" (Alexander 2005, 64). Thus, it makes sense that heteropatriarchy goes hand in hand with heteronormativity.

2. Conversely, decoupling lesbian rights from women's rights has enabled women's movements to silence critics, to curry favor with state actors, and to prove their racial and cultural authenticity (McFadden 2003; Tamale 2007). Not all African women's rights organizations shun lesbian rights publicly. Aili Mari Tripp (2006, 52) notes that at a 2004 conference about lesbian and gay rights in Uganda, "feminists were visible in discussing how to decriminalize homosexuality." Nevertheless, embracing lesbian rights can produce notoriety for feminist movement organizations, leading to an uncontrollable hypervisibility.

3. I use the term *antilesbian violence* to encompass corrective rape and other forms of violence directed at women because they are lesbians. Some South African LGBT activists have made compelling arguments against using the term *corrective rape,* which they believe prevents individuals, institutions, and state agencies from seeing antilesbian violence as part of a larger trend of gender-based violence (Anguita 2011).

4. Strategic orientations emerge organically from the choices activists make for the movement organization, but not all strategic orientations are planned. Activists may make choices that accrue into an unintentional strategic orientation that makes them more likely to select certain options and not to consider others. The meaning and content of strategic orientations are particular to the field in which a movement operates and contingent on cultural, political, historical, and geographic factors.

5. Lorway (2006, 2010) has documented the emergence of violence directed at LGBT persons in Namibia. While stories of violence circulated among Namibian LGBT activists while I observed Sister Namibia and TRP, anti-LGBT violence in Namibia was not as diffuse as it was in South Africa. In addition, although SWAPO leaders' antigay remarks instigated harassment and violence, these incidents appeared to be isolated. I do not deny a causal link between political homophobia and anti-LGBT hostility in Namibia; however, anti-LGBT violence did not materialize as a specter governing social interactions in the way it did in South Africa.

6. I am not implying that African feminisms are, by definition, insular and exclusive. In fact, some African feminists promoted African feminism as sensitive to and inclusive of African men (Mikell 1997). This strategy emerged partially out of feminists' efforts to preempt or undermine antifeminist sentiments alleging that African feminism was Western, un-African, and hostile to African men (Fallon 2008).

7. Toward the end of 1996, Ditsie (2006) founded Nkateko with several other GLOW members because they "felt that white men and women were dominating" GLOW (Gevisser 2000, 133). In Nkateko's first few months, members deliberated how to address homophobia, violence, homelessness, and coming out as "lesbian" (Shongwe

2006, 102). Nkateko's "strong presence" at the 1997 Pride March in Johannesburg elicited much interest from black lesbians (Shongwe 2006, 102). Apparently, Nkateko grew so rapidly that there were no structures in place to handle members' multiple needs, resulting in the group's demise (Shongwe 2006). Another lesbian organization, Sistahs Kopanang, emerged in the mid- to late 1990s (Bullington and Swarr 2010). According to FEW staff members who participated in the defunct group, Sistahs Kopanang folded because it lacked leadership and a clear vision of the content of lesbian organizing (Lindiwe, interview with the author, February 14, 2006). Bonnie, a black lesbian and FEW member, also attributed the group's demise to infighting and class conflicts (interview with the author, March 24, 2006).

8. Like other scholars, I understand antilesbian violence as both homophobic and misogynistic violence stemming from colonial- and apartheid-era inequalities (Gqola 2007; Muholi 2004). I also focus my discussion on violence in African communities, not to imply that they are more violent than white, Asian Indian, or coloured communities but because FEW worked with black constituents. Awareness of antilesbian violence dates back to the 1990s. A black lesbian interviewed by Tanya Chan Sam (1995, 187) recalled that the "Jackrollers [a notorious Soweto gang] targeted black lesbians for rape; she stated that 'when they catch one they say, "We'll put you right"'" (see also Wood 2005). In her documentary *Simon & I*, Ditsie recounts her ordeal with threats of antilesbian rape in the township in which she lived; these threats started after she appeared on television as an out lesbian (see also Morgan and Reid 2003).

9. Antigay hate speech is illegal in South Africa. In 2000, lawmakers passed the Promotion of Equality and Prevention of Unfair Discrimination Act, which outlawed hate speech (Reid and Dirsuweit 2002, 108). In 2011, the Johannesburg Equality Court found Jon Qwelane, a former newspaper columnist and the current South African ambassador to Uganda, guilty of antigay hate speech based on a 2008 column (*Mail & Guardian* 2011). Luis Abolafia Anguita (2011) documents the obstacles South African LGBT movement organizations encountered in involving the Commission for Gender Equality and South African Human Rights Commission in antilesbian-violence initiatives.

10. Of the forty-seven black lesbians Zanele Muholi (2004, 118) interviewed, twenty were raped because of their perceived gender and sexual transgression, seventeen were "physically assaulted (3 with a weapon)," eight experienced physical abuse, four survived attempted rape, and two were kidnapped; twenty-nine of these women "knew their attackers and only 16 reported these hate crimes to the police." Since 2006, several black lesbians have been raped and murdered (Tshabalala 2008). On July 7, 2007, Sizakele Sigasa and Salome Massooa, two lesbian activists, were found raped and murdered in Soweto; their murders sparked the formation of the 07–07–07 campaign by the JWG to stop violence against gender and sexual minorities (Hassim 2009a; Nel and Judge 2008). FEW was involved in this campaign (Anguita 2011).

In April 2008, Eudy Simelane, a member of Banyana Banyana, the national women's soccer team, was murdered (*Mail & Guardian* 2009). On April 24, 2011, Noxolo Nogwaza, a black lesbian activist, was murdered in KwaThema, a township outside of Johannesburg (Bryson 2011).

11. Police and media were slow to respond to Nkonyana's death. Glenn de Swardt of the Triangle Project stated that "the gay community is also to blame" for the delay in investigating her murder (Thamm 2006). He admitted that if the *Sunday Times* had not contacted him about "an unrelated gay issue around the time [he] heard about her funeral," then "it would have been just another murder in Khayelitsha" (Thamm 2006).

12. In discussions and interviews with staff and members about why antilesbian violence occurred, I got the impression that perpetrators were nonwhite. Survivors and FEW staff and members attributed the prevalence of violence against black lesbians to intolerance within townships.

13. Perpetrators often targeted butch lesbians with masculine appearances for attack (Kheswa 2005). Lesbians with feminine gender presentations slipped by undetected because observers interpreted their femininity as congruent with their female-sexed bodies (Swarr 2009). Black lesbians might also be recognizable by the language they use. Black South African women who use isiTsotsi, urban street speech, may be perceived as butch lesbians because this argot is customarily used by black South African township men (Rudwick, Nkomo, and Shange 2006).

14. This invisibility extends to antilesbian-violence statistics. Black lesbians in South Africa were hesitant to report violent crime to the police because they feared being further victimized by police, whom many believed would belittle their predicaments (Sebetoane 2011; Wells and Polders 2006).

15. Some black lesbians "found Johannesburg safer [than townships]. Expressing, or acting on an attraction to other women, was seen as less risky in Johannesburg than in a township environment" (Vetten and Dladla 2000, 71). However, "main roads, taxi ranks, bus stops, and railway stations" were unsafe public spaces for black lesbians who had to pass through these areas on their way from Johannesburg to their township homes (Wells and Polders 2006, 24). Some black lesbians reported having little difficulty living openly as lesbians in their families and communities, which suggests that there is "no one, monolithic" narrative of being a black lesbian woman in South Africa (Potgieter 2005, 178).

16. FEW did not block bisexual women from joining but did not zealously recruit them, from what I observed.

17. This term is also spelled *isitabane* and *stabane* (Hunter 2010, 175; Rankhotha 2005, 165).

18. I explore the Western dimensions of gender and sexual identity terminology in chapter 4.

19. I am not aware of any male-to-female transgender lesbian women who tried

to join FEW. In addition, some lesbians identified as transgender, but FEW staff understood them as lesbians, which granted them access to FEW (Matebeni 2009).

20. While I observed FEW, no South African LGBT movement organization publicly challenged FEW's choices about its membership.

21. Occasionally, white, Asian Indian, and coloured women frequented FEW and attended its public events if they were partners of FEW staff or members. However, these individuals exerted no observable influence on FEW's structure or strategic choices. A notable exception was the chairperson of FEW's executive board, who was a white lesbian and had important connections in the South African LGBT and feminist movements. The executive board seemed to supervise FEW from a distance. I did not observe executive board members openly or directly influencing FEW's daily operations.

22. Celia had been with FEW for a couple of years. It is possible that early in its formation, FEW members were more flexible about membership requirements, but over time, they tightened membership restrictions. I was unable to access FEW's historical documents, which kept me from confirming this hypothesis.

23. Under apartheid, black South Africans found themselves perpetually disadvantaged, whereas "Coloured and Asian Indian groups" were extended "specific rights of self-rule and government in townships and parliament" in 1983 and 1984 (Olzak, Beasley, and Olivier 2002, 30).

24. FEW received $461,539 in one multiyear grant (Espinoza 2007, 9). A report from Funders for Lesbian and Gay Issues does not provide details about the source(s) of this grant (Espinoza 2007). I was not granted access to FEW's internal memoranda and funding applications. It is my understanding that while I observed FEW, it did not receive state funding, though the state might have become a funding source for the organization since 2006.

25. Tours of Constitution Hill passed through the Old Fort and Women's Gaol by FEW's office, but guides accompanied tourists and kept them from disrupting FEW staff. One tour guide was a black lesbian *sangoma,* a spiritual healer (Nkabinde 2009).

26. Bullington and Swarr (2010) observed similar tensions that led to Sistahs Kopanang's disintegration.

27. Establishing a satellite township office was an option that some LGBT movement organizations in other cities had exercised with varying degrees of success. In 1996, the Triangle Project, a Cape Town–based organization, opened a satellite office in Guguletu township to provide counseling services for black gay and bisexual men (Tucker 2009). Instead of using the organization for social services, constituents utilized the space to socialize. Some constituents disliked the notion of frequenting a township office for counseling and preferred traveling to the Triangle Project's main office so that their concerns would not become public knowledge in township social networks (Tucker 2009).

FEW's office in Johannesburg also did not privilege one township over another. Some townships to Johannesburg's north were quite far from townships to the city's south. If members had to travel from a northern township to a southern one, it would have been prohibitively expensive for them because most minibus taxis passed through central Johannesburg and required passengers to change minibus taxis, thus forcing members to pay double the fare. Members who resided in Alexandra, a northern township, for instance, would not be alienated because FEW's office was located in Soweto, a southern township. FEW's central location avoided unduly straining members' material resources. FEW's office was within walking distance from the city's transportation hub, Park Station, which served short- and long-distance buses and trains, although it required constituents and staff to walk through Hillbrow. On more than one occasion, constituents and staff reported being hassled on the street by men and youths because of their visible gender nonconformity.

28. FEW worked with LGBT movement organizations on other campaigns, but during my period of observation, FEW's working relationships with feminist movement organizations were relatively new. FEW sometimes brought survivors of rape or violent attacks to People Opposing Woman Abuse for counseling and other social services (Sebetoane 2011).

29. Butch lesbians who were visitors or prospective members of FEW were often known by staff members and were not miscategorized as men. I neither observed nor heard stories of staff misrecognizing butch lesbians as men.

30. Some black gay men did not identify as transgender but rather as "ladies" (Reid 2005, 213). "Ladies are gay. To be a lady does not mean that you want to be a woman, although some pass quite successfully as women. . . . To be a lady is to be a gay and to be gay is to be socially effeminate and sexually passive" (Reid 2005, 213).

31. One FEW member had survived being raped by a man who told her early in their acquaintance that he was gay (Sebetoane 2011).

32. Staff let me attend the antiviolence workshop but asked me not to observe the small groups in which workshop attendees shared their violent ordeals. Staff worried that my presence as an outsider—a white, middle-class American female researcher—would inhibit an ethos of openness staff hoped to instill in the small groups; I complied with this request. After the small groups concluded their discussions, a representative from each small group summarized in broad strokes the type of violence and harassment that attendees had experienced. However, some attendees narrated in detail stories of violence. The attendee who narrated her cautionary tale of how a heterosexual woman set up her rape seemed to have little difficulty repeating her story in front of the larger group (and me), and I use it here because she intended the story to teach her peers about how to keep themselves safe.

33. Zuma became president of the ANC in December 2007 and president of the Republic of South Africa in May 2009.

34. Zuma's defense outraged HIV/AIDS activists, who participated in the protests. In his characterization of the rape as consensual sex, he claimed that he did not use a condom. He stated that he showered after having sex with the HIV-positive

survivor—herself an HIV/AIDS activist—as a precaution against HIV transmission. Activists accused Zuma of setting back HIV education a decade.

35. Khwezi was wearing a *kanga,* a knee-length piece of fabric fashioned to cover a woman's torso and tied above her breasts, which Zulu women often wore in the privacy of their rooms or homes. As was customary with the *kanga,* Khwezi was not wearing undergarments, which Zuma interpreted as part of her supposed invitation to have sex (Motsei 2007). Zuma also stated that Khwezi suggested that she wanted to have sex with him by confessing that "she was lonely without a partner because of her HIV status" and by permitting him to "give her a massage" (Hassim 2009b, 58).

36. The media did not report Khwezi's name, but Zuma supporters learned her identity and acquired her photograph.

37. The *toyi-toyi* is a boisterous protest tactic composed of dancing and chanting also used in antiapartheid protests (Bozzoli 2004; Seidman 2001).

38. Although FEW's director made most major strategic decisions, she did not control every aspect of staff members' work lives. Community representatives directed their own work in townships, although they reported their progress regularly to the director.

39. Several months after Zuma's acquittal in May 2006, Khwezi went into exile because of the threats she received in connection with the rape trial; her present exile mirrors the childhood she spent in exile with her ANC activist parents (Hassim 2009b). Since Zuma's rape trial, the One in Nine Campaign has monitored how courts handle rape trials and sponsored protests demanding justice for rape survivors. In May 2010, the campaign dropped a banner in front of a building close to the Johannesburg High Court that read, "Four years later, Zuma is President. Khwezi is in exile. Where is the justice?" Protestors with the One in Nine Campaign warned women that the High Court building was "unsafe" for women (*Mail & Guardian* 2010). For more information about the One in Nine Campaign, see the group's website (http://www. oneinnine.org.za/).

40. TRP has consistently obtained funding since 1999–2000 and showed no signs of fiscal weakness in 2006. In contrast, Sister Namibia experienced financial difficulty during the period of my ethnographic observation, as I explain later in this chapter.

41. Ovambos historically practiced gender nonconformity in adulthood rites, notably in girls' passage into womanhood through *efundula,* an initiation ritual (Becker 2004). Young women occupied "'male' roles" temporarily and adopted the "names of great warriors" (Becker 2004, 42). During this ritual, women could travel freely throughout Ovambo territory and "could mock at and beat every man they encountered," including men these women eventually married (Becker 2004, 42). Colonial rule and surveillance from Christian missions disrupted and affected this practice; however, *efundula* persists in the present as a transformed initiation ritual (Becker 2004). Yet SWAPO officials do not seem to recognize the historic

existence of "gender inversion" in *efundula* in Ovambo culture (Becker 2004, 42).

42. According to Elizabeth |Khaxas and Saskia Wieringa (2005, 149), there is no indigenous term for same-sex sexual desire, behavior, or identity in the Damara lexicon.

43. It is noteworthy that Sister Namibia cited a German anthropologist in the defense of homosexuality as an indigenous sexual practice. Kurt Falk (1998) conducted his research at the height of German colonialism. Antigay proponents could have rejected Falk's research out of hand because some anthropologists in the early twentieth century extracted information from indigenous communities so that colonialists could subjugate them more efficiently (Bleys 1995). Sister Namibia risked its reputation by siding with a German anthropologist over SWAPO but favored citing research in support of the position that homosexuality was African, even if the anthropologist was German and had conducted his research during the German occupation of Namibia. In this sense, Sister Namibia members were trying to make the point that homosexuality and Namibian national identity need not be antithetical, but the group could have experienced a backlash for this reason.

44. Sister Namibia's assertion that homophobia was a foreign, colonial import was similar to sentiments expressed by other southern African LGBT activists who alleged that homophobia, not same-sex sexuality, was introduced by European colonialists and Christian missionaries (Epprecht 2004, 2008; Hoad 2007).

45. In a 2002 interview with Gretchen Bauer (2004), former Minister of Health and Social Services Libertine Amathila used lesbian rights to differentiate the Namibian women's movement from Western feminist organizing. She stated, "European women tend to discuss issues like lesbianism and freedom to have sex that we haven't reached here. We haven't reached that yet . . . so I wouldn't say there is any influence on us" from Western feminism (Bauer 2004, 295).

46. See chapter 3 for a discussion of how this lawsuit affected TRP's legal mobilization.

47. State-funded media, such as the newspaper *New Era* and the Namibian Broadcasting Corporation, were under orders from the state not to give LGBT organizing favorable coverage. This ban prevented TRP from having a radio show on the independent KCR in 2002–3 because KCR rented space in a state-owned office building, and the landlord threatened to evict KCR if TRP broadcast its show there. TRP succeeded in getting its own radio show when KCR moved to a privately owned building in Katutura township.

48. Melber (2005) explains that Namibia's classification as a lower-middle-income African country masked deep-seated economic and racial inequalities stemming from the country's colonial and apartheid history. At the time of independence in 1990, the UN classified Namibia as a least developed country, according to Melber (2005). Namibia has one of the highest Gini coefficients in the world (0.707), if not the highest (CIA 2011). The Gini coefficient measures individual income inequality on

a scale of 0 to 1, where 0 refers to total income equality and 1 refers to total income inequality (Melber 2005, 318). Namibia's high Gini coefficient attests to dramatic income variation among different ethnic groups, suggesting that there is much social justice work to be done (Susser 2009).

3. Disappearing Acts

1. Judith Stacey (2011) offers a compelling look at the parallels between same-sex and polygamous marriage legislation in South Africa.

2. Representatives from LGBT movement organizations did attend a meeting in February 2006 sponsored by the South African Council of Churches (SACC) to discuss the Constitutional Court ruling on same-sex marriage (Raubenheimer 2006). SACC, not LGBT movement organizations, initiated this meeting. SACC and other Christian leaders joined forces in 2006 with "traditional leaders from polygamous South African cultures" to oppose same-sex marriage (Stacey 2011, 97).

3. The JWG met twice a year, usually in March and October. Quotations come from my ethnographic observations of JWG meetings, unless otherwise indicated.

4. This ban dates back at least to 1986, when posters placed in Natal province advised gay men not to give blood (Mbali 2008).

5. The GLA acquired the reputation among LGBT activists for being a front for a white gay man, Juan-Duval Uys. Between 1998 and 2006, LGBT movement organizations publicly disputed the GLA's existence, discredited it as a representative of the LGBT movement, and discounted its outlandish claims (Currier 2010b).

6. The GLA's leader condemned the meeting LGBT activists had with the SANBS and SABTS because of the composition of meeting attendees. He contended that since the blood-donation ban only affected men who have sex with men, they were best equipped to resolve the matter. He claimed in a nonsensical manner typical of GLA press releases, "One cannot expect any results when you have lesbians consulting on an issue that discriminates against gay men.... Whoever decided on lesbians to consult on behalf of gay men clearly lack basic human intelligence and should be tested without any delay for bird flue [sic]" (GLA press release, February 17, 2006).

7. Stacey (2011, 96, 103) observes that only "indigenous black" LGBT South Africans "have a constitutional basis to press for a right to plural marriage," owing to a history of polygamous arrangements in South Africa that accommodated same-sex relationships. Her interviews with four Constitutional Court justices revealed that they believed that this history could "sustain a bid for including same-sex marriage within the definition of an indigenous African tradition" and for allowing black lesbians and gay men access to polygamy (Stacey 2011, 103). Stacey also notes that despite this legal possibility, few LGBT activists had expressed interest in launching such a legal challenge.

8. Whether contemporary same-sex relationships that involve same-sex intimacy qualify for the same kind of cultural recognition as same-sex marriages, such as "woman–woman marriages," which scholars argue did not involve same-sex intimacy, remains hotly contested (Amadiume 1987; Bonthuys 2008; Wieringa 2005).

9. Hubbard (2007, 99–100) notes that "all laws in force at the date of independence remain in force until they are explicitly repealed or amended by Parliament, or declared unconstitutional by a competent court."

10. A Namibian newspaper article states that Frank's bid for permanent residency began in 1995 (Menges 2001b).

11. Details of TRP's involvement with NANGOF's Human Rights and Democracy sector came from my interviews and informal conversations with Johannes.

12. Stefan, a coloured gay man and TRP member, found TRP's office location in 2006 on Love Street ironic, not just because of the street's name, but also because of its proximity to Parliament and the president's home (interview with the author, June 28, 2006). Stefan stated, "When I found out that TRP moved to Love Street [from its downtown location], I asked myself, 'Isn't Love Street behind the President's house?' [Stefan laughs.] And, yes, Love Street is behind the President's house. And I asked myself, 'Wow, God, when is he [Nujoma] going to bomb those poor people?'" TRP did not experience problems related to the office's proximity to state landmarks.

13. According to Lorway (2008b, 82), in 1998, TRP received funding from the "Swedish International Development Agency, the Heinrich Böll Foundation based in Germany, and Mama Cash and HIVOS of the Netherlands."

4. Homosexuality *Is* African

1. By putting "African" in quotation marks, I recognize an intellectual tradition of African and Africanist scholarship documenting the social construction of "Africa" (Hoad 2007; Mudimbe 1988).

2. Adjudicating authenticity relies on appeals to essentialism. Emily S. Lee (2011, 259) recognizes that claims that individuals are inauthentic arise out of an "epistemic incongruity, a lack of correspondence between an image . . . and the embodiment" and actions of individuals whose group membership becomes questioned. To rejoin the group from which they have been exiled, maligned individuals may deploy essentialism strategically to emphasize their group membership. Gayatri Spivak (1987) has advanced this as a strategic possibility for marginalized groups trying to improve their social, political, and economic circumstances. I am less concerned with the perils of pursuing strategic essentialism, pitfalls that postcolonial feminist theorists have thoroughly documented, than I am with exposing how activists' actions can undercut their public appeals to racial, cultural, or national authenticity (Lee 2011).

3. Other social movement studies discuss authenticity in terms of reconciling one's interior self with public identifiers; LGBT activists in the United States have

used the language of authenticity when discussing the coming-out process in terms of using identity categories that accurately express one's interior gendered or sexual self (Armstrong 2002). Journalists look for "authenticity" in raw, unpolished performances offered by activists (Sobieraj 2011). Authenticity can also refer to how realistically—close to life—activists portray their grievances based on life experiences.

4. I treat these organizations racially as "African" in two ways. First, staff positions at all four organizations in question were held by a majority of black and coloured Namibians and South Africans of African descent, with the exception of a white lesbian at TRP, a white lesbian at Sister Namibia, and a white bisexual woman at Behind the Mask. Second, staff and members of these organizations regarded the majority of their constituents as black Africans.

5. Hakan Seckinelgin (2009, 104) asked a similar question when he interviewed an East African LGBT activist in 2007. The activist acknowledged that few Africans used the LGBT acronym, but he admitted to preferring it "because it is the international language. I have been going to regional meetings and it is their language. [The language] makes us part of the larger [international] group for the possibility of funding and support when we need it. But people, no, they don't really use LGBTI, even men who are talking to us, it takes some time before they call themselves gay." Using such rhetoric put African activists in touch with Western ideas and human rights frameworks and permitted them to access funding opportunities more easily. The supremacy of English as a language and Western nomenclature gives some queer scholars pause. They view this supremacy as cultural imperialism, forcing activists to sacrifice elements of their political projects to achieve intelligibility and influence in Western political circuits (Hoad 2007; Massad 2002).

6. Recent research illustrates the coexistence of complex lesbian and gay languages in Namibia and South Africa influenced by indigenous African and European languages (Cage 2003; Lorway 2008a, 2008b; Rudwick, Nkomo, and Shange 2006).

7. Astraea Lesbian Foundation is a U.S.-based philanthropic agency that provides "cash funding" to "lesbian led, LGBTI and progressive organisations" (Samelius and Wågberg 2005, 30, 65).

8. It may also have been difficult for Behind the Mask to obtain funding because it did not directly represent a set of constituents in the ways FEW and TRP did. Funders prioritized programs that directly improved the lives of individuals. Behind the Mask managed to secure Northern funding through Willem, a white gay man and former Behind the Mask director (interview with the author, October 25, 2005).

9. Scholars are critical of unequal Northern donor–Southern recipient relationships (Sperling, Ferree, and Risman 2001). Some contend that donor characterizations of these relationships as "partnerships" are misleading (Nzegwu 2002, 2–3). Many movement organizations experience difficulty satisfying donors' expectations for spending funds and submitting reports. This bureaucracy can be especially cumbersome for activists

who know little about accounting, grant writing, and recordkeeping (Britton 2006). Owing to reporting inconsistencies, donors were wary of new groups because of their experiences with recipients' financial mismanagement. For example, South African recipients found that donors' bureaucratic "requirements were a distraction from their real work, confusing, redundant, or destructive" (Bornstein 2006, 54). Namibian and South African LGBT movement organizations became involved with foreign donors within this circuit of power.

Feminist and social movement scholars express differing opinions about the funding and professionalization—the NGO-ization—of movement organizations in the global South (Alvarez 1998; Guenther 2011; Thayer 2009). Some feminists claim that funding can sustain gender and sexuality movements when public support wanes (Staggenborg 1988; Taylor 1989) and enhance a movement's success (Raeburn 2004; Seidman 1999; Viterna and Fallon 2008). Other feminists worry that if movements obtain funding from the state or from foreign donors, funders may attach demands to funding that deradicalize feminist activism and render movements increasingly reliant on foreign funding (Bulbeck 2007; Matthews 1995; Nzegwu 2002; Reinelt 1995).

10. It may seem hypocritical that some antigay opponents derided LGBT movement organizations for obtaining funding from Northern donors when, in fact, Northern donor assistance has been an important part of the postapartheid sociopolitical landscape in Namibia and South Africa (Ballard, Habib, and Valodia 2006; Melber 2005). However, I understand antigay opponents' criticism of LGBT activists' procurement of Northern funding as one element of their campaign to besmirch the reputation and visibility of LGBT movement organizations.

11. According to Samelius and Wågberg (2005, 30), Hivos, a Dutch NGO, financed "HIV prevention" and work with men who have sex with men. As a former antiapartheid organization, Hivos maintained a financial and political commitment to organizations in southern Africa (http://www.hivos.nl/). The Ford Foundation's East Africa Office funded this investigation through its "Education, Sexuality, and Religion program," which aimed to "build knowledge, develop policy and deepen public understanding of sexuality and its relationship to human fulfillment, culture, religion, and identity" (Kiragu and Nyong'o 2005, 41). My data come from interviews and informal conversations with key Behind the Mask and TRP members and from organizational documents.

12. It is possible that the Ford Foundation declined to fund Behind the Mask's proposal because Ford was focusing on East African initiatives and shifting funding away from more affluent southern African nations. In 2006, Namibian LGBT movement organizations found themselves in a similar funding bind when European countries decided to stop funding Namibian initiatives after the World Bank reclassified the country's economic status, which I discussed in the previous chapter.

13. Johannes described how GALZ and the NCGLE supported TRP's development through mentoring: "[GALZ and the NCGLE] were very actively involved in helping us strategizing and doing workshops . . . so that we could acquire the skills that were necessary in helping us understand the political landscape as it was unfolding in Namibia and helping us understand why we should not be tackling some laws and giving some attention to other[s]. . . . So in that sense they were really invaluable to us." The NCGLE played an especially significant role by advising TRP to pursue the decriminalization of sodomy cautiously from a position of protected visibility; a public decriminalization campaign might have provoked a repressive backlash from SWAPO leaders.

14. According to a Behind the Mask member, her organization had "strong contacts" in Namibia, Zambia, Botswana, Kenya, Uganda, Tanzania, Rwanda, Burundi, Ghana, and Sierra Leone; places in which she hoped Behind the Mask would develop more contacts included Ethiopia, Nigeria, and North Africa (interview with the author, November 1, 2005).

15. Interestingly, the reactions the leaders of Behind the Mask and TRP had to intramovement competition for funding differ from how South African organizations fighting violence against women competed for funding (Britton 2006). Similar to Chasin's (2000) concerns about the competition for funding and corporate sponsorship in the U.S. LGBT movement, Hannah Britton (2006, 155) finds that jostling for limited funding threatened "to pit women's organizations against each other, undermining the chances for a broad women's movement and jeopardizing the networking potential of many fledgling groups."

16. Whether member nations complied with the ACHPR's request was another matter altogether.

17. Ethnographic data, including quotations from meeting participants, come from my observation of this meeting, which took place on February 21, 2006, at Behind the Mask's office.

18. See Saiz (2004) for a discussion of the UN's historic silence on LGBT human rights violations. On June 17, 2011, the UN Human Rights Council adopted a declaration supporting LGBT rights and established a UN mechanism for documenting LGBT human rights abuses worldwide. The South African delegation to the UN sponsored the declaration, a move seen by some commentators as trying to ease African political opposition to LGBT rights (Jordans 2011).

19. Also see the International Gay and Lesbian Human Rights Commission (2006a, 2006b, 2007) reports on the proposed Nigerian legislation, which lawmakers passed late in 2011 (Awoniyi 2011). The legalization of same-sex marriage in South Africa affected LGBT organizing in other African nations (Judge et al. 2008b), suggesting a transnational "spillover effect" in African LGBT organizing (Meyer and Whittier 1994, 278).

20. A 1995 South African Constitutional Court ruling abolished the death penalty on the grounds that it was "contrary to the country's interim constitution" (Schabas 2002, 356).

21. In 1993, ILGA obtained consultative status on LGBT issues with ECOSOC. Consultative status permits NGOs "access to UN proceedings, presence at conferences, and rights to propose agenda items" (Mertus 2007, 1040). In 1994, ILGA lost its ECOSOC status after U.S. Senator Jesse Helms initiated a smear campaign that exposed the North American Man–Boy Love Association's (NAMBLA) membership in ILGA (Gamson 1997). In 2006, the United States and other countries asked ECOSOC not to hear the applications of ILGA and another LGBT organization for consultative status (Mertus 2007). "This was the first time in its history that [ECOSOC] . . . dismissed the application of [an NGO] without the hearings usually given to applicants. The US action was a reversal of policy, as it had voted for ILGA observer status in 2002" (Marks 2006, 36). In 2006, ECOSOC extended consultative status to ILGA-Europe. In July 2011, ECOSOC voted to reinstate ILGA's consultative status; the Namibian representative voted against the measure (International Lesbian and Gay Association 2011).

22. This test is under way within the continental LGBT movement. When news that same-sex marriage was legal in South Africa reached Kenya, Lourence Misedah, a Kenyan LGBT activist, explained that he and other activists would not seek to replicate the South African marriage-equality campaign. Emphasizing the importance of indigenous mobilization for same-sex marriage in Kenya, he stated, "We want Kenyans to see things in our context and know that we are Kenyans and not South Africans. . . . [T]hen they will not see gay and lesbian rights as an imported thing" (Judge et al. 2008b, 306).

Methodological Appendix

1. I confined my search to English-language newspapers in Namibia and South Africa because most LGBT activists interacted with the media in English. In addition, I do not speak Afrikaans, German, or indigenous African languages. I am unable to comment on trends in newspaper publishing about homosexuality or LGBT organizing in publications in these languages.

2. GALA's name changed to Gay and Lesbian Memory in Action in 2006.

3. Although LGBT movement organizations maintained a presence in Namibian and South African townships, at the time I initiated this study, I could find no LGBT movement organization solely based in Johannesburg or Windhoek townships.

4. Pinning my hopes to FEW was admittedly risky. FEW could have turned down my request to study the organization at any time. Because FEW appeared to be the only LGBT movement organization in South Africa working solely with black lesbians and on corrective rape in 2005, I believed it was worth the risk and investment of my time to continue trying to obtain permission to observe the organization.

Works Cited

Aarmo, Margrete. 1999. "How Homosexuality Became 'Un-African': The Case of Zimbabwe." In *Female Desires: Same-Sex Relations and Transgender Practices across Cultures,* ed. E. Blackwood and S. E. Wieringa, 255–80. New York: Columbia University Press.

Achmat, Taghmeda, and Theresa Raizenberg. 2003. "Midi and Theresa: Lesbian Activism in South Africa." *Feminist Studies* 29, no. 3: 643–51.

Achmat, Zackie. 1993. "'Apostles of Civilised Vice': 'Immoral Practices' and 'Unnatural Vice' in South African Prisons and Compounds, 1890–1920." *Social Dynamics* 19, no. 2: 92–110.

———. 1996. "That Banner: Not Particularly Funny nor Radical!" *Exit* 83: 10.

Adam, Barry D., Jan Willem Duyvendak, and André Krouwel. 1999. "Gay and Lesbian Movements beyond Borders?" In *The Global Emergence of Gay and Lesbian Politics: National Imprints of a Worldwide Movement,* ed. B. D. Adam, J. W. Duyvendak, and A. Krouwel, 344–71. Philadelphia: Temple University Press.

Alexander, M. Jacqui. 2005. *Pedagogies of Crossing: Meditations on Feminism, Sexual Politics, Memory, and the Sacred.* Durham, N.C.: Duke University Press.

Alexander, M. Jacqui, and Chandra Talpade Mohanty. 1997. *Feminist Genealogies, Colonial Legacies, Democratic Futures.* New York: Routledge.

Almeida, Paul D. 2003. "Opportunity Organizations and Threat-Induced Contention: Protest Waves in Authoritarian Settings." *American Journal of Sociology* 109, no. 2: 345–400.

Altman, Dennis. 1997. "Global Gaze/Global Gays." *GLQ* 3, no. 4: 417–36.

———. 2001. *Global Sex.* Chicago: University of Chicago Press.

Alvarez, Sonia E. 1998. "Latin American Feminisms 'Go Global': Trends of the 1990s and Challenges for the New Millennium." In *Cultures of Politics, Politics of Cultures: Re-visioning Latin American Social Movements,* ed. S. E. Alvarez, E. Dagnino, and A. Escobar, 293–324. Boulder, Colo.: Westview Press.

Amadiume, Ifi. 1987. *Male Daughters, Female Husbands: Gender and Sex in an African Society.* London: Zed.

Amupadhi, Tangeni. 2000. "Sister Namibia's Office Gutted in Suspected Anti-gay Attack." *Namibian,* July 11. http://allafrica.com/stories/200007120033.html.

Anguita, Luis Abolafia. 2011. "Tackling Corrective Rape in South Africa: The Engagement between LGBT CSOs and the NHRIs (CGE and SAHRC) and Its Role." *International Journal of Human Rights.* http://dx.doi.org/10.1080/13642987.2011.575054.

Angula, Conrad. 2000. "Ekandjo Faces Vote of No Confidence." *Namibian,* October 4. http://allafrica.com/stories/200010040047.html.

Armour, Mary, and Sheila Lapinsky. 1995. "'Lesbians in Love and in Compromising Situations': Lesbian Feminist Organising in the Western Cape." In *Defiant Desire: Gay and Lesbian Lives in South Africa,* ed. M. Gevisser and E. Cameron, 295–300. New York: Routledge.

Armstrong, Elizabeth A. 2002. *Forging Gay Identities: Organizing Sexuality in San Francisco, 1950–1994.* Chicago: University of Chicago Press.

Armstrong, Elizabeth A., and Mary Bernstein. 2008. "Culture, Power, and Institutions: A Multi-institutional Politics Approach to Social Movements." *Sociological Theory* 26, no. 1: 74–99.

Arnfred, Signe, ed. 2004. *Re-thinking Sexualities in Africa.* Uppsala, Sweden: Nordic Africa Institute.

Auerbach, Carl F., and Louise B. Silverstein. 2003. *Qualitative Data: An Introduction to Coding and Analysis.* New York: New York University Press.

Awondo, Patrick. 2010. "The Politicisation of Sexuality and Rise of Homosexual Movements in Post-Colonial Cameroon." *Review of African Political Economy* 37, no. 125: 315–28.

Awoniyi, Ola. 2011. "Nigeria Slams Critics, Hustles Anti-gay Law through Parliament." *Mail & Guardian,* December 8. http://mg.co.za/article/2011-12-08-nigerias-antigay-bill-forced-through-despite-opposition.

Ayanda. 2006. "My First Thought Was That She Had Been Shot." In *Pride: Protest and Celebration,* ed. S. de Waal and A. Manion, 172. Johannesburg: Jacana.

Bacchetta, Paola. 2002. "Rescaling Transnational 'Queerdom': Lesbian and 'Lesbian' Identitary-Positionalities in Delhi in the 1980s." *Antipode* 34, no. 5: 947–73.

Ballard, Richard, Adam Habib, and Imraan Valodia, eds. 2006. *Voices of Protest: Social Movements in Post-apartheid South Africa.* Scottsville, South Africa: University of KwaZulu-Natal Press.

Baraka, Nancy, with Ruth Morgan. 2005. "'I Want to Marry the Woman of My Choice without Fear of Being Stoned': Female Marriages and Bisexual Women in Kenya." In *Tommy Boys, Lesbian Men, and Ancestral Wives: Female Same-Sex Practices in Africa,* ed. R. Morgan and S. E. Wieringa, 25–50. Johannesburg: Jacana.

Barnard, Ian. 2004. *Queer Race: Cultural Interventions in the Racial Politics of Queer Theory.* New York: Peter Lang.

Bauer, Gretchen. 1998. *Labor and Democracy in Namibia, 1971–1996.* Athens: Ohio University Press.

———. 2001. "Namibia in the First Decade of Independence: How Democratic?" *Journal of Southern African Studies* 27, no. 1: 33–55.

———. 2004. "'The Hand That Stirs the Pot Can Also Run the Country': Electing Women to Parliament in Namibia." *Journal of Modern African Studies* 42, no. 4: 479–509.

Beauchamp, Toby. 2009. "Artful Concealment and Strategic Visibility: Transgender Bodies and U.S. State Surveillance after 9/11." *Surveillance & Society* 6, no. 4: 356–66.

Becker, Heike. 1995. *The Namibian Women's Movement, 1980 to 1992: From Anti-colonial Resistance to Reconstruction.* Frankfurt, Germany: IKO-Verlag für Interkulterelle Kommunikation.

———. 2004. "*Efundula*: Women's Initiation, Gender, and Sexual Identities in Colonial and Post-colonial Northern Namibia." In *Re-thinking Sexualities in Africa,* ed. S. Arnfred, 35–56. Uppsala, Sweden: Nordic Africa Institute.

———. 2006. "'New Things after Independence': Gender and Traditional Authorities in Postcolonial Namibia." *Journal of Southern African Studies* 32, no. 1: 29–48.

———. 2007. "Making History: A Historical Perspective on Gender in Namibia." In *Unravelling Taboos: Gender and Sexuality in Namibia,* ed. S. LaFont and D. Hubbard, 22–38. Windhoek: LAC.

Benford, Robert D., and David A. Snow. 2000. "Framing Processes and Social Movements: An Overview and Assessment." *Annual Review of Sociology* 26: 611–39.

Berger, Jonathan. 2008. "Getting to the Constitutional Court on Time: A Litigation History of Same-Sex Marriage." In *To Have and to Hold: The Making of Same-Sex Marriage in South Africa,* ed. M. Judge, A. Manion, and S. de Waal, 17–41. Johannesburg: Fanele.

Berlant, Lauren, and Michael Warner. 1998. "Sex in Public." *Critical Inquiry* 24, no. 2: 547–66.

Bernstein, Mary. 1997. "Celebration and Suppression: The Strategic Uses of Identity by the Lesbian and Gay Movement." *American Journal of Sociology* 103, no. 3: 531–65.

———. 2005. "Identity Politics." *Annual Review of Sociology* 31: 47–74.

———. 2008. "The Analytic Dimensions of Identity: A Political Identity Framework." In *Identity Work in Social Movements,* ed. J. Reger, D. J. Myers, and R. L. Einwohner, 277–301. Minneapolis: University of Minnesota Press.

Bettcher, Talia Mae. 2007. "Evil Deceivers and Make-Believers: On Transphobic Violence and the Politics of Illusion." *Hypatia* 22, no. 3: 43–65.

Bhabha, Homi K. 1994. *The Location of Culture.* New York: Routledge.

Bhaskaran, Suparna. 2004. *Made in India: Decolonizations, Queer Sexualities, Trans/National Projects.* New York: Palgrave Macmillan.

Binnie, Jon. 2004. *The Globalization of Sexuality.* Thousand Oaks, Calif.: Sage.

Blackwood, Evelyn. 2002. "Reading Sexualities across Cultures: Anthropology and Theories of Sexuality." In *Out in Theory: The Emergence of Lesbian and Gay Anthropology,* ed. E. Lewin and W. L. Leap, 69–92. Urbana: University of Illinois Press.

———. 2004. "Conference Report: The Women's Same-Sex Forum and African Women's Life History Project of Sex and Secrecy." *Sexuality Research and Social Policy* 1, no. 1: 104–7.

———. 2005. "Transnational Sexualities in One Place: Indonesian Readings." *Gender & Society* 19, no. 2: 221–42.

———. 2008. "Transnational Discourses and Circuits of Queer Knowledge in Indonesia." *GLQ* 14, no. 4: 481–507.

Blee, Kathleen M. 2002. *Inside Organized Racism: Women in the Hate Movement.* Berkeley: University of California Press.

Blee, Kathleen M., and Ashley Currier. 2005. "Character-Building: The Dynamics of Emerging Social Movement Groups." *Mobilization: An International Journal* 10, no. 1: 101–16.

———. 2006. "How Local Social Movement Groups Handle a Presidential Election." *Qualitative Sociology* 29, no. 3: 261–80.

Blee, Kathleen M., and Verta Taylor. 2002. "Semi-structured Interviewing in Social Movement Research." In *Methods of Social Movement Research,* ed. B. Klandermans and S. Staggenborg, 92–117. Minneapolis: University of Minnesota Press.

Bleys, Rudi C. 1995. *The Geography of Perversion: Male-to-Male Sexual Behavior outside the West and the Ethnographic Imagination.* New York: New York University Press.

Blignaut, Charl, and Swapna Prabhakaran. 1997. "Gay Coalition Claims Victory over Omar." *Mail & Guardian,* November 7, 12.

Bob, Clifford. 2005. *The Marketing of Rebellion: Insurgents, Media, and International Activism.* Cambridge: Cambridge University Press.

Boellstorff, Tom. 2005. *The Gay Archipelago: Sexuality and Nation in Indonesia.* Princeton, N.J.: Princeton University Press.

———. 2007. *A Coincidence of Desires: Anthropology, Queer Studies, Indonesia.* Durham, N.C.: Duke University Press.

———. 2008. "Queer Trajectories of the Postcolonial." *Postcolonial Studies* 11, no. 1: 113–17.

Bonthuys, Elsje. 2008. "Possibilities Foreclosed: The Civil Union Act and Lesbian and Gay Identity in Southern Africa." *Sexualities* 11, no. 6: 726–39.

Borland, Elizabeth, and Barbara Sutton. 2007. "Quotidian Disruption and Women's Activism in Times of Crisis, Argentina 2002–2003." *Gender & Society* 21, no. 5: 700–22.

Bornstein, Lisa. 2006. "Systems of Accountability, Webs of Deceit? Monitoring and Evaluation in South African NGOs." *Development* 49, no. 2: 52–61.

Botha, Kevan. 2005a. "A Lesson Well Worth Learning." In *Sex and Politics in South Africa,* ed. N. Hoad, K. Martin, and G. Reid, 50–53. Cape Town: Double Storey Books.

———. 2005b. "Address at Simon Nkoli's Memorial Service." In *Sex and Politics in South Africa,* ed. N. Hoad, K. Martin, and G. Reid, 166–67. Cape Town: Double Storey Books.

Botha, Kevan, and Edwin Cameron. 1997. "South Africa." In *Sociolegal Control of Homosexuality: A Multi-nation Comparison,* ed. D. J. West and R. Green, 5–42. New York: Plenum.

Bozzoli, Belinda. 2004. *Theatres of Struggle and the End of Apartheid.* Athens: University of Ohio Press.

Brighenti, Andrea Mubi. 2010. *Visibility in Social Theory and Social Research.* New York: Palgrave Macmillan.

Britton, Hannah. 2006. "Organising against Gender Violence in South Africa." *Journal of Southern African Studies* 32, no. 1: 145–63.

Bryson, Donna. 2011. "Only a Matter of Time before Next 'Corrective Rape.'" *Mail & Guardian,* May 11. http://mg.co.za/article/2011–05–11-only-a-matter-of-time-before-next-corrective-rape.

Bulbeck, Chilla. 2007. "Hailing the 'Authentic Other': Constructing the Third World Woman as Aid Recipient in Donor NGO Agendas." *Advances in Gender Research* 11: 59–73.

Bullington, Sam, and Amanda Lock Swarr. 2010. "Conflicts and Collaborations: Building Trust in Transnational South Africa." In *Critical Transnational Feminist Praxis,* ed. A. L. Swarr and R. Nagar, 87–104. Albany: State University of New York Press.

Butler, Judith. 1991. "Imitation and Gender Insubordination." In *Inside/Out: Lesbian Theories, Gay Theories,* ed. D. Fuss, 13–31. New York: Routledge.

———. 1993. *Bodies That Matter: On the Discursive Limits of "Sex."* New York: Routledge.

———. 2004. *Undoing Gender.* New York: Routledge.

———. 2006. *Gender Trouble: Feminism and the Subversion of Identity.* 2nd ed. New York: Routledge.

Cage, Ken. 2003. *Gayle: The Language of Kinks and Queens: A History and Dictionary of Gay Language in South Africa.* Johannesburg: Jacana.

Carter, Julian B. 2007. *The Heart of Whiteness: Normal Sexuality and Race in America, 1880–1940.* Durham, N.C.: Duke University Press.

Casper, Monica J., and Lisa Jean Moore. 2009. *Missing Bodies: The Politics of Visibility.* New York: New York University Press.

Central Intelligence Agency. 2011. "World Factbook 2011: Distribution of Family Income—Gini Index." https://www.cia.gov/library/publications/the-world-factbook/fields/2172.html.

Chabot, Sean, and Jan Willem Duyvendak. 2002. "Globalization and Transnational Diffusion between Social Movements: Reconceptualizing the Dissemination of the Gandhian Repertoire and the 'Coming Out' Routine." *Theory and Society* 31, no. 6: 697–740.

Chan Sam, Tanya. 1995. "Five Women: Black Lesbian Life on the Reef." In *Defiant Desire: Gay and Lesbian Lives in South Africa,* ed. M. Gevisser and E. Cameron, 186–92. New York: Routledge.

Chasin, Alexandra. 2000. *Selling Out: The Gay and Lesbian Movement Goes to Market.* New York: Palgrave Macmillan.

Chetty, Dhianaraj. 1995. "A Drag at Madame Costello's: Cape *Moffie* Life and the Popular Press in the 1950s and 1960s." In *Defiant Desire: Gay and Lesbian Lives in South Africa,* ed. M. Gevisser and E. Cameron, 115–27. New York: Routledge.

Clarke, Eric O. 2000. *Virtuous Vice: Homoeroticism and the Public Sphere.* Durham, N.C.: Duke University Press.

Cock, Jacklyn. 2003. "Engendering Gay and Lesbian Rights: The Equality Clause in the South African Constitution." *Women's Studies International Forum* 26, no. 1: 35–45.

Conway, Daniel. 2008. "The Masculine State in Crisis: State Response to War Resistance in Apartheid South Africa." *Men and Masculinities* 10, no. 4: 422–39.

———. 2009. "Queering Apartheid: The National Party's 1987 'Gay Rights' Election Campaign in Hillbrow." *Journal of Southern African Studies* 35, no. 4: 849–63.

Council of the European Union. 2001. "Declaration by the Presidency on Behalf of the European Union on Human Rights in Namibia." http://europa.eu/rapid/pressReleasesAction.do?reference=PESC/01/81&format=HTML&aged=1&language=EN&guiLanguage=en.

Cress, Daniel M., and David A. Snow. 1996. "Mobilization at the Margins: Resources, Benefactors, and the Viability of Homeless Social Movement Organizations." *American Sociological Review* 61, no. 6: 1089–1109.

Croucher, Sheila. 2002. "South Africa's Democratisation and the Politics of Gay Liberation." *Journal of Southern African Studies* 28, no. 2: 315–30.

Currier, Ashley. 2010a. "Behind the Mask: Developing LGBTI Visibility in Africa." In *Development, Sexual Rights, and Global Governance,* ed. A. Lind, 155–68. New York: Routledge.

———. 2010b. "Political Homophobia in Postcolonial Namibia." *Gender & Society* 24, no. 1: 110–29.

———. 2010c. "The Strategy of Normalization in the South African LGBT Movement." *Mobilization* 15, no. 1: 45–62.

———. 2011. "Representing Gender and Sexual Dissidence in Southern Africa." *Qualitative Sociology* 34, no. 3: 463–81.

———. 2012. "The Aftermath of Decolonization: Gender and Sexual Dissidence in Postindependence Namibia." *Signs: Journal of Women in Culture and Society* 37, no. 2: 441–67.

Daniels, Glenda. 1997. "No Rights for Gays When It Comes to the Law." *Star,* September 10, 11.

Decena, Carlos Ulises. 2008. "Profiles, Compulsory Disclosure, and Ethical Sexual Citizenship in the Contemporary USA." *Sexualities* 11, no. 4: 397–413.

de la Dehesa, Rafael. 2010. *Queering the Public Sphere in Mexico and Brazil: Sexual Rights Movements in Emerging Democracies.* Durham, N.C.: Duke University Press.

della Porta, Donatella, and Mario Diani. 1999. *Social Movements: An Introduction.* Malden, Mass.: Blackwell.

Delport, Christelle, and Raven Delport. 2008. "'I Didn't Marry the Body, I Married the Person Inside': Interview with Christelle Delport and Raven Delport." In *To Have and to Hold: The Making of Same-Sex Marriage in South Africa,* ed. M. Judge, A. Manion, and S. de Waal, 335–37. Johannesburg: Fanele.

Dentlinger, Lindsay. 2004. "Justice Minister Scorns Homosexuality as 'Criminal.'" *Namibian,* May 7. http://allafrica.com/stories/200405070159.html.

de Swardt, Glenn. 2008. "Counting the Gay Faces." In *To Have and to Hold: The Making of Same-Sex Marriage in South Africa,* ed. M. Judge, A. Manion, and S. de Waal, 111–14. Johannesburg: Fanele.

de Vos, Pierre. 2004. "Same-Sex Sexual Desire and the Re-imagining of the South African Family." *South African Journal of Human Rights* 20, no. 2: 179–206.

———. 2006. "Gays and Lesbians Now 'Separate but Equal.'" *Mail & Guardian,* September 17. http://www.mg.co.za/article/2006-09-17-gays-and-lesbians-now-separate-but-equal.

———. 2008. "Difference and Belonging: The Constitutional Court and the Adoption of the Civil Union Act." In *To Have and to Hold: The Making of Same-Sex Marriage in South Africa,* ed. M. Judge, A. Manion, and S. de Waal, 29–41. Johannesburg: Fanele.

de Waal, Shaun, and Anthony Manion. 2006. Introduction to *Pride: Protest and Celebration,* ed. S. de Waal and A. Manion, 6–10. Johannesburg: Jacana.

Diamond, Larry Jay, and Marc F. Plattner, eds. 2010. *Democratization in Africa: Progress and Retreat.* Baltimore: The Johns Hopkins University Press.

Diescho, Joseph. 1994. *The Namibian Constitution in Perspective.* Windhoek: Gamsberg Macmillan.

Dirlik, Arif. 2007. "Global South: Predicament and Promise." *The Global South* 1, nos. 1–2: 12–23.

Dirsuweit, Teresa. 2002. "Johannesburg: Fearful City?" *Urban Forum* 13, no. 3: 3–19.

———. 2006. "The Problem of Identities: The Lesbian, Gay, Bisexual, Transgender, and Intersex Social Movement in South Africa." In *Voices of Protest: Social Movements in Post-apartheid South Africa*, ed. R. Ballard, A. Habib, and I. Valodia, 325–47. Scottsville, South Africa: University of KwaZulu-Natal Press.

Ditsie, Beverly Palesa. 2006. "Today We Are Making History." In *Pride: Protest and Celebration*, ed. S. de Waal and A. Manion, 19–20. Johannesburg: Jacana.

Dobell, Lauren. 1998. *SWAPO's Struggle for Namibia, 1960–1991: War by Other Means*. Basel, Switzerland: Basler Afrika Bibliographien.

Donham, Donald L. 1998. "Freeing South Africa: The 'Modernization' of Male–Male Sexuality in Soweto." *Cultural Anthropology* 13, no. 1: 3–21.

Downey, Dennis J., and Deana A. Rohlinger. 2008. "Linking Strategic Choice with Macro-organizational Dynamics: Strategy and Social Movement Articulation." *Research in Social Movements, Conflicts, and Change* 28: 3–38.

Dubow, Saul. 1992. "Afrikaner Nationalism, Apartheid, and the Conceptualization of 'Race.'" *Journal of African History* 33, no. 2: 209–37.

Dugan, Kimberly B. 2008. "Just Like You: The Dimensions of Identity Presentations in an Antigay Contested Context." In *Identity Work in Social Movements*, ed. J. Reger, D. J. Myers, and R. L. Einwohner, 21–46. Minneapolis: University of Minnesota Press.

Duggan, Lisa. 2003. *The Twilight of Equality? Neoliberalism, Cultural Politics, and the Attack on Democracy*. Boston: Beacon Press.

Dunton, Chris, and Mai Palmberg. 1996. *Human Rights and Homosexuality in Southern Africa*. Uppsala, Sweden: Nordic African Institute.

du Pisani, André. 2004. "The Role of the Military in the Formation and Consolidation of the Namibian State." In *Demilitarisation and Peace-Building in Southern Africa: The Role of the Military in State Formation and Nation-Building*, vol. 3, ed. P. Batchelor, K. Kingma, and G. Lamb, 62–84. Burlington, Vt.: Ashgate.

Dykes, Kevin. 2004. "New Urban Social Movements in Cape Town and Johannesburg." *Urban Forum* 15, no. 2: 162–79.

Earl, Jennifer. 2003. "Tanks, Tear Gas, and Taxes: Toward a Theory of Movement Repression." *Sociological Theory* 21, no. 1: 45–68.

———. 2004. "Controlling Protest: New Directions for Research on the Social Control of Protest." *Research in Social Movements, Conflicts, and Change* 25: 55–83.

Earl, Jennifer, Andrew Martin, John D. McCarthy, and Sarah A. Soule. 2004. "The Use of Newspaper Data in the Study of Collective Action." *Annual Review of Sociology* 30: 65–80.

Eastlick, Megan. 2002. "*Sister Namibia* Editor Fights for Lesbian Rights Post-apartheid." *Off Our Backs* 32, nos. 3–4: 30–33.

Einwohner, Rachel L. 2006. "Identity Work and Collective Action in a Repressive Context: Jewish Resistance on the 'Aryan Side' of the Warsaw Ghetto." *Social Problems* 53, no. 1: 38–56.

Einwohner, Rachel L., Jo Reger, and Daniel J. Myers. 2008. "Identity Work, Sameness, and Difference in Social Movements." In *Identity Work in Social Movements,* ed. J. Reger, D. J. Myers, and R. L. Einwohner, 1–17. Minneapolis: University of Minnesota Press.

Elder, Glen S. 1995. "Of Moffies, Kaffirs, and Perverts: Male Homosexuality and the Discourse of Moral Order in the Apartheid State." In *Mapping Desire: Geographies of Sexualities,* ed. D. Bell and G. Valentine, 56–65. New York: Routledge.

———. 2003. *Hostels, Sexuality, and the Apartheid Legacy: Malevolent Geographies.* Athens: University of Ohio Press.

Epprecht, Marc. 1998. "The 'Unsaying' of Indigenous Homosexualities in Zimbabwe: Mapping a Blindspot in African Masculinity." *Journal of Southern African Studies* 24, no. 4: 631–51.

———. 2001a. "'Unnaturel Vice' in South Africa: The 1907 Commission of History." *International Journal of African Historical Studies* 34, no. 1: 121–40.

———. 2001b. "'What an Abomination, a Rottenness of Culture': Reflections upon the Gay Rights Movement in Southern Africa." *Canadian Journal of Development Studies* 22, no. 2: 1089–1107.

———. 2004. *Hungochani: The History of a Dissident Sexuality in Southern Africa.* Montreal, Canada: McGill-Queen's University Press.

———. 2005. "Black Skin, 'Cowboy' Masculinity: A Genealogy of Homophobia in the African Nationalist Movement in Zimbabwe to 1983." *Culture, Health & Sexuality* 7, no. 3: 253–66.

———. 2008. *Heterosexual Africa? The History of an Idea from the Age of Exploration to the Age of AIDS.* Athens: Ohio University Press.

Eschle, Catherine, and Neil Stammers. 2004. "Taking Part: Social Movements, INGOs, and Global Change." *Alternatives* 29, no. 3: 333–72.

Espinoza, Robert. 2007. "A Global Gaze: Lesbian, Gay, Bisexual, Transgender, and Intersex Grantmaking in the Global South and East." Funders for Lesbian and Gay Issues. http://www.lgbtfunders.org/files/FLGI%20LGBTI_GFRprWeb.pdf.

Evans, Jenni, and Riaan Wolmarans. 2006. "Timeline of the Jacob Zuma Rape Trial." *Mail & Guardian,* March 21. http://mg.co.za/article/2006-03-21-timeline-of-the-jacob-zuma-rape-trial.

Evans, Sara M., and Harry C. Boyte. 1992. *Free Spaces: The Sources of Democratic Change in America.* New York: Harper and Row.

Exit. 1996. "The Coalition's Equal Rights Project Starts." 81: 3.

Falk, Kurt. 1998. "Homosexuality among the Natives of Southwest Africa." In *Boy-Wives and Female Husbands: Studies in African Homosexualities,* ed. S. O. Murray and W. Roscoe, 187–96. New York: St. Martin's Press.

Fallon, Kathleen M. 2008. *Democracy and the Rise of Women's Movements in Sub-Saharan Africa.* Baltimore: The Johns Hopkins University Press.

Farred, Grant. 2004. "The Not-Yet Counterpartisan: A New Politics of Oppositionality." *South Atlantic Quarterly* 103, no. 4: 589–605.

Fenwick, Colin. 2006. "Labour Law in Namibia: Towards an 'Indigenous Solution.'" *South African Law Journal* 123: 665–99.

Ferguson, James. 2006. *Global Shadows: Africa in the Neoliberal World Order.* Durham, N.C.: Duke University Press.

Ferree, Myra Marx. 1994. "'The Time of Chaos Was the Best': Feminist Mobilization and Demobilization in East Germany." *Gender & Society* 8, no. 4: 597–623.

———. 2004. "Soft Repression: Ridicule, Stigma, and Silencing in Gender-Based Movements." *Research in Social Movements, Conflict, and Change* 25: 85–101.

Fetner, Tina. 2008. *How the Religious Right Shaped Lesbian and Gay Activism.* Minneapolis: University of Minnesota Press.

Fine, Derrick, and Julia Nicol. 1995. "The Lavender Lobby: Working for Lesbian and Gay Rights within the Liberation Movement." In *Defiant Desire: Gay and Lesbian Lives in South Africa,* ed. M. Gevisser and E. Cameron, 269–77. New York: Routledge.

Forrest, Joshua Bernard. 1994. "Namibia—The First Postapartheid Democracy." *Journal of Democracy* 5, no. 3: 88–100.

———. 2000. "Democracy and Development in Post-independence Namibia." In *The Uncertain Promise of Southern Africa,* ed. Y. Bradshaw and S. N. Ndegwa, 94–114. Bloomington: Indiana University Press.

Fosse, Leif John. 1997. "Negotiating the Nation: Ethnicity, Nationalism, and Nation-Building in Independent Namibia." *Nations and Nationalism* 3, no. 3: 427–50.

Foucault, Michel. 1977. *Discipline and Punish: The Birth of the Prison.* New York: Vintage.

———. 1978. *The History of Sexuality, Volume 1: An Introduction.* New York: Vintage.

Frank, Liz, and Elizabeth |Khaxas. 1996. "Lesbians in Namibia." In *Amazon to Zami: Towards a Global Lesbian Feminism,* ed. M. Reinfelder, 109–17. London: Cassell.

———. 2006. "Sister Namibia: Fighting for All Human Rights for All Women." *Feminist Africa* 6: 83–87.

Frankenberg, Ruth. 1993. *White Women, Race Matters: The Social Construction of Whiteness.* Minneapolis: University of Minnesota Press.

Fraser, Nancy. 1997. *Justice Interruptus: Critical Reflections on the "Postsocialist" Condition.* New York: Routledge.

Fredrickson, George M. 2002. *Racism: A Short History.* Princeton, N.J.: Princeton University Press.

Friedman, Debra, and Doug McAdam. 1992. "Collective Identity and Activism: Networks, Choices, and the Life of a Social Movement." In *Frontiers in Social Movement Theory,* ed. A. D. Morris and C. M. Mueller, 156–73. New Haven, Conn.: Yale University Press.

Gaitskell, Deborah, and Elaine Unterhalter. 1989. "Mothers of the Nation: A Comparative Analysis of Nation, Race, and Motherhood in Afrikaner Nationalism and the African National Congress." In *Woman-Nation-State,* ed. N. Yuval-Davis and F. Anthias, 58–78. New York: St. Martin's Press.

Gallagher, Christina. 2006. "Gay Organisation Launches Blood War." *Star,* January 14. http://www.iol.co.za/news/south-africa/gay-organisation-launches-blood-war-1.263644.

Galli, Peter, and Luis Rafael. 1995. "Johannesburg's 'Health Clubs': Places of Erotic Languor or Prison-Houses of Desire." In *Defiant Desire: Gay and Lesbian Lives in South Africa,* ed. M. Gevisser and E. Cameron, 134–39. New York: Routledge.

Gamson, Joshua. 1997. "Messages of Exclusion: Gender, Movements, and Symbolic Boundaries." *Gender & Society* 11, no. 2: 178–99.

Gamson, William A. 1975. *The Strategy of Social Protest.* Homewood, Ill.: Dorsey Press.

———. 1996. "Safe Spaces and Social Movements." *Perspectives on Social Problems* 8: 27–38.

Gamson, William A., and David S. Meyer. 1996. "Framing Political Opportunity." In *Comparative Perspectives on Social Movements: Political Opportunities, Mobilizing Structures, and Cultural Framings,* ed. D. McAdam, J. D. McCarthy, and M. N. Zald, 275–90. Cambridge: Cambridge University Press.

Gamson, William A., and Gadi Wolfsfeld. 1993. "Movements and Media as Interacting Systems." *Annals of the American Academy of Political and Social Science* 528: 114–25.

Ganz, Marshall. 2000. "Resources and Resourcefulness: Strategic Capacity in the Unionization of California Agriculture, 1959–1966." *American Journal of Sociology* 105, no. 4: 1003–62.

Geisler, Gisela. 2004. *Women and the Remaking of Politics in Southern Africa: Negotiating Autonomy, Incorporation, and Representation.* Uppsala, Sweden: Nordic Africa Institute.

Gevisser, Mark. 1995. "A Different Fight for Freedom: A History of South African Lesbian and Gay Organisation from the 1950s to the 1990s." In *Defiant Desire: Gay and Lesbian Lives in South Africa,* ed. M. Gevisser and E. Cameron, 14–88. New York: Routledge.

———. 2000. "Mandela's Stepchildren: Homosexual Identity in Post-apartheid South Africa." In *Different Rainbows,* ed. P. Drucker, 111–36. London: Gay Men's Press.

———. 2004. "From the Ruins: The Constitution Hill Project." *Public Culture* 16, no. 3: 507–19.

Gevisser, Mark, and Graeme Reid. 1995. "Pride or Protest? Drag Queens, Comrades and the Lesbian and Gay Pride March." In *Defiant Desire: Gay and Lesbian Lives in South Africa,* ed. M. Gevisser and E. Cameron, 278–83. New York: Routledge.

Ghaziani, Amin. 2008. *The Dividends of Dissent: How Conflict and Culture Work in Lesbian and Gay Marches on Washington.* Chicago: University of Chicago Press.

Gibson, James L., and Amanda Gouws. 2003. *Overcoming Intolerance in South Africa: Experiments in Democratic Persuasion.* Cambridge: Cambridge University Press.

Gilman, Lisa. 2009. *The Dance of Politics: Gender, Performance, and Democratization in Malawi.* Philadelphia: Temple University Press.

Gitlin, Todd. 2003. *The Whole World Is Watching: Mass Media in the Making and Unmaking of the New Left.* Berkeley: University of California Press.

Goddard, Keith. 2004. "A Fair Representation: GALZ and the History of the Gay Movement in Zimbabwe." *Journal of Gay and Lesbian Social Services* 16, no. 1: 75–98.

Goffman, Erving. 1959. *The Presentation of Self in Everyday Life.* New York: Doubleday.

———. 1986. *Stigma: Notes on the Management of Spoiled Identity.* New York: Simon and Schuster.

Goldberg, David Theo. 2002. *The Racial State.* Malden, Mass.: Blackwell.

Gomez, Mario. 1995. "Social Economic Rights and Human Rights Commissions." *Human Rights Quarterly* 17, no. 1: 155–69.

Goodman, Ryan. 2001. "Unenforced Sodomy Laws and South Africa: Social Effects of Criminalizing Homosexuality." PhD dissertation, Department of Sociology, Yale University, New Haven, Conn.

Gordon, Avery F. 2008. *Ghostly Matters: Haunting and the Sociological Imagination.* Minneapolis: University of Minnesota Press.

Gordon, Robert J. 2002. "Unsettled Settlers: Internal Pacification and Vagrancy in Namibia." In *Ethnography in Unstable Places: Everyday Lives in Contexts of Dramatic Political Change,* ed. C. J. Greenhouse, E. Mertz, and K. B. Warren, 61–84. Durham, N.C.: Duke University Press.

Govender, Pregs. 2006. "You Have Struck a Woman, You Have Struck a Rock." *Mail & Guardian,* March 8. http://mg.co.za/article/2006-03-17-you-have-struck-a-woman-rock.

Gqola, Pumla Dineo. 2007. "How the 'Cult of Femininity' and Violent Masculinities Support Endemic Gender Based Violence in Contemporary South Africa." *African Identities* 5, no. 1: 111–24.

Gqola, Pumla Dineo, and Wendy Isaack. 2006. "Pumla Dineo Gqola Speaks with Wendy Isaack." *Feminist Africa* 6: 91–100.

Graig, Augetto. 2005. "Deputy Minister's 'Hate Speech' Slammed." *Namibian,* September 12. http://allafrica.com/stories/200509120527.html.

Gray, Herman, and Macarena Gómez-Barris, eds. 2010. *Toward a Sociology of the Trace*. Minneapolis: University of Minnesota Press.

Grewal, Inderpal, and Caren Kaplan. 2001. "Global Identities: Theorizing Transnational Studies of Sexuality." *GLQ* 7, no. 4: 663–79.

Guenther, Katja M. 2011. "The Possibilities and Pitfalls of NGO Feminism: Insights from Postsocialist Eastern Europe." *Signs* 36, no. 4: 863–87.

Guidry, John A. 2003. "The Struggle to Be Seen: Social Movements and the Public Sphere in Brazil." *International Journal of Politics, Culture, and Society* 16, no. 4: 493–524.

Gunkel, Henriette. 2010. *The Cultural Politics of Female Sexuality in South Africa*. New York: Routledge.

Günzel, Erhard. 1996. "Nujoma Blasts Gays." *Windhoek Advertiser*, December 12, 1.

———. 1997. "Nujoma Wants Gays behind Shut Doors." *Windhoek Advertiser*, April 28, 1.

Haffajee, Ferral. 2006. "Jacob Zuma Rape Trial: What Now?" *Mail & Guardian*, February 26, 26–27.

Haines, Herbert H. 1984. "Black Radicalization and the Funding of Civil Rights: 1957–1970." *Social Problems* 32, no. 1: 31–43.

———. 2006. "Dangerous Issues and Public Identities: The Negotiation of Controversy in Two Movement Organizations." *Sociological Inquiry* 76, no. 2: 231–63.

Halley, Janet. 2000. "'Like Race' Arguments." In *What's Left of Theory? New Work on the Politics of Literary Theory*, ed. J. Butler, J. Guillory, and K. Thomas, 40–74. New York: Routledge.

Hamata, Max. 2000. "Namibian Minister Elaborates on Anti-gay Stance." *Namibian*, November 3. http://www.afrol.com/Categories/Gay/q001/q002_nam_elaborate.htm.

———. 2001. "SFF Launch Earring 'Purge.'" *Namibian*, May 2. http://allafrica.com/stories/200105020082.html.

Hammersley, Martyn, and Paul Atkinson. 1995. *Ethnography: Principles in Practice*. New York: Routledge.

Hammonds, Evelynn M. 1994. "Black (W)holes and the Geometry of Black Female Sexuality." *Differences* 6, nos. 2–3: 126–45.

Haraway, Donna. 1988. "Situated Knowledges: The Science Question in Feminism and the Privilege of Partial Perspective." *Feminist Studies* 14, no. 3: 575–99.

Harries, Patrick. 1990. "Symbols and Sexuality: Culture and Identity on the Early Witwatersrand Gold Mines." *Gender & History* 2, no. 3: 318–36.

Hassim, Shireen. 2005. *Women's Organizations and Democracy in South Africa: Contesting Authority*. Madison: University of Wisconsin Press.

———. 2009a. "After Apartheid: Consensus, Contention, and Gender in South Africa's Public Sphere." *International Journal of Politics, Culture, and Society* 22, no. 4: 453–64.

———. 2009b. "Democracy's Shadows: Sexual Rights and Gender Politics in the Rape Trial of Jacob Zuma." *African Studies* 68, no. 1: 57–77.

Hemmings, Clare. 2007. "What's in a Name? Bisexuality, Transnational Sexuality Studies, and Western Colonial Legacies." *International Journal of Human Rights* 11, nos. 1–2: 13–32.

Hennessy, Rosemary. 1994. "Queer Visibility in Commodity Culture." *Cultural Critique* 29: 31–76.

Hill Collins, Patricia. 2000. *Black Feminist Thought: Knowledge, Consciousness, and the Politics of Empowerment.* Rev. 10th anniversary ed. New York: Routledge.

Hoad, Neville. 2007. *African Intimacies: Race, Homosexuality, and Globalization.* Minneapolis: University of Minnesota Press.

Hobson, Barbara, ed. 2003. *Recognition Struggles and Social Movements: Contested Identities, Agency, and Power.* Cambridge: Cambridge University Press.

Hollander, Michael. 2009. "Gay Rights in Uganda: Seeking to Overturn Uganda's Anti-sodomy Laws." *Virginia Journal of International Law* 50, no. 1: 219–66.

Holmes, Rachel. 1995. "'White Rapists Made Coloureds (and Homosexuals)': The Winnie Mandela Trial and the Politics of Race and Sexuality." In *Defiant Desire: Gay and Lesbian Lives in South Africa,* ed. M. Gevisser and E. Cameron, 284–94. New York: Routledge.

———. 1997. "Queer Comrades: Winnie Mandela and the Moffies." *Social Text* 52/53, nos. 3–4: 161–80.

Hubbard, Dianne. 2007. "Gender and Sexuality: The Law Reform Landscape." In *Unravelling Taboos: Gender and Sexuality in Namibia,* ed. S. LaFont and D. Hubbard, 99–128. Windhoek: LAC.

Hubbard, Dianne, and Collette Solomon. 1995. "The Many Faces of Feminism in Namibia." In *The Challenge of Local Feminisms: Women's Movements in Global Perspective,* ed. A. Basu, 163–86. Boulder, Colo.: Westview Press.

Huisman, Biénne. 2006. "Teen Beaten to Death for Being a Lesbian." *Sunday Independent,* February 19, 6.

Human Rights Watch. 2005. "Uganda: Same-Sex Marriage Ban Deepens Repression." http://www.hrw.org/en/news/2005/07/11/uganda-same-sex-marriage-ban-deepens-repression.

Human Rights Watch and the International Gay and Lesbian Rights Commission. 2003. "More Than a Name: State-Sponsored Homophobia and Its Consequences in Southern Africa." http://www.iglhrc.org/binary-data/ATTACHMENT/file/000/000/160-1.pdf.

Hunter, Mark. 2010. *Love in the Time of AIDS: Inequality, Gender, and Rights in South Africa.* Bloomington: Indiana University Press.

Incite! Women of Color against Violence, ed. 2009. *The Revolution Will Not Be Funded: Beyond the Non-profit Industrial Complex.* Boston: South End Press.

International Gay and Lesbian Human Rights Commission. 1997. "A Celebration of Courage: Felipa de Souza Award Recipient 1997—Sister Namibia." http://www.iglhrc.org/cgi-bin/iowa/article/support/cocarchives/96.html.

———. 2000. "Making the Mountain Move: An Activist's Guide to How International Human Rights Mechanisms Can Work for You." http://www.iglhrc.org/binary-data/ATTACHMENT/file/000/000/179-1.pdf.

———. 2006a. "Annual Report." http://www.iglhrc.org/binary-data/ATTACHMENT/file/000/000/25-1.pdf.

———. 2006b. "Voices from Nigeria: Gays, Lesbians, Bisexuals, and Transgenders Speak Out about the Same-Sex Bill." http://www.iglhrc.org/binary-data/ATTACHMENT/file/000/000/131-1.pdf.

———. 2007. "Annual Report." http://www.iglhrc.org/binary-data/ATTACHMENT/file/000/000/24-1.pdf.

———. 2009. "A Celebration of Courage: Helem Wins 2009 Felipa de Souza Award." http://www.iglhrc.org/cgi-bin/iowa/article/support/coc2009/850.html.

International Lesbian and Gay Association. 2006a. "ECOSOC Unfairly Dismisses ILGA and LBL." http://ilga.org/ilga/en/article/741.

———. 2006b. "Lesbian and Bisexual Women's Health: Control over Women's Bodies." http://doc.ilga.org/ilga/publications/publications_in_english/other_publications/lesbian_and_bisexual_women_s_health_report.

———. 2011. "ECOSOC Council Vote Grants Consultative Status to ILGA." http://ilga.org/ilga/en/article/n5GebHB1PY.

Isaacks, Madelene, with Ruth Morgan. 2005. "'I Don't Force My Feelings for Other Women, My Feelings Have to Force Me': Same-Sexuality amongst Ovambo Women in Namibia." In *Tommy Boys, Lesbian Men, and Ancestral Wives: Female Same-Sex Practices in Africa,* ed. R. Morgan and S. Wieringa, 77–120. Johannesburg: Jacana.

Isaacs, Gordon, and Brian McKendrick. 1992. *Male Homosexuality in South Africa: Identity Formation, Culture, and Crisis.* Oxford: Oxford University Press.

Jara, Mazibuko, and Sheila Lapinsky. 1998. "Forging a Representative Gay Liberation Movement in South Africa." *Development Update* 2, no. 2: 44–56.

Jasper, James M. 1997. *The Art of Moral Protest: Culture, Biography, and Creativity in Social Movements.* Chicago: University of Chicago Press.

———. 2004. "A Strategic Approach to Collective Action: Looking for Agency in Social-Movement Choices." *Mobilization* 9, no. 1: 1–16.

———. 2006. *Getting Your Way: Strategic Dilemmas in the Real World.* Chicago: University of Chicago Press.

Jasper, James M., and Jane Poulsen. 1993. "Fighting Back: Vulnerabilities, Blunders, and Countermobilization by the Targets in Three Animal Rights Campaigns." *Sociological Forum* 8, no. 4: 639–57.

Jasson da Costa, Wendy. 2006. "Rape Complainant Has Been Victimised." *Star*, February 15, 3.

Jewkes, Rachel, and Naeema Abrahams. 2002. "The Epidemiology of Rape and Sexual Coercion in South Africa: An Overview." *Social Science & Medicine* 55, no. 7: 1231–44.

Jewkes, Rachel, Kristin Dunkle, Mary P. Koss, Jonathan B. Levin, Mzikazi Nduna, Nwabisa Jama, and Yandisa Sikweyiya. 2006. "Rape Perpetration by Young, Rural South African Men: Prevalence, Patterns, and Risk Factors." *Social Science & Medicine* 63, no. 11: 2949–61.

Johnson, Krista. 2003. "Liberal or Liberation Framework? The Contradictions of ANC Rule in South Africa." In *Limits to Liberation in Southern Africa: The Unfinished Business of Democratic Consolidation*, ed. H. Melber, 200–23. Cape Town: HSRC Press.

Johnston, Hank, Enrique Laraña, and Joseph Gusfield. 1994. "Identities, Grievances, and New Social Movements." In *New Social Movements: From Ideology to Identity*, ed. E. Laraña, H. Johnston, and J. Gusfield, 3–35. Philadelphia: Temple University Press.

Joint Working Group. 2008. "A Letter of Complaint about Hate Speech." In *To Have and to Hold: The Making of Same-Sex Marriage in South Africa*, ed. M. Judge, A. Manion, and S. de Waal, 133–34. Johannesburg: Fanele.

Jones, Tiffany F. 2008. "Averting White Male (Ab)normality: Psychiatric Representations and Treatment of 'Homosexuality' in 1960s South Africa." *Journal of Southern African Studies* 34, no. 2: 397–410.

Jordans, Frank. 2011. "UN Backs Gay Rights for First Time Ever." Associated Press, June 17. http://hosted2.ap.org/APDEFAULT/privacy/Article_2011–06–17-UN-Gay%20Rights/id-64b2c88829ea46199211e9bc6d4c31ae.

Joubert, Pearlie. 2006. "Home Affairs Committee 'Homophobic.'" *Mail & Guardian*, October 22. http://www.mg.co.za/article/2006-10-22-home-affairs-committee-homophobic.

Judge, Melanie, Anthony Manion, and Shaun de Waal, eds. 2008a. Introduction to *To Have and to Hold: The Making of Same-Sex Marriage in South Africa*. Johannesburg: Fanele.

———. 2008b. "'We First Need to Be Recognized': Activists Reflect on Same-Sex Marriage and LGBTI Rights in Africa." In *To Have and to Hold: The Making of Same-Sex Marriage in South Africa*, ed. M. Judge, A. Manion, and S. de Waal, 300–6. Johannesburg: Fanele.

Kandirikirira, Niki. 2002. "Deconstructing Domination: Gender Disempowerment and the Legacy of Colonialism and Apartheid in Omaheke, Namibia." In *Masculinities Matter! Men, Gender, and Development*, ed. F. Cleaver, 112–37. London: Zed.

Katyal, Sonia. 2002. "Exporting Identity." *Yale Journal of Law and Feminism* 14, no. 1: 97–176.

Katz, Jonathan Ned. 2007. *The Invention of Heterosexuality.* Chicago: University of Chicago Press.

Keck, Margaret E., and Kathryn Sikkink. 1998. *Activists beyond Borders: Advocacy Networks in International Politics.* Ithaca, N.Y.: Cornell University Press.

Keegan, Timothy. 2001. "Gender, Degeneration, and Sexual Danger: Imagining Race and Class in South Africa, ca. 1912." *Journal of Southern African Studies* 27, no. 3: 459–77.

Kendall, Kathryn Limakatso. 1999. "Women in Lesotho and the (Western) Construction of Homophobia." In *Female Desires: Same-Sex Relations and Transgender Practices across Cultures,* ed. E. Blackwood and S. E. Wieringa, 157–78. New York: Columbia University Press.

|Khaxas, Elizabeth, with Saskia Wieringa. 2005. "'I Am a Pet Goat, I Will Not Be Slaughtered': Female Masculinity and Femme Strength amongst the Damara in Namibia." In *Tommy Boys, Lesbian Men, and Ancestral Wives: Female Same-Sex Practices in Africa,* ed. R. Morgan and S. E. Wieringa, 123–96. Johannesburg: Jacana.

Kheswa, Busi, with Saskia Wieringa. 2005. "'My Attitude Is Manly . . . a Girl Needs to Walk on the Aisle': Butch-Femme Subculture in Johannesburg, South Africa." In *Tommy Boys, Lesbian Men, and Ancestral Wives: Female Same-Sex Practices in Africa,* ed. R. Morgan and S. E. Wieringa, 199–229. Johannesburg: Jacana.

Kim-Puri, H. J. 2005. "Conceptualizing Gender-Sexuality-State-Nation." *Gender & Society* 19, no. 2: 137–59.

Kiragu, Jane, and Zawadi Nyong'o. 2005. *LGBTI Organizing in East Africa: The True Test for Human Rights Defenders.* Nairobi: Urgent Action Fund–Africa.

Klandermans, Bert. 2004. "The Demand and Supply of Participation: Social–Psychological Correlates of Participation in Social Movements." In *The Blackwell Companion to Social Movements,* ed. D. A. Snow, S. A. Soule, and H. Kriesi, 360–79. Malden, Mass.: Blackwell.

Klein, Thamar. 2008. "Querying Medical and Legal Discourses of Queer Sexes and Genders in South Africa." *Anthropology Matters* 10, no. 2: 1–17.

Koopmans, Ruud. 2004. "Movements and Media: Selection Processes and Evolutionary Dynamics in the Public Sphere." *Theory and Society* 33, nos. 3–4: 367–91.

Kowalchuk, Lisa. 2005. "The Discourse of Demobilization: Shifts in Activist Priorities and the Framing of Political Opportunities in a Peasant Land Struggle." *The Sociological Quarterly* 46, no. 2: 237–61.

Kraak, Gerald. 2005. "Homosexuality and the South African Left: The Ambiguities of Exile." In *Sex and Politics in South Africa,* ed. N. Hoad, K. Martin, and G. Reid, 118–35. Cape Town: Double Storey Books.

Kurzman, Charles. 1996. "Structural Opportunity and Perceived Opportunity in Social-Movement Theory: The Iranian Revolution of 1979." *American Sociological Review* 61, no. 1: 153–70.

Kuteeue, Petros. 2003. "Nujoma Renews Attacks on Whites, Gays, Media as His Retirement Debate Heats Up." *Namibian,* September 1. http://allafrica.com/stories/200309020430.html.

Kwesi, Busi, and Naomi Webster. 1997. "Black, Lesbian, and Speaking Out." *Agenda* 36: 90–93.

LaFont, Suzanne. 2007. "Decolonising Sexuality." In *Transitions in Namibia: Which Changes for Whom?,* ed. H. Melber, 245–60. Uppsala, Sweden: Nordic Africa Institute.

Lee, Emily S. 2011. "The Epistemology of the Question of Authenticity, in Place of Strategic Essentialism." *Hypatia* 26, no. 2: 258–79.

Levitsky, Sandra. 2007. "Niche Activism: Constructing a Unified Movement Identity in a Heterogeneous Organizational Field." *Mobilization* 12, no. 3: 271–86.

Lewis, Desiree. 2007. "The Coverage of Sexuality by the South African Print Media." Africa Regional Sexuality Resource Centre. http://www.arsrc.org/downloads/sim/Sexualityinthe%20MediaNoveDec2005South%20Africa.pdf.

———. 2011. "Representing African Sexualities." In *African Sexualities: A Reader,* ed. S. Tamale, 199–216. Cape Town: Pambazuka.

Lewis, Jack, and Francois Loots. 1995. "'Moffies en Manvroue': Gay and Lesbian Life Histories in Contemporary Cape Town." In *Defiant Desire: Gay and Lesbian Lives in South Africa,* ed. M. Gevisser and E. Cameron, 140–57. New York: Routledge.

Leys, Colin, and John S. Saul. 1994. "Liberation without Democracy? The SWAPO Crisis of 1976." *Journal of Southern African Studies* 20, no. 1: 123–47.

———. 1995. *Namibia's Liberation Struggle: The Two-Edged Sword.* Athens: University of Ohio Press.

Lind, Amy. 2009. "Governing Intimacy, Struggling for Sexual Rights: Challenging Heteronormativity in the Global Development Industry." *Development* 52, no. 1: 34–42.

———, ed. 2010. *Development, Sexual Rights, and Global Governance.* New York: Routledge.

Lindeke, William A. 1995. "Democratization in Namibia: Soft State, Hard Choices." *Studies in Comparative International Development* 30, no. 1: 3–29.

Linington, E. H. 2006. "*Saturday Star* 'Did Not Check Its Facts.'" *Saturday Star,* January 28, 1.

Lorway, Robert. 2006. "Dispelling 'Heterosexual African AIDS' in Namibia: Same-Sex Sexuality in the Township of Katutura." *Culture, Health & Sexuality* 8, no. 5: 435–49.

———. 2007. "Breaking a Public Health Silence: HIV Risk and Male–Male Sexual Practices in the Windhoek Urban Area." In *Unravelling Taboos: Gender and Sexuality in Namibia,* ed. S. LaFont and D. Hubbard, 276–95. Windhoek: LAC.

———. 2008a. "Defiant Desire in Namibia: Female Sexual-Gender Transgression and the Making of Political Being." *American Ethnologist* 35, no. 1: 20–33.

———. 2008b. "'Where Can I Be Deported?' Thinking through the 'Foreigner Fetish' in Namibia." *Medical Anthropology* 27, no. 1: 70–97.

———. 2010. "Beyond Pseudo-Homosexuality: Corrective Rape, Transactional Sex, and the Undoing of Lesbian Identities in Namibia." In *Routledge Handbook of Sexuality, Health, and Rights,* ed. P. Aggleton and R. Parker, 324–35. New York: Routledge.

Louw, Ronald. 2001. "Mkhumbane and New Traditions of (Un)African Same-Sex Weddings." In *Changing Men in Southern Africa,* ed. R. Morrell, 287–96. London: Zed.

Luirink, Bart. 2000. *Moffies: Gay Life in Southern Africa.* Cape Town: David Philip.

Lynch, Gabrielle, and Gordon Crawford. 2011. "Democratization in Africa 1990–2010: An Assessment." *Democratization* 18, no. 2: 275–310.

MacDonald, Michael. 2006. *Why Race Matters in South Africa.* Cambridge, Mass.: Harvard University Press.

Maclennan, Ben. 2006. "Home Affairs Reassures Christians on Marriage Bill." *Mail & Guardian,* September 16. http://mg.co.za/article/2006-09-16-home-affairs-reassures-christians-on-marriage-bill.

Maffeis, Sonia. 1997. "Gay Community Speaks Out." *Namibian,* March 27, B3.

Magaziner, Daniel R. 2010. *The Law and the Prophets: Black Consciousness in South Africa, 1968–1977.* Athens: Ohio University Press.

Mail & Guardian. 2006a. "'Marriage' Stays in Civil Unions Bill." November 8. http://mg.co.za/article/2006-11-08-marriage-stays-in-civil-unions-bill.

———. 2006b. "Zuma Found Not Guilty." May 8. http://mg.co.za/article/2006-05-08-zuma-found-not-guilty.

———. 2009. "Gang-Rape Killer of Lesbian Footballer Gets Life." September 23. http://mg.co.za/article/2009–09–23-gangrape-killer-of-lesbian-footballer-gets-life.

———. 2010. "One in Nine Campaign for Khwezi." May 11. http://www.mg.co.za/multimedia/2010-05-12-one-in-nine-campaign-for-khwezi.

———. 2011. "Jon Qwelane Guilty of Hate Speech." May 31. http://mg.co.za/article/2011-05-31-jon-qwelane-guilty-of-hate-speech.

Maletsky, Christof. 1998. "Government Planning to Criminalise Gays." *Namibian,* November 9. http://allafrica.com/stories/199811090086.html.

———. 1999. "New Call for Anti-gay Law." *Namibian,* April 21, 5.

Mamdani, Mahmood. 1996. *Citizen and Subject: Contemporary Africa and the Legacy of Late Colonialism.* Princeton, N.J.: Princeton University Press.

Manalansan, Martin F., IV. 1995. "In the Shadows of Stonewall: Examining Gay Transnational Politics and the Diasporic Dilemma." *GLQ* 2, no. 4: 425–38.

———. 2005. "Race, Violence, and Neoliberal Spatial Politics in the Global City." *Social Text* 84–85: 141–55.

Manion, Anthony, and Ruth Morgan. 2006. "The Gay and Lesbian Archives: Documenting Same-Sexuality in an African Context." *Agenda* 67: 29–35.

Markowitz, Lisa, and Karen W. Tice. 2002. "Paradoxes of Professionalization: Parallel

Dilemmas in Women's Organizations in the Americas." *Gender & Society* 16, no. 6: 941–58.

Marks, Suzanne M. 2006. "Global Recognition of Human Rights for Lesbian, Gay, Bisexual, and Transgender People." *Health and Human Rights* 9, no. 1: 33–42.

Marrian, Natasha. 2006. "Gay Blood Row Compromise." *Citizen,* February 21, 6.

Marx, Anthony T. 1992. *Lessons of Struggle: South African Internal Opposition, 1960–1990.* Oxford: Oxford University Press.

Mason, Jennifer. 2002. *Qualitative Researching.* 2nd ed. Thousand Oaks, Calif.: Sage.

Massad, Joseph. 2002. "Re-orienting Desire: The Gay International and the Arab World." *Public Culture* 14, no. 2: 361–86.

Massaquoi, Notisha. 2008. "The Continent as a Closet: The Making of an African Queer Theory." *Outliers* 1, no. 1: 50–60.

Massoud, Mark F. 2003. "The Evolution of Gay Rights in South Africa." *Peace Review* 15, no. 3: 301–7.

Matebeni, Zethu. 2008. "Blissful Complexities: Black Lesbians Reflect on Same-Sex Marriage and the Civil Union Act." In *To Have and to Hold: The Making of Same-Sex Marriage in South Africa,* ed. M. Judge, A. Manion, and S. de Waal, 249–57. Johannesburg: Fanele.

———. 2009. "Feminizing Lesbians, Degendering Transgender Men: A Model for Building Lesbian Feminist Thinkers and Leaders in Africa?" *Souls* 11, no. 3: 347–54.

Mattes, Robert. 2002. "South Africa: Democracy without the People?" *Journal of Democracy* 14, no. 1: 22–36.

Matthews, Nancy A. 1994. *Confronting Rape: The Feminist Anti-rape Movement and the State.* New York: Routledge.

———. 1995. "Feminist Clashes with the State: Tactical Choices by State-Funded Rape Crisis Centers." In *Feminist Organizations: Harvest of the New Women's Movement,* ed. M. M. Ferree and P. Y. Martin, 291–305. Philadelphia: Temple University Press.

Mbali, Mandisa. 2008. "Gender, Sexuality, and Global Linkages in the History of South African AIDS Activism, 1982–94." In *The Politics of AIDS: Globalization, the State, and Civil Society,* ed. M. Follér and H. Thörn, 177–98. New York: Palgrave Macmillan.

Mbembe, Achille. 2001. *On the Postcolony.* Berkeley: University of California Press.

McAdam, Doug. 1999. *Political Process and the Development of Black Insurgency, 1930–1970.* 2nd ed. Chicago: University of Chicago Press.

McAdam, Doug, Sidney Tarrow, and Charles Tilly. 2001. *Dynamics of Contention.* Cambridge: Cambridge University Press.

McCammon, Holly J., Soma Chaudhuri, Lyndi Hewitt, Courtney Sanders Muse, and Harmony D. Newman. 2008. "Becoming Full Citizens: The U.S. Women's Jury Rights Campaigns, the Pace of Reform, and Strategic Adaptation." *American Journal of Sociology* 113, no. 4: 1104–47.

McCarthy, John D., and Mayer N. Zald. 1977. "Resource Mobilization and Social Movements: A Partial Theory." *American Journal of Sociology* 82, no. 6: 1212–41.

McClintock, Anne. 1995. *Imperial Leather: Race, Gender, and Sexuality in the Colonial Context.* New York: Routledge.

McCulloch, Jock. 2000. *Black Peril, White Virtue: Sexual Crime in Southern Rhodesia, 1902–1935.* Bloomington: Indiana University Press.

McFadden, Patricia. 1996. "Editorial: Sexuality, Identity, and Change." *Southern African Feminist Review* 2, no. 1: vii–xiii.

———. 2003. "Sexual Pleasure as Feminist Choice." *Feminist Africa* 2. http://www.feministafrica.org/index.php/sexual-pleasure-as-feminist-choice.

McLean, Hugh, and Linda Ngcobo. 1995. "*Abangibhamayo Bathi Ngimnandi* (Those Who Fuck Me Say I'm Tasty): Gay Sexuality in Reef Townships." In *Defiant Desire: Gay and Lesbian Lives in South Africa,* ed. M. Gevisser and E. Cameron, 158–92. New York: Routledge.

Meer, Fatima. 1984. "South Africa: New Constitution, Old Ideology." *Race & Class* 25, no. 3: 81–86.

Melber, Henning. 2003a. "From Controlled Change to Changed Control: The Case of Namibia." In *Limits to Liberation in Southern Africa: The Unfinished Business of Democratic Consolidation,* ed. H. Melber, 134–55. Cape Town: HSRC Press.

———. 2003b. "Limits to Liberation: An Introduction to Namibia's Postcolonial Political Culture." In *Re-examining Liberation in Namibia: Political Culture since Independence,* ed. H. Melber, 9–24. Uppsala, Sweden: Nordic Africa Institute.

———. 2004. "Decolonization and Democratization: The United Nations and Namibia's Transition to Democracy." In *The UN Role in Promoting Democracy: Between Ideals and Reality,* ed. E. Newman and R. Rich, 233–57. New York: United Nations University Press.

———. 2005. "Namibia's Post-colonial Socio-economic (Non-)Transformation: Business as Usual?" *Nord-Süd Aktuell* 3, no. 4: 306–21.

———. 2006a. "Liberation Movements as Governments: The Unfinished Business of Decolonization." In *Outside the Ballot Box: Preconditions for Elections in Southern Africa,* ed. J. Minnie, 19–31. Windhoek: MISA.

———. 2006b. "'Presidential Indispensability' in Namibia: Moving Out of Office but Staying in Power?" In *Legacies of Power: Leadership Change and Former Presidents in African Politics,* ed. R. Southall and H. Melber, 98–119. Cape Town: HSRC Press.

———. 2007. "'SWAPO Is the Nation, and the Nation Is SWAPO': Government and Opposition in a Dominant Party State: The Case of Namibia." In *Political Opposition in African Countries: The Cases of Kenya, Namibia, Zambia, and Zimbabwe,* ed. H. Melber, 61–81. Uppsala, Sweden: Nordic Africa Institute.

Meli, Francis. 1988. *South Africa Belongs to Us: A History of the ANC.* Bloomington: Indiana University Press.

Melucci, Alberto. 1989. *Nomads of the Present: Social Movements and Individual Needs in Contemporary Society.* Philadelphia: Temple University Press.

Menges, Werner. 2001a. "Gay-Bashing Likened to 'Cancer of Racism.'" *Namibian,* March 22. http://allafrica.com/stories/200103220160.html.

———. 2001b. "Gay Rights Dealt Blow." *Namibian,* March 6. http://allafrica.com/stories/200103060058.html.

———. 2001c. "Nujoma's Gay Tirade 'Has No Legal Basis.'" *Namibian,* March 23. http://allafrica.com/stories/200103230147.html.

Merry, Sally Engle. 1990. *Getting Justice and Getting Even: Legal Consciousness among Working-Class Americans.* Chicago: University of Chicago Press.

Mertus, Julie. 2007. "The Rejection of Human Rights Framings: The Case of LGBT Advocacy in the US." *Human Rights Quarterly* 29, no. 4: 1036–64.

Meyer, David S., and Debra C. Minkoff. 2004. "Conceptualizing Political Opportunity." *Social Forces* 82, no. 4: 1457–92.

Meyer, David S., and Nancy Whittier. 1994. "Social Movement Spillover." *Social Problems* 41, no. 2: 277–98.

Michael, Sarah. 2004. *Undermining Development: The Absence of Power among Local NGOs in Africa.* Bloomington: Indiana University Press.

Mikell, Gwendolyn. 1997. Introduction to *African Feminism: The Politics of Survival in Sub-Saharan Africa,* ed. G. Mikell. Philadelphia: University of Pennsylvania Press.

Mindry, Deborah. 2001. "Nongovernmental Organizations, 'Grassroots,' and the Politics of Virtue." *Signs* 26, no. 4: 1187–1211.

Minkoff, Debra C., and John D. McCarthy. 2005. "Reinvigorating the Study of Organizational Processes in Social Movements." *Mobilization* 10, no. 2: 289–308.

Mkhize, Nonhlanhla. 2001. "Durban Gays Protest Attacks." *Namibian,* April 10. http://allafrica.com/stories/200104110129.html.

———. 2008. "(Not) in My Culture: Thoughts on Same-Sex Marriage and African Practices." In *To Have and to Hold: The Making of Same-Sex Marriage in South Africa,* ed. M. Judge, A. Manion, and S. de Waal, 97–106. Johannesburg: Fanele.

Mkhize, Nonhlanhla, Jane Bennett, Vasu Reddy, and Relebohile Moletsane. 2010. *The Country We Want to Live In: Hate Crimes and Homophobia in the Lives of Black Lesbian South Africans.* Cape Town: HSRC Press.

Moffett, Helen. 2009. "Sexual Violence, Civil Society, and the New Constitution." In *Women's Activism in South Africa: Working across Divides,* ed. H. Britton, J. Fish, and S. Meintjes, 155–84. Scottsville, South Africa: University of KwaZulu-Natal Press.

Mohanty, Chandra Talpade. 2003. *Feminism without Borders: Decolonizing Theory, Practicing Solidarity.* Durham, N.C.: Duke University Press.

Moodie, T. Dunbar. 2002. "Mobilization on the South African Gold Mines." In *Social Movements: Identity, Culture, and the State,* ed. D. S. Meyer, N. Whittier, and B. Robnett, 47–64. Oxford: Oxford University Press.

Moodie, T. Dunbar, with Vivienne Ndatshe and British Sibuyi. 1988. "Migrancy and

Male Sexuality on the South African Gold Mines." *Journal of Southern African Studies* 14, no. 2: 228–56.

Mooney, Katie. 1998. "'Ducktails, Flick-Knives, and Pugnacity': Subcultural and Hegemonic Masculinities in South Africa, 1948–1960." *Journal of Southern African Studies* 24, no. 4: 753–74.

Moothoo-Padayachie, Nitasha. 2004. "Lesbian Violence Explored." *Agenda* 60: 81–86.

Morgan, Ruth, and Graeme Reid. 2003. "'I've Got Two Men and One Woman': Ancestors, Sexuality, and Identity among Same-Sex Identified Women Traditional Healers in South Africa." *Culture, Health & Sexuality* 5, no. 5: 375–91.

Morrell, Robert. 1998. "Of Boys and Men: Masculinity and Gender in Southern African Studies." *Journal of Southern African Studies* 24, no. 4: 605–30.

Morris, Aldon. 1984. *The Origins of the Civil Rights Movement: Black Communities Organizing for Change.* New York: Free Press.

Motsei, Mmatshilo. 2007. *The Kanga and the Kangaroo Court: Reflections on the Rape Trial of Jacob Zuma.* Johannesburg: Jacana.

Moya, Fikile-Ntsikelelo. 2006. "100% Zuluboy." *Mail & Guardian,* April 7–12, 4–5.

Mudimbe, V. Y. 1988. *The Invention of Africa: Gnosis, Philosophy, and the Order of Knowledge.* Bloomington: Indiana University Press.

Mugabe, Robert. 1995. "Opening Speech of the Zimbabwe International Book Fair." August 1. http://www.qrd.org/QRD/world/africa/zimbabwe/excerpt.of.mugabe.speech-08.03.95.

Muholi, Zanele. 2004. "Thinking through Lesbian Rape." *Agenda* 61: 116–25.

Mulvey, Laura. 1975. "Visual Pleasure and Narrative Cinema." *Screen* 16, no. 3: 6–18.

Munamava, Rajah. 1995. "Gays, Lesbians to End Silence: Ostracised, Isolated, the 'Oddity' Demands Recognition." *New Era,* June 8–14, 24.

Murray, Martin J. 2008. *Taming the Disorderly City: The Spatial Landscape of Johannesburg after Apartheid.* Ithaca, N.Y.: Cornell University Press.

———. 2011. *City of Extremes: The Spatial Politics of Johannesburg.* Durham, N.C.: Duke University Press.

Murray, Rachel, and Frans Viljoen. 2007. "Towards Non-discrimination on the Basis of Sexual Orientation: The Normative Basis and Procedural Possibilities before the African Commission on Human and Peoples' Rights and the African Union." *Human Rights Quarterly* 29, no. 1: 86–111.

Murray, Stephen O. 1998. "Sexual Politics in Contemporary Southern Africa." In *Boy-Wives and Female Husbands: Studies in African Homosexualities,* ed. S. O. Murray and W. Roscoe, 243–54. New York: St. Martin's Press.

Mutikani, Lucia. 1996. "No Free Condoms for Prisoners." *Windhoek Advertiser,* June 14, 1.

Mwilima, Fred. 1995. "Hishongwa Blasts Gays: Homosexuality Is Like Cancer or the AIDS Scourge." *New Era,* October 5–11, 2.

Nagadya, Marie, with Ruth Morgan. 2005. "'Some Say I Am Hermaphrodite Just because I Put on Trousers': Lesbians and Tommy Boys in Kampala, Uganda." In *Tommy Boys, Lesbian Men, and Ancestral Wives: Female Same-Sex Practices in Africa,* ed. R. Morgan and S. E. Wieringa, 65–77. Johannesburg: Jacana.

Nagel, Joane. 1994. "Constructing Ethnicity: Creating and Recreating Ethnic Identity and Culture." *Social Problems* 41, no. 1: 152–76.

Naidoo, Prishani, and Zanele Muholi. 2010. "Women's Bodies and the World of Football in South Africa." In *The Race to Transform: Sport in Post-apartheid South Africa,* ed. A. Desai, 105–45. Cape Town: HSRC Press.

Namibian. 1997a. "Alpheus Comes Out on Gay Issue." January 24, 3.

———. 1997b. "EU Concern on Anti-Gay Attacks." February 3, 1–2.

———. 1997c. "Gay Rights Group Take Their Concerns to Ombudswoman." June 6, 4.

———. 1997d. "Geingob Steps into Gay Fray." February 4, 1–2.

———. 1997e. "Nujoma Renews Gay Attack." April 28, 1.

———. 2000. "Jerry in New Anti-gay Rant." October 2. http://allafrica.com/stories/200010020039.html.

———. 2001a. "Black Radicals Slam Gay Outbursts." May 8. http://allafrica.com/stories/200105080034.html.

———. 2001b. "President Nujoma Urges 'Gay Purge.'" March 20. http://allafrica.com/stories/200103200214.html.

Naples, Nancy A. 2003. *Feminism and Method: Ethnography, Discourse Analysis, and Activist Research.* New York: Routledge.

National Coalition for Gay and Lesbian Equality. 1995. "Submission to Constitutional Assembly Theme Committee 4 on Fundamental Rights: The Right to Equality." February 20. Gay and Lesbian Archives AM 2615.

Nattrass, Nicoli. 2008. "AIDS and the Scientific Governance of Medicine in Post-apartheid South Africa." *African Affairs* 107, no. 427: 157–76.

Ndegwa, Stephen N. 2001. "A Decade of Democracy in Africa." *Journal of Asian and African Studies* 36, no. 1: 1–16.

Nel, Juan A., and Melanie Judge. 2008. "Exploring Homophobic Victimisation in Gauteng, South Africa: Issues, Impacts, and Responses." *Acta Criminologica* 21, no. 3: 19–36.

Nel, Tanya. 1997. "Face Reality—Amathila." *Windhoek Advertiser,* February 5, 3.

Nell, Marion, and Janet Shapiro. 2006. "Reviving the Equality Project." Presentation at the Joint Working Group meeting, Johannesburg, South Africa, March 5.

New Era. 1997. "This Lesbian Issue." February 10–13, 8.

News24. 2006. "Lesbian 'Khwezi' Names 5 Men." March 9. http://www.news24.com/SouthAfrica/Archives/ZumaFiles/Lesbian-Khwezi-names-5-men-20060309.

Nghidinwa, Maria Mboono. 2008. *Women Journalists in Namibia's Liberation Struggle, 1985–1990.* Basel, Switzerland: Basler Africa Bibliographien.

Nguaiko, Amos. 1995. "Prisons Not for Sodomy—Hausiku." *New Era,* December 10–13, 7.

Nicol, Julia. 2005. "If We Can't Dance to It, It's Not Our Revolution." In *Sex and Politics in South Africa,* ed. N. Hoad, K. Martin, and G. Reid, 72–84. Cape Town: Double Storey Books.

Nkabinde, Nkunzi Zandile. 2009. *Black Bull, Ancestors, and Me: My Life as a Lesbian Sangoma.* Johannesburg: Jacana.

Nkoli, Simon. 1995. "Wardrobes: Coming Out as a Black Gay Activist in South Africa." In *Defiant Desire: Gay and Lesbian Lives in South Africa,* ed. M. Gevisser and E. Cameron, 249–57. New York: Routledge.

Nzegwu, Nkiru. 2002. "Questions of Agency: Development, Donors, and Women of the South." *Jenda: A Journal of Culture and African Women Studies* 2, no. 1: 1–28.

Oliver, Pamela, and Daniel J. Myers. 2002. "The Coevolution of Social Movements." *Mobilization* 8, no. 1: 1–24.

Olzak, Susan, Maya Beasley, and Johan L. Olivier. 2002. "The Impact of State Reforms on Protest against Apartheid in South Africa." *Mobilization* 8, no. 1: 27–50.

Oswin, Natalie. 2007. "Producing Homonormativity in Neoliberal South Africa: Recognition, Redistribution, and the Equality Project." *Signs* 32, no. 3: 649–69.

Outright. 2000. "Change of Face at the Coalition." March–April, 10.

Oyěwùmí, Oyèrónké. 1997. *The Invention of Women: Making an African Sense of Western Gender Discourses.* Minneapolis: University of Minnesota Press.

Palmberg, Mai. 1999. "Emerging Visibility of Gays and Lesbians in Southern Africa." In *The Global Emergence of Gay and Lesbian Politics: National Imprints of a Worldwide Movement,* ed. B. D. Adam, J. W. Duyvendak, and A. Krouwel, 266–92. Philadelphia: Temple University Press.

Phelan, Shane. 2001. *Sexual Strangers: Gays and Lesbians and Dilemmas of Citizenship.* Philadelphia: Temple University Press.

Phillips, Oliver. 1997. "Zimbabwean Law and the Production of a White Man's Disease." *Social & Legal Studies* 6, no. 4: 471–91.

———. 2000. "Constituting the Global Gay: Issues of Individual Subjectivity and Sexuality in Southern Africa." In *Law and Sexuality: The Global Arena,* ed. D. Herman and C. F. Stychin, 17–34. Minneapolis: University of Minnesota Press.

———. 2006. "Gender, Justice, and Human Rights in Post-colonial Zimbabwe and South Africa." In *Gender and Justice: New Concepts and Approaches,* ed. F. Heidensohn, 243–79. Portland, Oreg.: Willan.

———. 2011. "The 'Perils' of Sex and the Panics of Race: The Dangers of Interracial Sex in Colonial Southern Rhodesia." In *African Sexualities: A Reader,* ed. S. Tamale, 101–15. Cape Town: Pambazuka.

Polletta, Francesca. 1999. "Free Spaces in Collective Action." *Theory and Society* 28, no. 1: 1–28.

Polletta, Francesca, and James M. Jasper. 2001. "Collective Identity and Social Movements." *Annual Review of Sociology* 27: 283–305.

Posel, Deborah. 1987. "The Meaning of Apartheid before 1948: Conflicting Interests and Forces within the Afrikaner Nationalist Alliance." *Journal of Southern African Studies* 14, no. 1: 123–39.

———. 2001. "Race as Common Sense: Racial Classification in Twentieth-Century South Africa." *African Studies Review* 44, no. 2: 87–113.

———. 2005. "Sex, Death, and the Fate of the Nation: Reflections on the Politicization of Sexuality in Post-apartheid South Africa." *Africa* 75, no. 2: 125–53.

Potgieter, Cheryl. 2005. "Sexualities? Hey, This Is What Black South African Lesbians Have to Say about Relationships with Men, the Family, Heterosexual Women, and Culture." In *Performing Queer: Shaping Sexualities, 1994–2004*, vol. 1, ed. M. van Zyl and M. Steyn, 177–92. Cape Town: Kwela Books.

Powers, Cathy. 1997. "Gay-Rights Supporters Dress for Success at Court." *Star*, November 26, 3.

Przeworski, Adam. 2010. *Democracy and the Limits of Self-Government*. Cambridge: Cambridge University Press.

Puar, Jasbir K. 2001. "Global Circuits: Transnational Sexualities and Trinidad." *Signs* 26, no. 4: 1039–65.

———. 2007. *Terrorist Assemblages: Homonationalism in Queer Times*. Durham, N.C.: Duke University Press.

Raeburn, Nicole. 2004. *Changing Corporate America from Inside Out: Lesbian and Gay Workplace Rights*. Minneapolis: University of Minnesota Press.

Rainbow Project. 1996. "Rainbow Project Speaks Its Mind." *Namibian*, December 20, 11.

———. 1998. "The Way Forward: Strategic Planning Workshop of the Rainbow Project." Meeting minutes.

———. 2000. "The Truth about Gay People." *Namibian*, July 14, 11.

Rankhotha, Sylvester Charles. 2005. "How Black Men Involved in Same-Sex Relationships Construct Their Masculinities." In *Performing Queer: Shaping Sexualities, 1994–2004*, vol. 1, ed. M. van Zyl and M. Steyn, 165–75. Cape Town: Kwela Books.

Ratele, Kopano. 2008. "Analysing Males in Africa: Certain Useful Elements in Considering Ruling Masculinities." *African and Asian Studies* 7, no. 4: 515–36.

Raubenheimer, Louis. 2006. "Clergy Split over Gays." *Nova*, February 8, 1.

Ray, Raka. 1999. *Fields of Protest: Women's Movements in India*. Minneapolis: University of Minnesota Press.

Reddy, Vasu. 1998. "Negotiating Gay Masculinities." *Agenda* 37: 65–70.

———. 2001. "Institutionalizing Sexuality: Theorizing Queer in Post-apartheid South Africa." In *The Greatest Taboo: Homosexuality in Black Communities*, ed. D. Constantine-Simons, 163–84. Los Angeles, Calif.: Alyson Books.

———. 2002. "Perverts and Sodomites: Homophobia as Hate Speech in Africa." *Southern African Linguistics and Applied Language Studies* 20: 163–75.

———. 2006. "Decriminalisation of Homosexuality in Post-apartheid South Africa: A Brief Legal Case History Review from Sodomy to Marriage." *Agenda* 67: 146–57.

———. 2009. "Queer Marriage: Sexualising Citizenship and the Development of Freedoms in South Africa." In *The Price and the Prize: Shaping Sexualities in South Africa*, ed. M. Steyn and M. van Zyl, 341–63. Cape Town: HSRC Press.

Reddy, Vasu, and Zethu Cakata. 2007. "'Even Animals of the Same Sex Don't Take This Route': Politics, Rights, and Identity about Same-Sex Marriage in South Africa." *Sexuality in Africa* 4, no. 1: 7–9.

Reger, Jo. 2002. "Organizational Dynamics and Construction of Multiple Feminist Identities in the National Organization for Women." *Gender & Society* 16, no. 5: 710–27.

Reid, Graeme. 2002. "'The History of the Past Is the Trust of the Present': Preservation and Excavation in the Gay and Lesbian Archives of South Africa." In *Refiguring the Archive*, ed. C. Hamilton, V. Harris, M. Pickover, G. Reid, R. Saleh, and J. Taylor, 193–207. Cape Town: David Philip.

———. 2005. "'A Man Is a Man Completely and a Wife Is a Wife Completely': Gender Classification and Performance amongst 'Ladies' and 'Gents' in Ermelo, Mpumalanga." In *Men Behaving Differently: South African Men since 1944*, ed. G. Reid and L. Walker, 205–27. Cape Town: Double Storey Books.

Reid, Graeme, and Teresa Dirsuweit. 2002. "Understanding Systemic Violence: Homophobic Attacks in Johannesburg and Its Surrounds." *Urban Forum* 13, no. 3: 99–126.

Reinelt, Claire. 1995. "Moving onto the Terrain of the State: The Battered Women's Movement and the Politics of Engagement." In *Feminist Organizations: Harvest of the New Women's Movement*, ed. M. M. Ferree and P. Y. Martin, 84–104. Philadelphia: Temple University Press.

Reinharz, Shulamit. 1992. *Feminist Methods in Social Research*. Oxford: Oxford University Press.

Republic of South Africa. 1996. *Constitution of the Republic of South Africa No. 108 of 1996*. http://www.info.gov.za/documents/constitution/1996/a108-96.pdf.

Retief, Glen. 1995. "Keeping Sodom out of the Laager: State Repression of Homosexuality in Apartheid South Africa." In *Defiant Desire: Gay and Lesbian Lives in South Africa*, ed. M. Gevisser and E. Cameron, 99–111. New York: Routledge.

Richardson, Diane. 2005. "Desiring Sameness? The Rise of a Neoliberal Politics of Normalisation." *Antipode* 37, no. 3: 515–35.

Robins, Steven L. 2008. *From Revolution to Rights in South Africa: Social Movements, NGOs, and Popular Politics after Apartheid*. Pietermaritzburg, South Africa: University of KwaZulu-Natal Press.

Rohlinger, Deana A. 2006. "Friends and Foes: Media, Politics, and Tactics in the Abortion War." *Social Problems* 53, no. 4: 537–61.

Rothschild, Cynthia. 2005. *Written Out: How Sexuality Is Used to Attack Women's*

Organizing. New York: IGLHRC and Center for Women's Global Leadership.

Rudwick, Stephanie, Khathala Nkomo, and Magcino Shange. 2006. "*Ulimi Iwen-kululeko*: Township 'Women's Language of Empowerment' and Homosexual Linguistic Identities." *Agenda* 67: 57–65.

Rupp, Leila J. 2001. "Toward a Global History of Same-Sex Sexuality." *Journal of the History of Sexuality* 10, no. 2: 287–302.

Russell, Alec. 2009. *Bring Me My Machine Gun: The Battle for the Soul of South Africa, from Mandela to Zuma.* New York: PublicAffairs.

Ryan, Charlotte. 1991. *Prime Time Activism: Media Strategies for Grassroots Organizing.* Boston: South End Press.

Rydström, Jens. 2005. "Solidarity—with Whom? The International Gay and Lesbian Rights Movement and Apartheid." In *Sex and Politics in South Africa,* ed. N. Hoad, K. Martin, and G. Reid, 34–49. Cape Town: Double Storey Books.

Saiz, Ignacio. 2004. "Bracketing Sexuality: Human Rights and Sexual Orientation—A Decade of Development and Denial at the UN." *Health and Human Rights* 7, no. 2: 48–80.

Salih, M. A. Mohamed. 2007. "African Liberation Movement Governments and Democracy." *Democratization* 14, no. 4: 669–85.

Samara, Tony Roshan. 2011. *Cape Town after Apartheid: Crime and Governance in the Divided City.* Minneapolis: University of Minnesota Press.

Samelius, Lotta, and Eric Wågberg. 2005. "Sexual Orientation and Gender Identity Issues in Development: A Study of Swedish Policy and Administration of Lesbian, Gay, Bisexual, and Transgender Issues in International Development." Swedish International Development Cooperation Agency. http://www.ilga-europe.org/europe/guide/country_by_country/sweden/sexual_orientation_and_gender_identity_issues_in_development.

Sandberg, Eve. 2000. "Theories of Democratization and the Case of Donor-Assisted Democratization in Namibia." In *Handbook of Global Political Policy,* ed. S. S. Nagel, 87–104. New York: Marcel Dekker.

Sandbrook, Timothy. 2000. *Closing the Circle: Democratization and Development in Africa.* London: Zed.

Sanger, Nadia. 2010. "'The Real Problems Need to Be Fixed First': Public Discourses on Sexuality and Gender in South Africa." *Agenda* 83: 114–25.

Sawyers, Traci M., and David S. Meyer. 1999. "Missed Opportunities: Social Movement Abeyance and Public Policy." *Social Problems* 46, no. 2: 187–206.

Schabas, William. 2002. *The Abolition of the Death Penalty in International Law.* Cambridge: Cambridge University Press.

Scott, James C. 1990. *Weapons of the Weak: Everyday Forms of Peasant Resistance.* New Haven, Conn.: Yale University Press.

Scott, Joan Wallach. 2007. *The Politics of the Veil.* Princeton, N.J.: Princeton University Press.

Sebetoane, Keba. 2011. "Who Are You to Tell Me Who I Am?" In *Reclaiming the L-Word: Sappho's Daughters Out in Africa,* ed. A. Diesel, 91–94. Athlone, South Africa: Modjaji Books.

Seckinelgin, Hakan. 2009. "Global Activism and Sexualities in the Time of HIV/ AIDS." *Contemporary Politics* 15, no. 1: 103–18.

Sedgwick, Eve Kosofsky. 1990. *Epistemology of the Closet.* Berkeley: University of California Press.

Seidman, Gay W. 1994. *Manufacturing Militance: Workers' Movements in Brazil and South Africa, 1970–1985.* Berkeley: University of California Press.

———. 1999. "Is South Africa Different? Sociological Comparisons and Theoretical Contributions from the Land of Apartheid." *Annual Review of Sociology* 25: 419–40.

———. 2001. "Guerrillas in Their Midst: Armed Struggle in the South African Anti-apartheid Movement." *Mobilization* 6, no. 2: 111–27.

Shigwedha, Absalom. 2004. "There Are Two Namibias: Activist." *Namibian,* March 3. http://allafrica.com/stories/200403030196.html.

Shongwe, Zodwa. 2006. "It Was Magic." In *Pride: Protest and Celebration,* ed. S. de Waal and A. Manion, 101–3. Johannesburg: Jacana.

Simi, Pete, and Robert Futrell. 2009. "Negotiating White Power Activist Stigma." *Social Problems* 56, no. 1: 89–110.

Simon, David. 1986. "Desegregation in Namibia: The Demise of Urban Apartheid?" *Geoforum* 17, no. 2: 289–307.

———. 1996. "Restructuring the Local State in Post-apartheid Cities: Namibian Experience and Lessons for South Africa." *African Affairs* 95, no. 378: 51–84.

Sinnott, Megan. 2004. *Toms and Dees: Transgender Identity and Female Same-Sex Relationships in Thailand.* Honolulu: University of Hawaii Press.

Sister Namibia. 1995. "Sister Namibia Responds to Ministers' Remarks." *Die Republikein,* October 9, 4.

———. 1999. *Namibian Women's Manifesto.* Windhoek: Sister Namibia.

———. 2001. "Dear Readers." *Sister Namibia* 13, no. 2: 2.

———. 2003. "Who We Are." *Sister Namibia* 12, nos. 5–6: 2.

Smith, Ann. 2005. "Where Was I in the Eighties?" In *Sex and Politics in South Africa,* ed. N. Hoad, K. Martin, and G. Reid, 58–62. Cape Town: Double Storey Books.

Snow, David A., and Robert D. Benford. 1999. "Alternative Types of Cross-National Diffusion in the Social Movement Arena." In *Social Movements in a Globalizing World,* ed. D. della Porta, H. Kriesi, and D. Rucht, 23–39. New York: Palgrave Macmillan.

Snow, David A., and Doug McAdam. 2000. "Identity Work Processes in the Context of Social Movements: Clarifying the Identity/Movement Nexus." In *Self, Identity, and Social Movements,* ed. S. Stryker, T. J. Owens, and R. W. White, 41–67. Minneapolis: University of Minnesota Press.

Sobieraj, Sarah. 2011. *Soundbitten: The Perils of Media-Centered Political Activism.* New York: New York University Press.

Somerville, Daniel. 2006. "It's Very Easy to Criticise the Organisers of Pride, and Very Difficult to Pull Off the Parade." In *Pride: Protest and Celebration,* ed. S. de Waal and A. Manion, 136–37. Johannesburg: Fanele.

Somerville, Siobhan B. 1994. "Scientific Racism and the Emergence of the Homosexual Body." *Journal of the History of Sexuality* 5, no. 2: 243–66.

Southall, Roger. 2007. "The ANC, Black Economic Empowerment, and State-Owned Enterprises: A Recycling of History?" In *State of the Nation: South Africa 2007,* ed. S. Buhlungu, J. Daniel, R. Southall, and J. Lutchman, 201–25. Cape Town: HSRC Press.

Sow, Fatou. 1997. "The Social Sciences in Africa and Gender Analysis." In *Engendering African Social Sciences,* ed. A. Imam, A. Mama, and F. Sow, 31–60. Dakar: Codesria.

Sperling, Valerie, Myra Marx Ferree, and Barbara Risman. 2001. "Constructing Global Feminism: Transnational Advocacy Networks and Russian Women's Activism." *Signs* 26, no. 4: 1155–86.

Spivak, Gayatri Chakravorty. 1987. *In Other Worlds: Essay in Cultural Politics.* New York: Routledge.

Spurlin, William J. 2006. *Imperialism within the Margins: Queer Representation and the Politics of Culture in Southern Africa.* New York: Palgrave Macmillan.

Stacey, Judith. 2011. *Unhitched: Love, Marriage, and Family Values from West Hollywood to Western China.* New York: New York University Press.

Staggenborg, Suzanne. 1988. "The Consequences of Professionalization and Formalization in the Pro-choice Movement." *American Sociological Review* 53, no. 4: 585–605.

Statistics South Africa. 2011. "Mid-year Population Estimates: 2011." July 27. http://www.statssa.gov.za/publications/P0302/P03022011.pdf.

Steinbugler, Amy C. 2005. "Visibility as Privilege and Danger: Heterosexual and Same-Sex Interracial Intimacy in the 21st Century." *Sexualities* 8, no. 4: 425–43.

Steyn, Melissa. 2001. *"Whiteness Just Isn't What It Used to Be": White Identity in a Changing South Africa.* Albany: State University of New York Press.

Stobbs, Paul. 2006. "Welcome . . . the Rest Is Up to You." In *Pride: Protest and Celebration,* ed. S. de Waal and A. Manion, 84–89. Johannesburg: Fanele.

Stobie, Cheryl. 2007. *Somewhere in the Double Rainbow: Representations of Bisexuality in Post-apartheid Novels.* Scottsville, South Africa: University of KwaZulu-Natal Press.

Stockdill, Brett C. 2003. *Activism against AIDS: At the Intersections of Sexuality, Race, Gender, and Class.* Boulder, Colo.: Lynne Rienner.

Stoecker, Randy. 1995. "Community, Movement, Organization: The Problem of Identity Convergence in Collective Action." *Sociological Quarterly* 36, no. 1: 111–30.

Stychin, Carl F. 1996. "Constituting Sexuality: The Struggle for Sexual Orientation in the South African Bill of Rights." *Journal of Law and Society* 23, no. 4: 455–83.

———. 2001. "The Globalization of Sexual Identities: Universality, Tradition, and the

(Post)Colonial Encounter." In *Between Law and Culture: Relocating Legal Studies,* ed. D. T. Goldberg, M. Musheno, and L. C. Bower, 275–87. Minneapolis: University of Minnesota Press.

Suh, Doowon. 2001. "How Do Political Opportunities Matter for Social Movements? Political Opportunity, Misframing, Pseudosuccess, and Pseudofailure." *Sociological Quarterly* 42, no. 3: 437–60.

Susser, Ida. 2009. *AIDS, Sex, and Culture: Global Politics and Survival in Southern Africa.* Malden, Mass.: Blackwell.

Swarr, Amanda Lock. 2003. "South African Transgendered Subjectivities: Exploring the Boundaries of Sex, Gender, and Race." PhD dissertation, Department of Gender, Women, and Sexuality Studies, University of Minnesota, Minneapolis.

———. 2009. "*Stabane,* Intersexuality, and Same-Sex Relationships in South Africa." *Feminist Studies* 35, no. 3: 524–48.

Swarr, Amanda Lock, and Richa Nagar. 2003. "Dismantling Assumptions: Interrogating 'Lesbian' Struggles for Identity and Survival in India and South Africa." *Signs* 29, no. 2: 491–516.

Swart, Werner. 2006. "Zuma Trial 'a Sad Day for the Sexes.'" *Citizen,* February 16, 4.

Talavera, Philippe. 2002. *Challenging the Namibian Perception of Sexuality: A Case Study of the Ovahimba and Ovaherero Culturo-Sexual Models in Kunene North in an HIV/AIDS Context.* Windhoek: Gamsberg Macmillan.

———. 2007. "Past and Present Practices: Sexual Development in Namibia." In *Unravelling Taboos: Gender and Sexuality in Namibia,* ed. S. LaFont and D. Hubbard, 39–57. Windhoek: LAC.

Tamale, Sylvia. 2007. "Out of the Closet: Unveiling Sexuality Discourses in Uganda." In *Africa after Gender?,* ed. C. M. Cole, T. Manuh, and S. F. Miescher, 17–29. Bloomington: Indiana University Press.

Tan, Chong Kee. 2001. "Transcending Sexual Nationalism and Colonialism: Cultural Hybridization as Process of Sexual Politics in '90s Taiwan." In *Postcolonial, Queer: Theoretical Intersections,* ed. J. C. Hawley, 123–37. Albany: State University of New York Press.

Tarrow, Sidney. 2005. *The New Transnational Activism.* Cambridge: Cambridge University Press.

———. 2011. *Power in Movement: Social Movements and Contentious Politics.* 3rd ed. Cambridge: Cambridge University Press.

Tatchell, Peter. 2005. "The Moment the ANC Embraced Gay Rights." In *Sex and Politics in South Africa,* ed. N. Hoad, K. Martin, and G. Reid, 140–47. Cape Town: Double Storey Books.

Taylor, Verta. 1989. "Social Movement Continuity: The Women's Movement in Abeyance." *American Sociological Review* 54, no. 5: 761–75.

Taylor, Verta, and Nella Van Dyke. 2004. "'Get Up, Stand Up': Tactical Repertoires of

Social Movements." In *The Blackwell Companion to Social Movements*, ed. D. A. Snow, S. A. Soule, and H. Kriesi, 262–93. Malden, Mass.: Blackwell.

Taylor, Verta, and Nancy E. Whittier. 1992. "Collective Identity in Social Movement Communities: Lesbian Feminist Mobilization." In *Frontiers in Social Movement Theory*, ed. A. D. Morris and C. M. Mueller, 104–29. New Haven, Conn.: Yale University Press.

Thamm, Marianne. 2006. "Not Just Another Murder." *Mail & Guardian*, February 26, 7.

Thayer, Millie. 2009. *Making Transnational Feminism: Rural Women, NGO Activists, and Northern Donors in Brazil*. New York: Routledge.

Thomas, Greg. 2007. *The Sexual Demon of Colonial Power: Pan-African Embodiment and Erotic Schemes of Empire*. Bloomington: Indiana University Press.

Thompson, Leonard. 2001. *A History of South Africa*. New Haven, Conn.: Yale University Press.

Thoreson, Ryan Richard. 2008. "Somewhere over the Rainbow Nation: Gay, Lesbian, and Bisexual Activism in South Africa." *Journal of Southern African Studies* 34, no. 3: 679–97.

Thornton, Robert J. 2008. *Unimagined Community: Sex, Networks, and AIDS in Uganda and South Africa*. Chicago: University of Chicago Press.

Tibinyane, Natasha. 1998. "Homosexuals Vow to Remain as They Are." *New Era*, February 13–15, 20.

———. 1999. "Sexual Choice for Inmates." *New Era*, June 14–17, 1–2.

Tilly, Charles. 2004. *Social Movements, 1768–2004*. Boulder, Colo.: Paradigm.

Tripp, Aili Mari. 2006. "The Evolution of Transnational Feminisms: Consensus, Conflict, and New Dynamics." In *Global Feminisms: Transnational Women's Activism, Organizing, and Human Rights*, ed. M. M. Ferree and A. M. Tripp, 51–75. New York: New York University Press.

Tripp, Aili Mari, Isabel Casimiro, Joy Kwesiga, and Alice Mungwa. 2009. *African Women's Movements: Transforming Political Landscapes*. Cambridge: Cambridge University Press.

Tshabalala, Themelihle. 2008. "Growing Anti-lesbian Violence." *Mail & Guardian*, May 18. http://www.mg.co.za/article/2008-05-16-growing-anti-lesbian-violence.

Tucker, Andrew. 2009. *Queer Visibilities: Space, Identity, and Interaction in Cape Town*. Malden, Mass.: Blackwell.

Tutu, Desmond. 2000. *No Future without Forgiveness*. New York: Random House.

van der Westhuizen, Christi. 2006. "The Real Blood Wars." *Out News*, March 1.

Van Dyke, Nella, Sarah A. Soule, and Verta A. Taylor. 2004. "The Targets of Social Movements: Beyond a Focus on the State." *Research in Social Movements, Conflicts, and Change* 25: 27–51.

van Zyl, Mikki. 2005. "Shaping Sexualities—Per(trans)forming Queer." In *Performing*

Queer: Shaping Sexualities, 1994–2004, vol. 1, ed. M. van Zyl and M. Steyn, 19–38. Cape Town: Kwela Books.

———. 2009. "Beyond the Constitution: From Sexual Rights to Belonging." In *The Prize and the Price: Shaping Sexualities in South Africa,* ed. M. Steyn and M. van Zyl, 364–87. Cape Town: HSRC Press.

———. 2011. "A Step Too Far? Five Cape Town Lesbian Couples Speak about Being Married." *Agenda* 25, no. 1: 53–64.

van Zyl, Mikki, Jeanelle de Gruchy, Sheila Lapinsky, Simon Lewin, and Graeme Reid. 1999. "The aVersion Project: Human Rights Abuses of Gays and Lesbians in the SADF by Health Workers during the Apartheid Era." Cape Town: Simply Said and Done.

Vetten, Lisa. 2007. "Violence against Women in South Africa." In *State of the Nation: South Africa 2007,* ed. S. Buhlungu, J. Daniel, R. Southall, and J. Lutchman, 425–47. Cape Town: HSRC Press.

Vetten, Lisa, and Joy Dladla. 2000. "Women's Fear and Survival in Inner-City Johannesburg." *Agenda* 45: 70–75.

Vilakazi, Fikile. 2008. "Lobbying for Same-Sex Marriage: An Activist's Reflections." In *To Have and to Hold: The Making of Same-Sex Marriage in South Africa,* ed. M. Judge, A. Manion, and S. de Waal, 87–96. Johannesburg: Fanele.

Vilakazi, Fikile, and Veneshree Chetty. 2006. "We Want to Get Married, and That Was Very Much in Our Minds That Day." In *Pride: Protest and Celebration,* ed. S. de Waal and A. Manion, 166–67. Johannesburg: Fanele.

Viterna, Jocelyn, and Kathleen M. Fallon. 2008. "Democratization, Women's Movements, and Gender-Equitable States: A Framework for Comparison." *American Sociological Review* 73, no. 4: 668–89.

Vliegenthart, Rens, Dirk Oegema, and Bert Klandermans. 2005. "Media Coverage and Organizational Support in the Dutch Environmental Movement." *Mobilization* 10, no. 3: 365–81.

Walker, Liz. 2005. "Negotiating the Boundaries of Masculinity in Post-apartheid South Africa." In *Men Behaving Differently: South African Men since 1944,* ed. G. Reid and L. Walker, 161–82. Cape Town: Double Storey Books.

Ward, Jane. 2008. *Respectably Queer: Diversity Culture in LGBT Activist Organizations.* Nashville, Tenn.: Vanderbilt University Press.

Warner, Michael. 1999. *The Trouble with Normal: Sex, Politics, and the Ethics of Queer Life.* New York: Free Press.

———. 2002. *Publics and Counterpublics.* New York: Zone Books.

Weidlich, Brigitte. 1998. "Ekandjo Compares Homosexuality with Satanism." *Windhoek Observer,* November 14, 8.

Wells, Helen, and Louise Polders. 2006. "Anti-gay Hate Crimes in South Africa: Prevalence, Reporting Practices, and Experiences of the Police." *Agenda* 67: 20–28.

Welsh, Frank. 2000. *A History of South Africa*. London: HarperCollins.

Whittier, Nancy. 2009. *The Politics of Child Sexual Abuse: Emotion, Social Movements, and the State*. Oxford: Oxford University Press.

Wieringa, Saskia. 2005. "Women Marriages and Other Same-Sex Practices: Historical Reflections on African Women's Same-Sex Relations." In *Tommy Boys, Lesbian Men, and Ancestral Wives: Female Same-Sex Practices in Africa*, ed. R. Morgan and S. Wieringa, 281–307. Johannesburg: Jacana.

Williams, Rhys H. 1995. "Constructing the Public Good: Social Movements and Cultural Resources." *Social Problems* 42, no. 1: 124–44.

Windhoek Observer. 1999. "Manifesto Gets the Tag of Homosexuality." October 16, 12.

———. 2001. "Lesbian Love Plays Key Role in Condonation Matter Filed by Immigration Chief." March 10, 18–19.

Winnubst, Shannon. 2006. *Queering Freedom*. Bloomington: Indiana University Press.

Wise, Sheila J. 2007. "The Male 'Powersexual': An Exploratory Study of Manhood, Power and Sexual Behaviour among Elite Afrikaner and Owambo Men in Windhoek." In *Unravelling Taboos: Gender and Sexuality in Namibia*, ed. S. LaFont and D. Hubbard, 330–43. Windhoek: LAC.

Wood, Kate. 2005. "Contextualizing Group Rape in Post-apartheid South Africa." *Culture, Health & Sexuality* 7, no. 4: 303–17.

World Bank. 2008. "Population 2008." http://siteresources.worldbank.org/DATA-STATISTICS/Resources/POP.pdf.

Woubshet, Dagmawi. 2007. "Figurations of Catastrophe: The Poetics and Politics of AIDS Loss." PhD dissertation, Committee on Higher Degrees in the History of American Civilization, Harvard University, Cambridge, Mass.

Wright, Timothy. 2000. "Gay Organizations, NGOs, and the Globalization of Sexual Identity: The Case of Bolivia." *Journal of Latin American Anthropology* 5, no. 2: 89–111.

Young, Crawford. 2004. "The End of the Post-colonial State in Africa? Reflections on Changing African Political Dynamics." *African Affairs* 103, no. 410: 23–49.

Younis, Mona N. 2000. *Liberation and Democratization: The South African and Palestinian National Movements*. Minneapolis: University of Minnesota Press.

Zald, Mayer N., and Roberta Ash. 1966. "Social Movement Organizations: Growth, Decay, and Change." *Social Forces* 44, no. 3: 327–41.

Zuern, Elke. 2011. *The Politics of Necessity: Community Organizing and Democracy in South Africa*. Madison: University of Wisconsin Press.

Zulu, Xoliswa. 2006. "Gay Blood Carries No Greater Risk." *Star*, October 3. http://www.iol.co.za/news/south-africa/gay-blood-carries-no-greater-risk-1.295994.

Archival Sources Consulted

Gay and Lesbian Archives (GALA), University of the Witwatersrand, Johannesburg,
    South Africa:
ACTIVATE (AM 2648)
Association of Bisexuals, Gays, and Lesbians (AM 2802, AM 2993)
Equality Foundation (AM 2688)
Forum for the Empowerment of Women (AM 3161)
GALA Press Clippings (AM 2704)
Namibia (AM 2641)
Nkateko (AM 2661)
The Rainbow Project (AM 2974, AM 3186)

Index

Continued from page ii

ASHLEY CURRIER is assistant professor of women's, gender, and sexuality studies at the University of Cincinnati.